Microsoft® Office Visio® 2007 Step by Step

Judy Lemke and Resources Online

PUBLISHED BY
Microsoft Press
A Division of Microsoft Corporation
One Microsoft Way
Redmond, Washington 98052-6399

Library of Congress Control Number: 2006938195

ISBN: 978-0-7356-2357-6

5 6 7 8 9 10 11 12 13 14 QGT 6 5 4 3 2 1

Printed and bound in the United States of America.

Microsoft Press books are available through booksellers and distributors worldwide. For further information about international editions, contact your local Microsoft Corporation office or contact Microsoft Press International directly at fax (425) 936-7329. Visit our Web site at www.microsoft.com/mspress. Send comments to mspinput@ microsoft.com.

Acquisitions Editor: Juliana Aldous Atkinson
Developmental Editor: Sandra Haynes
Project Editor: Rosemary Caperton
Editorial Production: Custom Editorial Productions, Inc.
Technical Editor: Mitch Tulloch

Body Part No. X13-24137

[2011-08-19]

Your All-in-One Resource

On the CD that accompanies this book, you'll find additional resources to extend your learning.

The reference library includes the following fully searchable titles:

- *Microsoft Computer Dictionary*, 5th ed.
- *First Look 2007 Microsoft Office System* by Katherine Murray
- Windows Vista Product Guide

Also provided are a sample chapter and poster from *Look Both Ways: Help Protect Your Family on the Internet* by Linda Criddle

The CD interface has a new look. You can use the tabs for an assortment of tasks:

- Check for book updates (if you have Internet access)
- Install the book's practice file
- Go online for product support or CD support
- Send us feedback

The following screen shot gives you a glimpse of the new interface.

Contents

What do you think of this book? We want to hear from you!

Microsoft is interested in hearing your feedback so we can continually improve our books and learning resources for you. To participate in a brief online survey, please visit:

microsoft.com/learning/booksurvey

> **Important** Chapters 9 through 12 are included on the CD that accompanies this book. These fully searchable and printable PDFs include more advanced tasks than are covered in Chapters 1 through 8 and topics specific to Microsoft Office Visio Professional 2007. See Appendix A for a complete list of the topics covered in those chapters.

What do you think of this book? We want to hear from you!

Microsoft is interested in hearing your feedback so we can continually improve our books and learning resources for you. To participate in a brief online survey, please visit:

microsoft.com/learning/booksurvey

What's New in Visio 2007?

You'll notice some changes as soon as you start Microsoft Office Visio 2007. The Getting Started window appears immediately with a list of simplified template categories, thumbnail previews of templates and documents you opened recently, and large thumbnail previews of every template included in the product. All this helps you choose the right template and get you started diagramming on the right track. But the features that are new or improved in this version of Visio go beyond just changes in appearance. Some changes won't be apparent until you start using Visio. For example, Visio Professional 2007 also includes a new Data menu that includes new Data Link, Data Refresh, and Data Graphics features that enable you to more easily visualize data in Visio diagrams.

The following table lists the new features that you might be interested in, as well as the chapters in which those features are discussed.

> **Important** Chapters 9 through 12 are included on the CD that accompanies this book. These fully searchable and printable PDFs include more advanced tasks than are covered in Chapters 1 through 8 and topics specific to Microsoft Office Visio Professional 2007. See Appendix A for a complete list of the topics covered in those chapters.

To learn how to	See
Quickly find the right template for your diagram by using the new Getting Started window	Chapter 1
Search the entire Microsoft Office Online Web site directly from within Visio by using the new Visio Help window, find answers to your questions, tips and tricks, in-depth articles about using Visio, answers to frequently asked questions, and more templates	Chapter 1
Design professional-looking Visio diagrams by choosing a color or effect theme from the Theme—Colors task pane and Theme—Effects task pane, or to choose from the built-in themes included with Visio, or create your own custom themes	Chapter 3
Let Visio automatically connect, distribute, and align shapes in diagrams for you using new AutoConnect functionality	Chapter 4

To learn how to	See
Integrate data with any Visio diagram by using the new Data Link features on the Data menu in Visio Professional 2007	Chapter 9
View data linked to diagrams in spreadsheet format by viewing the External Data window	Chapter 9
With Visio Professional 2007, open sample, data-connected diagrams from the new Samples category in the Getting Started window to get ideas for creating and designing your own diagrams	Chapter 9
Link data to shapes to easily display data on the drawing page by using various, intuitive methods, including the new Automatic Link wizard	Chapter 9
Visualize data in Visio diagrams as text, data bars, and icons by using the new Data Graphics task pane in Visio Professional 2007 and even color code shapes according to data values	Chapter 9
Easily refresh data in diagrams by using the new Data Refresh feature, and, using the new Refresh Conflicts task pane, deal with data conflicts that might arise when the data source changes	Chapter 9
Create PivotDiagrams (that show data groups and totals in a tree structure) with the new PivotDiagram template included with Visio Professional 2007	Chapter 10
See sample PivotDiagrams included with Visio Professional 2007 and use as them as models for your own	Chapter 10
Drill down into complex business data and show different views of it using the PivotDiagram template	Chapter 10
Track data trends in PivotDiagrams by using the new Data Graphics task pane in Visio Professional 2007	Chapter 10

Some new features are beyond the scope of this book. However, you can easily find out more about them. In Visio, type the name of the feature in the Type A Question For Help box in the upper right corner of the Visio window, and then press the Enter key.

Feature	Description
Value Stream template	Visualize manufacturing processes based on Lean Methodology to facilitate efficiency gains.
ITIL template	Diagram IT service processes with the new ITIL (Information Technology Infrastructure Library) template.

Feature	Description
Insert PivotDiagrams into Visio diagrams	Insert PivotDiagrams into any Visio diagram to provide metrics and reports that help you track the progress of a process or system.
Generate PivotDiagrams from other programs	More effectively track and report on resources and projects managed in Microsoft Office SharePoint Server 2007 and Microsoft Office Project 2007 by generating visual reports from those programs in PivotDiagram form.
Enhanced Work Flow shapes	Design more dynamic workflows with the enhanced 3-D Work Flow shapes that were designed with the new built-in Visio themes in mind.
Trust Center	Adjust security and privacy settings for all 2007 Microsoft Office system programs, including Visio, using the new Trust Center. On the Tools menu, click Trust Center.
Save diagrams in more file types	Save Visio diagrams as PDFs and in the new Microsoft XPS file format to make them more portable and able to reach broader audiences. To save Visio diagrams as PDF or XPS files, first, you need to install an add-in. For more information, go to Microsoft Office Online and search for "save as PDF or XPS."
Microsoft Office SharePoint Server site integration	Share diagrams and collaborate using Document Workspaces. Check Visio diagrams and XML files in and out from SharePoint sites.
Visual reporting with Visio diagrams generated from Microsoft Office SharePoint Server 2007 and Microsoft Office Project 2007	Track and report on projects managed with SharePoint Server and Project by generating visual reports from those programs in PivotDiagram form.
Microsoft Office Outlook 2007 integration	Create, format, and share calendars from Office Outlook. View Office Visio diagram attachments directly in an Office Outlook e-mail message.
Multiple language and Unicode support	Work with character sets in 21 languages. Visio 2007 is now fully Unicode-compliant and includes support for Arabic, Hebrew, Turkish, and Russian.
Language-neutral installation support	Visio 2007 includes support for the new Microsoft Office language-neutral deployment architecture, which facilitates deployment of multiple languages.

Feature	Description
Developer-related features	Create custom data-connected solutions that take advantage of the new Visio Professional 2007 data visualization features by using the new application programming interfaces (APIs). Go to the Microsoft Developer Network (MSDN) to find the software development kit (SDK), documentation, articles, and other assistance for developing Microsoft Office solutions. In Visio, on the Help menu, click Developer Reference.

For more information about Visio products, visit the Microsoft Office Online Web site (*www.office.microsoft.com/*) or in Visio, on the Help menu, click Microsoft Office Online.

Features and Conventions of This Book

This book has been designed to lead you step-by-step through all the tasks you are most likely to want to perform in Microsoft Office Visio 2007. If you start at the beginning and work your way through all the exercises, you will gain enough proficiency to be able to create and work with Visio files. However, each topic is self contained. If you have worked with a previous version of Visio, or if you completed all the exercises and later need help remembering how to perform a procedure, the following features of this book will help you look up specific tasks in Visio 2007:

- Detailed table of contents. Get an overview of which topics are discussed in which chapters.
- Chapter thumb tabs. Easily open the book at the beginning of the chapter you want.
- Topic-specific running heads. Within a chapter, quickly locate the topic you want by looking at the running head of odd-numbered pages.
- Quick Reference. Refresh your memory about a task while working with your own documents.
- Detailed index. Look up specific tasks and features in the index, which has been carefully crafted with the reader in mind.
- Companion CD. Use to install the practice files needed for the step-by-step exercises, but also as a source of other useful information, including an online, searchable version of this book and four extra chapters of more advanced material, including subjects relating specifically to Office Visio Professional 2007.

In addition, we provide a glossary of terms for those times when you need to look up the meaning of a word or the definition of a concept.

You can save time when you use this book by understanding how the Step by Step series shows special instructions, keys to press, buttons to click, and so on.

Convention	Meaning
(CD icon)	This icon indicates a reference to the book's companion CD.
BE SURE TO	This paragraph preceding or following a step-by-step exercise indicates any prerequisite requirements that you should attend to before beginning the exercise, or actions you should take to restore your system after completing the exercise.
OPEN	This paragraph preceding a step-by-step exercise indicates files that you should open before beginning the exercise.
CLOSE	This paragraph following a step-by-step exercise provides instructions for closing open files or programs before moving on to another topic.
1 2	Blue numbered steps guide you through step-by-step exercises and procedures in the "Quick Reference."
1 **2**	Black numbered steps guide you through procedures in sidebars and topic introductions.
●	A single solid blue circle indicates an exercise that has only one step.
See Also	These paragraphs direct you to more information about a given topic in this book or elsewhere.
Troubleshooting	These paragraphs explain how to fix a common problem that might prevent you from continuing with an exercise.
Tip	These paragraphs provide a helpful hint or shortcut that makes working through a task easier, or information about other available options.
Important	These paragraphs point out information that you need to know to complete a procedure.
(Save button icon) Save	The first time you are told to click a button in an exercise, a picture of the button appears in the left margin. If the name of the button does not appear on the button itself, the name appears under the picture.
Enter	In step-by-step exercises, keys you must press appear in key-shaped boxes.
Ctrl + Home	A plus sign (+) between two key names means that you must hold down the first key while you press the second key. For example, "press Ctrl+Home" means "hold down the Ctrl key while you press the Home key."
Program interface elements	In steps, the names of program elements, such as buttons, commands, and dialog boxes, are shown in black bold characters.
User input	Anything you are supposed to type appears in blue bold characters.
Glossary terms	Terms that are explained in the glossary at the end of the book are shown in blue italic characters.

Getting Help

Every effort has been made to ensure the accuracy of this book and the contents of its CD. If you do run into problems, please contact the appropriate source for help and assistance.

Getting Help with This Book and Its CD

If your question or issue concerns the content of this book or its companion CD, please first search the online Microsoft Knowledge Base, which provides support information for known errors in or corrections to this book, at the following Web site:

www.microsoft.com/mspress/support/search.asp

If you do not find your answer at the online Knowledge Base, send your comments or questions to Microsoft Press Technical Support at:

mspinput@microsoft.com

Getting Help with Microsoft Office Visio 2007

If your question is about Microsoft Office Visio 2007, and not about the content of this Microsoft Press book, your first recourse is the Visio Help system. This system is a combination of help tools and files stored on your computer when you installed Visio 2007 and, if your computer is connected to the Internet, help files available from Microsoft Office Online. When you have a question about using Visio, you can type your question in the Type A Question For Help box at the right end of the Visio menu bar, and then press the Enter key to display a list of Help topics from which you can select the one that most closely relates to your question.

If you want to practice getting help, you can work through this exercise, which demonstrates two ways to get help.

1. Start Visio. At the right end of the Visio menu bar, in the **Type a question for help** box, type Sample diagrams, and press Enter.

   A list of topics that relate to your question appears in the Visio Help window.

> **Note** If you're not connected to the Internet when using Visio Help, Visio 2007 searches the Help topics installed with Visio on your computer. To find the most up-to-date Help topics, connect to the Internet while searching for Help so Visio 2007 searches Microsoft Office Online for Help topics in addition to the files on your computer.

2. In the Visio Help window, click **Work with sample diagrams and data**.

The Visio Help topic appears in the Visio Help window.

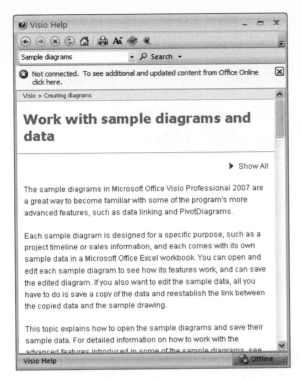

Close

3. In the upper-right corner of the Visio Help window, click the **Close** button to close the window.

4. On the **Help** menu, click **Microsoft Office Visio Help**.

The Visio Help window appears and lists categories of information.

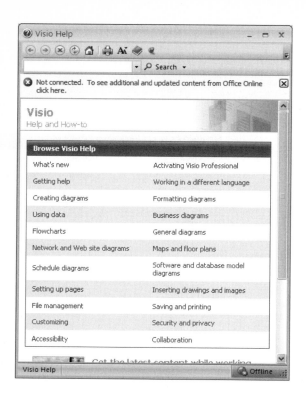

> **Tip** You can easily view the information on the Microsoft Office Online Web site. Just click Microsoft Office Online on the Help menu.

Show Table of Contents

5. In the Visio Help window, click the **Show Table of Contents** button.

The Table of Contents appears in the left portion of the Visio Help window.

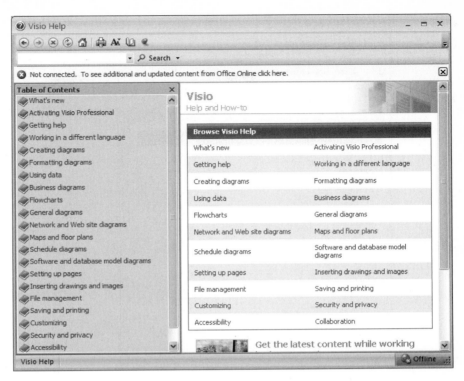

6. Under **Table of Contents**, click **Creating diagrams**.

   The section opens and displays Visio Help topics.

7. In the **Creating diagrams** section, click **Work with sample diagrams and data**.

   The Visio Help topic appears in the Visio Help window.

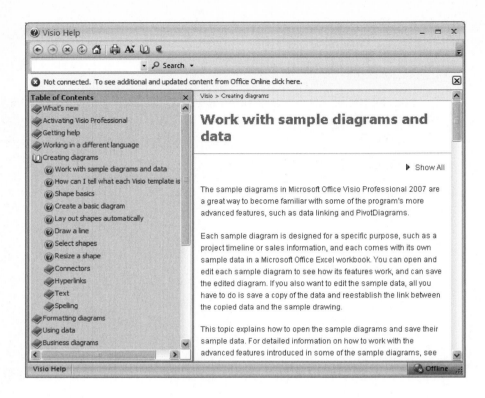

> **Tip** You can also search for Help by typing keywords in the Search box in the Visio Help window.

8. In the upper-right corner of the Visio Help window, click the **Close** button to close the window.

9. On the **File** menu, click **Exit** to exit Visio.

More Information

If your question is about a Microsoft software product, including Visio 2007, and not about the content of this Microsoft Press book, please search the appropriate product support center or the Microsoft Knowledge Base at:

support.microsoft.com

In the United States, Microsoft software product support issues not covered by the Microsoft Knowledge Base are addressed by Microsoft Product Support Services. The

Microsoft software support options available from Microsoft Product Support Services are listed at:

support.microsoft.com

Outside the United States, for support information specific to your location, please refer to the Worldwide Support menu on the Microsoft Product Support Services Web site for the site specific to your country:

support.microsoft.comsupport.microsoft.com/gp/selfoverview/

Using the Book's CD-ROM

The CD inside the back cover of this book contains the following files and software:

- Electronic version of the book (eBook)
- Setup to install the practice files
- Microsoft Office System Reference Pack eBooks:
  - ❏ Introducing the Tablet PC eBook
  - ❏ Microsoft Computer Dictionary, Fifth Edition eBook
  - ❏ Insider's Guide to Microsoft Office OneNote 2003 eBook
  - ❏ Microsoft Office System Quick Reference eBook
- Link to Microsoft Learning Technical Support

> **Important** You must install the trial or full version of Microsoft Office Visio 2007 before attempting the exercises in this book. For Chapter 9, "Visualizing Data in Diagrams," and Chapter 10, "Analyzing Business Data in PivotDiagrams," you must install the trial or full version of Microsoft Office Visio Professional 2007 to complete the exercises. To find information about Visio 2007 trial software availability in your country or region, visit the Microsoft Office System Worldwide Web site: *www.microsoft.com/office/worldwide.mspx*. If you want to order a 30-day trial of Visio Professional 2007, visit the Visio 2007 Trial Software Web site: *www.microsoft.com /office/visio/prodinfo/trial.mspx*.

For further information about using the CD, consult the Readme (Readme.txt) on the book's CD.

Minimum System Requirements

To complete the exercises in this book, you will need:

- Computer/Processor

  Computer with a 500-megahertz (MHz) or higher processor
- Operating System

  Microsoft Windows XP with Service Pack (SP) 2, Windows Server 2003 SP 1, or later operating system
- Memory

  256 megabytes (MB) of RAM or higher

- Hard Disk

    1.5 gigabyte (GB); Hard disk space requirements vary depending on configuration; custom installation choices may require more or less hard disk space; 5 MB of hard disk space is required for installing the practice files

- Drive

    CD-ROM or DVD drive

- Display

    1024 x 768 or higher-resolution monitor

- Peripherals

    Microsoft Mouse, Microsoft IntelliMouse, or compatible pointing device

- Programs

    Microsoft Office Visio Standard 2007, Visio Professional 2007, and Microsoft Office Word 2007. Microsoft Office Project and Microsoft Office Excel are recommended.

- Microsoft Internet Explorer 6.0 or later browser

- Internet access recommended

Installing the Practice Files

You must install the practice files before you can use them in the exercises in this book. Follow these steps to prepare the CD's files for your use:

1. Insert the CD into the CD drive of your computer.

    A menu screen appears.

    > **Important** If the menu screen does not appear, start Windows Explorer. In the left pane, locate the icon for your CD and click this icon. In the right pane, double-click the StartCD file.

2. Click **Install Practice Files**.

3. Click **Next** on the first screen, and then click **Yes** to accept the license agreement on the next screen.

4. If you want to install the practice files to a location other than the default folder (Documents\Microsoft Press\Visio 2007 SBS), click the **Browse** button, select the new drive and path, and then click **OK**.

> **Important** If you install the practice files to a location other than the default folder, go to that location when an exercise in this book instructs you to open a practice file instead of the default location. Also, you might need to reestablish the data link between data sources and practice files used in Chapter 9, "Visualizing Data in Diagrams," and Chapter 10, "Analyzing Business Data in PivotDiagrams." (Both of these chapters are included on the CD that accompanies the book.) For more information about reestablishing the link between a Visio diagram and data source, see either of those chapters.

5. Click **Next** on the **Choose Destination Location** screen, click **Next** on the **Select Features** screen, and then click **Next** on the **Start Copying Files** screen to install the selected practice files.

6. After the practice files have been installed, click **Finish**.

    Within the installation folder are subfolders for each chapter in the book.

Using the Practice Files

Each exercise in this book is preceded by a paragraph that lists the files needed for the exercise. The following table lists each chapter's practice files.

> **Important** Chapters 9 through 12 are included on the CD that accompanies this book. These fully searchable and printable PDFs cover more advanced tasks than are covered in Chapters 1 through 8 and topics specific to Microsoft Office Visio Professional 2007. See Appendix A for a complete list of the topics covered in those chapters.

Chapter	Folder	Files
Chapter 1: Getting Started with Visio 2007	01_Start	BasicSave
		GettingStarted
Chapter 2: Adding Shapes to Diagrams	02_Shapes	BlockFind
		BlockMove
		BlockPictures
		BlockText
		Logo
Chapter 3: Formatting Shapes and Diagrams	03_Format	FormatDecorate
		FormatShapes
		FormatTheme
Chapter 4: Connecting Shapes	04_Connect	ConnectLayout
		ConnectModify

Chapter	Folder	Files
Chapter 5: Creating Project Schedules	05_Schedules	NewGantt Timeline TimelineData
Chapter 6: Creating Organization Charts	06_OrgCharts	OrgChart OrgChartLayout Employees
Chapter 7: Laying Out Office Spaces	07_OfficeLayouts	OfficeFurnished OfficeWalls
Chapter 8: Creating Network Diagrams	08_Networks	NetworkReport NetworkStore
Chapter 9: Visualizing Data in Diagrams	09_Data	AppPayWorkflow AppPayWorkflow_Refresh DataGraphics LinkToDiagram LinkToShapes RefreshData
Chapter 10: Analyzing Business Data in PivotDiagrams	10_PivotDiagrams	CustomizePD SalesPipeline TrackData TreeStructure
Chapter 11: Using Visio Diagrams with the Microsoft Office System	11_OfficeSystem	PlanPhase Proposal
Chapter 12: Creating Shapes, Stencils, and Templates	12_Create	CreateStencil Garden Perennials Garden Plan GroupShapes ModifyShapes Perennials

Uninstalling the Practice Files

After you finish the exercises in this book, you can uninstall the practice files to free up hard disk space.

1. On the Windows taskbar, click the **Start** button, and then click **Control Panel**.
2. In Control Panel, click **Add or Remove Programs**.

3. In the list of installed programs, click **Microsoft Office Visio 2007 Step by Step**, and then click the **Remove** button.

   The Uninstall dialog box appears.

4. In the **Uninstall** dialog box, click **OK**.

5. After the files are uninstalled, click **Finish**, and then close the Add or Remove Programs window and Control Panel.

> **Important** If you need additional help installing or uninstalling the practice files, please see the Getting Help section earlier in this book. Microsoft product support does not provide support for this book or CD.

Quick Reference

1   Getting Started with Visio 2007

To start a new diagram using a template

1. On the **File** menu, point to **New**, and then click **Getting Started**.
2. In the **Template Categories** list, click a category, and then in the **Template** area, double-click the template you want to open.

To show the shapes on a stencil in the Shapes window

- Click the stencil's title bar.

To add a shape from a stencil to the drawing page

- Drag the shape from the stencil to the drawing page.

To see a shape's shortcut menu

- Right-click the shape.

To zoom in or out of the drawing page

- On the Standard toolbar, click the **Zoom** down arrow, and then click a zoom percentage.

To zoom out of the drawing page using a keyboard shortcut

- Hold down Shift + Ctrl while you right-click once.

To zoom in to the drawing page using a keyboard shortcut

- Hold down Shift + Ctrl while you left-click once.

To zoom in to a selected area on the drawing page using a keyboard shortcut

- Hold down Shift + Ctrl while you drag a selection net around the area you want to zoom in to.

To pan the drawing page

- Hold down Shift + Ctrl while you drag with the right mouse button.

To zoom out of the drawing page to view the whole page using a keyboard shortcut

● Press `Ctrl`+`W`.

To insert a page in a drawing file

1. Right-click a page tab at the bottom of the drawing window, and then click **Insert Page** on the shortcut menu.

2. In the **Page Setup** dialog box, click **OK**.

To change the size of a drawing page

● On the **File** menu, click **Page Setup**.

To view a page in a drawing file

● Click a page tab at the bottom of the drawing window.

To rename a page

1. Double-click the page tab for the page you want to rename. Or, right-click the page tab and then click **Rename Page**.

2. Type the new page name to replace the old one.

To open or close the task pane

● On the **View** menu, click **Task Pane**.

To see a specific task pane

● Click the task pane title bar, and then click the name of the task pane.

To preview a drawing before you print it

● On the **File** menu, click **Print Preview**.

To close the Print Preview window

● On the Print Preview toolbar, click **Close**.

To print a drawing from the Print Preview window

● On the Print Preview toolbar, click **Print**.

To print the current drawing page

● On the Standard toolbar, click the **Print Page** button.

To print a diagram

1. On the **File** menu, click **Print**.

2. Choose the options you want, and then click **OK**.

To change the drawing page size to match the printer's settings

1. On the **File** menu, click **Page Setup**.

2. Click the **Page Size** tab, select the **Same as printer paper size** option, and then click **OK**.

To change the printed page settings to match your diagram

1. On the **File** menu, click **Page Setup**.

2. Click the **Print Setup** tab, and then in the **Printer paper** area, select the option that matches the preview of the drawing page shown in the preview area of the dialog box, and then click **OK**.

To save a drawing file for the first time

1. On the Standard toolbar, click the **Save** button. Or, on the **File** menu, click **Save**.

2. In the **File name** box, type a name for the drawing file.

3. Click **Save**.

To enter properties about a drawing file

1. On the **File** menu, click **Properties**.

2. Enter the information you want, and then click **OK**.

To save a drawing as an image you can use on the Web

1. On the Standard toolbar, click the **Save** button.

2. In the **Save As** dialog box, in the **Save as type** box, scroll the file list to see the available file formats, such as **JPEG File Interchange Format (*.jpg)**.

To open a Visio drawing file

● On the **File** menu, click **Open**, find the diagram you want to open, and then click **OK**.

To hide or show the rulers

● On the **View** menu, click **Rulers**.

To hide or show the grid on the drawing page

● On the **View** menu, click **Grid**.

To display the Pan & Zoom window

- On the **View** menu, click **Pan & Zoom Window**.

To zoom in on a portion of the drawing page using the Pan & Zoom window

- Drag to draw a selection rectangle around

To turn autohide on or off for a window

- On the title bar of the window, click the **AutoHide** button, and then move the pointer away from the window.

To show a window that's been automatically hidden

- Point to the window's title bar.

To open a stencil

- On the Standard toolbar, click the **Shapes** button, point to a category, and then click the stencil you want to open.

To see a stencil's menu

- On the stencil title bar, click the stencil icon in the upper left corner.

To change how shapes appear on a stencil

1. On the stencil title bar, click the stencil icon in the upper left corner.
2. Point to **View**, and then click **Icons and Names**, **Names Under Icons**, **Icons Only**, **Names Only**, or **Icons and Details**.

To close a stencil

- On the stencil title bar, click the stencil icon in the upper left corner, and then click **Close**.

To customize various aspects of the Visio environment

- On the **Tools** menu, click **Options**.

To see sample diagrams for several diagram types in Visio Professional 2007

1. On the **File** menu, point to **New**, and then click **Getting Started**.
2. In the **Template Categories** list, click **Samples**.

To find answers to your questions by using keywords

1. Type a keyword in the "Type a question for help" box on the Visio menu bar, and then press the ⌷Enter⌷ key.
2. In the list of topics that appears, click a topic.

To browse the Visio Help topics

- On the **Help** menu, click **Microsoft Office Visio Help** to show the Visio Help window.

To find information on each option in a dialog box

- In a dialog box, click the **Help** button in the lower-left corner of the dialog box.

To find information on Microsoft Office Online

- On the **Help** menu, click **Microsoft Office Online**.

2 Adding Shapes to Diagrams

To select a shape

- Click the shape.

To deselect a shape

- Click a blank area of the drawing page or pasteboard, or press the Esc key.

To determine what a control handle does

- Pause the pointer over the control handle until its ScreenTip appears.

To add text to a shape

- Select the shape, and then type.

To correct a misspelled word

- Right-click the word, and then click the correct spelling on the shortcut menu.

To exit the text mode

- Click a blank area of the drawing page or pasteboard, or press the Esc key.

To modify existing text

- On the Standard toolbar, click the **Text Tool** button, click the text block you want to modify, and then select only the text you want to modify.

To change the size of all the text in a shape or text-only shape

1. Select the shape or text-only shape.
2. On the Formatting toolbar, click the **Font Size** down arrow, and then click a font size.

To add a text-only shape to the drawing page

● On the Standard toolbar, click the **Text Tool** button, click in the location on the drawing page where you want the text, and then type.

To save changes to a drawing file

● On the Standard toolbar, click the **Save** button.

To resize a shape

● Select a shape, and then drag one of its selection handles.

To move a shape

● Drag the shape.

To select more than one shape at once

● Hold down the Shift key while you click the shapes you want to select.

To move multiple shapes at one time

● Select the shapes you want to move, and then drag them to the new location.

To constrain the direction of shape movement horizontally or vertically

● Hold down the Shift key while you drag one or more shapes.

To nudge a shape

● Select a shape, and then use the arrows on the keyboard to move the shape horizontally or vertically.

To rotate a shape

● Select the shape, and then drag its rotation handle in either direction.

To copy a shape and position the copy in one action

1. Hold down the Ctrl key while you drag a shape.
2. Release the mouse button, and then release the Ctrl key.

To flip a shape horizontally or vertically

● On the **Shape** menu, point to **Rotate or Flip**, and then click **Flip Horizontal** or **Flip Vertical**.

To subselect a shape in a group

● Select the group, and then click the shape within the group.

To add text to a shape in a group

- Select the group, click the shape within the group, and then type.

To change the color of a shape in a group

1. Select the group, and then click the shape within the group.
2. On the Formatting toolbar, click the **Fill Color** down arrow, and then click a color.

To find a shape for a diagram by using a keyword and then add it to the drawing page

1. In the Shapes window, in the **Search For Shapes** box, type the keyword, and then click the arrow to the right of the **Search For Shapes** box.
2. From the new stencil that appears in the Shapes window, drag the shape onto the drawing page.

To insert a picture created in a different program into a diagram

1. On the **Insert** menu, point to **Picture**, and then click **From File**.
2. Find the picture you want to insert, and then click **Insert**.

To change a picture's properties

- On the Picture toolbar, click the button for the property you want to change.

To insert clip art into a diagram

1. On the **View** menu, click **Task Pane**.
2. Click the down arrow on the task pane title bar, and then click **Clip Art**.
3. In the **Search for** box, type a keyword, and then click the **Go** button to the right of the **Search for** box.
4. From the **Search Results** task pane, drag the clip art onto the drawing page.

3   Formatting Shapes and Diagrams

To change a shape's fill color

1. Select the shape.
2. On the Formatting toolbar, click the **Fill Color** down arrow.
3. Click a color, and then click **OK**.

To change a shape's thickness

1. Select the shape.
2. On the Formatting toolbar, click the **Line Weight** down arrow.
3. Click a weight, and then click **OK**.

To copy one shape's formatting to another shape

1. Select the shape that has the formatting you want to copy.
2. On the Standard toolbar, click the **Format Painter** button.
3. Click the shape to which you want to copy the formatting.

To copy one shape's formatting to multiple shapes

1. Select the shape that has the formatting you want to copy.
2. On the Standard toolbar, double-click the **Format Painter** button.
3. Click each shape—one at a time—to which you want to copy the formatting.
4. When you are finished, press the Esc key.

To select multiple shapes that are close together

● With the Pointer Tool, drag a selection net around the shapes you want to select.

To change a shape's text color

1. Select the shape.
2. On the Formatting toolbar, click the **Text Color** down arrow.
3. Click a color, and then click **OK**.

To add a border or title to a diagram

● From the Borders and Titles stencil, drag a border or title shape onto the drawing page.

To add a background to a diagram

● From the Backgrounds stencil, drag a background shape onto the drawing page.

To show the Theme – Colors task pane

● On the **Format** menu, click **Theme**.

To allow or forbid themes for a shape

● Right-click a shape, point to **Format**, and then click **Allow Themes** to check or uncheck the option.

To apply a color theme to a drawing

- In the **Theme – Colors** task pane, click a color theme.

To show the Theme – Effects task pane

- Click the task pane's title bar, and then click **Theme – Effects**.

To apply an effect theme to a drawing

- In the **Theme – Effects** task pane, click an effect theme.

To apply a color or effect theme to all the pages in a drawing file

- Right-click a theme, and then on the shortcut menu that appears, click Apply To All Pages.

To create a new effect theme

- At the bottom of the **Theme – Effects** task pane, click **New Theme Effects**.

To create a new color theme

- At the bottom of the **Theme – Colors** task pane, click **New Theme Colors**.

4   Connecting Shapes

To AutoConnect shapes by dragging a shape onto the drawing page

- Drag a shape onto another shape on the drawing page, and when blue arrows appear around the shape on the drawing page, position the shape over one of the arrows.

To AutoConnect shapes by clicking a shape on a stencil

1. Click a shape on a stencil, and then position the pointer over a shape on the drawing page.
2. When blue arrows appear around the shape on the drawing page, click one of them.

To AutoConnect neighboring shapes on the drawing page

1. Pause the pointer over a shape on the drawing page, and when blue arrows appear around the shape, pause the pointer over the blue arrow closest to the neighboring shape to which you want to connect.
2. When the blue arrow turns dark blue, a red box appears around the neighboring shape to which you can connect, and a Connect to Neighboring Shape ScreenTip appears, click the blue arrow to connect the two shapes.

To connect shapes as you drag them onto the drawing page using the Connector tool

- Click the Connector tool, and then drag shapes onto the drawing page. Each new shape is connected to the selected shape on the drawing page.

To connect shapes that are already on the drawing page using the Connector tool

- Position the pointer over a shape on the drawing page, and then drag to another shape to draw a connector between the two shapes. Or, position the pointer over a shape's connection point, and then drag to another shape's connection point to draw a connector between two shapes.

To connect shapes that are already on the drawing page using the Connect Shapes command

1. Hold down the [Shift] key, select all the shapes you want to connect, in the order you want to connect them.
2. On the **Shape** menu, click **Connect Shapes**.

To connect shapes that are already on the drawing page using a shape from a stencil

- Drag a connector from a stencil on to the drawing page, position one endpoint on a connection point on one shape, and then position the other endpoint on the connection point on the other shape.

To number the shapes in a flowchart

- On the **Tools** menu, point to **Add-Ons**, point to **Visio Extras**, and then click **Number Shapes**.

To add text to a connector

- Select the connector, and then type.

To insert a shape between two shapes that are already connected in a flowchart

- Drag the new shape between the two shapes that are already connected.

To delete all the text from a connector

- Select the connector, press [F2] to open the text block, and then press [Del] to delete the text.

To delete a connector

- Select the connector, and then press [Del].

To create a point-to-point connection

- With the Connector Tool, point to a connection point on the first shape, and then when a red border appears around the connection point, drag to a connection point on the second shape.

To move a segment of a connector

- Position the pointer over a midpoint on a segment of a connector, and then drag the midpoint.

To change the layout of a flowchart

1. On the **Shape** menu, click **Configure Layout**.
2. In the **Configure Layout** dialog box, in the **Placement** area, click an option in the **Style** list.
3. Click an option in the **Direction** list.
4. Click **OK**.

To center a drawing on the page

- On the **Shape** menu, click **Center Drawing**.

To distribute shapes evenly

1. Select three or more shapes.
2. On the **Shape** menu, click **Distribute Shapes**.
3. In the **Distribute Shapes** dialog box, click the option you want.
4. Click **OK**.

To align shapes

1. Select two or more shapes, making sure the first shape you select is the one you want the others to align with.
2. On the **Shape** menu, click **Align Shapes**.
3. In the **Align Shapes** dialog box, click the option you want.
4. Click **OK**.

To display the Action toolbar

- Right-click the toolbar area, and then click **Action** on the shortcut menu.

5   Creating Project Schedules

To create a timeline

1. On the **File** menu, point to **New**, point to **Schedule**, and then click **Timeline**.
2. Drag a timeline shape from the **Timeline Shapes** stencil onto the drawing page.
3. In the **Configure Timeline** dialog box, set the date range, scale, and format, and then click **OK**.
4. From the **Timeline Shapes** stencil, drag milestone and interval shapes onto the timeline.

To add an arrowhead to the right end of the timeline

● Right-click the timeline, and then click **Show Finish Arrowhead**.

To add interval markers to a timeline

1. From the **Timeline Shapes** stencil, drag an interval shape onto the timeline.
2. In the **Configure Interval** dialog box, choose the interval start date, finish date, and date format, type the interval description, and then click **OK**.

To add milestones to a timeline

1. From the **Timeline Shapes** stencil, drag a milestone shape onto the timeline.
2. In the **Configure Milestone** dialog box, enter the milestone date and description, select a date format, and then click **OK**.

To reconfigure the milestone

● Right-click the milestone, and then click **Configure Milestone**.

To change the milestone type

1. Right-click the milestone, and then click **Set Milestone Type**.
2. In the **Milestone Shape** list, click an option, and then click **OK**.

To quickly modify the milestone description

● Select the shape, press the F2 key to open the shape's text block, and type a new description.

To add an expanded timeline to the drawing page

1. From the **Timeline Shapes** stencil, drag the **Expanded timeline** shape onto the drawing page.

2. In the **Configure Timeline** dialog box, set the date range, scale, and format, and then click **OK**.

To show the percentage complete for an interval marker

1. Right-click the interval marker, and click **Set Percent Complete** on the shortcut menu.

2. In the **Percent Complete** box, type the percentage (without the percentage symbol), and then click **OK**.

3. Right-click the interval marker again, and click **Show Percent Complete** on the shortcut menu.

To export a timeline

1. Click the border of the timeline you want to export to select it.

2. On the **Timeline** menu, click **Export Timeline Data**.

3. Follow the instructions on the wizard pages to export the timeline.

To import timeline data to create a Gantt chart

1. On the **File** menu, point to **New**, point to **Schedule**, and then click **Gantt Chart**.

2. In the **Gantt Chart Options** dialog box, click **Cancel**.

3. On the **Gantt Chart** menu, click **Import**.

4. Follow the instructions on the wizard pages to import the timeline data and create the Gantt chart.

To create a Gantt chart

1. On the **File** menu, point to **New**, point to **Schedule**, and then click **Gantt Chart**.

2. On the **Date** tab, type a number in the **Number of tasks** box.

3. Choose options for **Time units**, **Duration options**, and **Timescale range**, and then click **OK**.

4. Enter task names, start dates, finish dates, and durations in the chart.

5. Add tasks and milestones, and then link tasks.

To create task dependencies

1. Select two or more tasks in the order of their dependency.

2. On the **Gantt Chart** menu, click **Link Tasks**.

To add a column for resource names to a Gantt chart

1. Right-click a column in the Gantt chart, and then click **Insert Column**.
2. In the **Column Type** list, click **Resource Names**.
3. Click **OK**.

To add a new task to a Gantt chart

● Right-click a cell in the row below the task you want to insert, and then click **New Task**.

To modify duration information in a Gantt chart

1. Click the cell that contains the duration you want to change.
2. Type the new duration using the following abbreviations: m for minutes, h for hours, d for days, and w for weeks.

To transform a task into a milestone

● Select the **Duration** cell for the task, and then type 0.

To change the milestone type for all the milestones in the Gantt chart

1. On the **Gantt Chart** menu, click **Options**.
2. On the **Format** tab, click a milestone in the **Shape** box, and then click **OK**.

6   Creating Organization Charts

To generate an organization chart from data

1. On the **File** menu, point to **New**, point to **Business**, and then click **Organization Chart Wizard**.
2. Follow the instructions on the wizard pages to import the organization data and create an organization chart from the data.

To create an organization chart

1. On the **File** menu, point to **New**, point to **Business**, and then click **Organization Chart**.
2. From the **Organization Chart Shapes** stencil, drag the **Executive** shape onto the drawing page, and then type the name and title of the executive in the shape.
3. From the **Organization Chart Shapes** stencil, drag a **Manager** shape directly onto the **Executive** shape, and then type the name and title of the manager in the shape. Repeat this step until you've added all the managers.

4. From the **Organization Chart Shapes** stencil, drag a **Position** shape onto a manager shape, and then type the name and title of the employee in the shape. Repeat this step until you've added all the employees.

To add shapes and create the hierarchy for an organization chart

1. From the **Organization Chart Shapes** stencil, drag a shape onto another shape on the drawing page, and then type the name and title of the employee.

2. Repeat the previous step until you've added all the employees you want.

To enter names and titles in organization chart shapes

1. Select an organization chart shape.

2. Type the person's name, press the Enter key, and then type the person's title.

3. Press the Esc key or click outside the shape.

To open the Shape Data window

● On the **View** menu, click **Shape Data Window**.

To see the shape data for a shape in the Shape Data window

1. On the **View** menu, click **Shape Data Window** to open it.

2. Select a shape.

To change a the shape data for a shape or add new data using the Shape Data window

1. On the **View** menu, click **Shape Data Window** to open it.

2. Select a shape.

3. In the Shape Data window, click the box for the shape data you want to change, and then type to replace or add new data.

4. Press the Enter key.

To change the information shown in organization chart shapes

1. On the **Organization Chart** menu, click **Options**.

2. Click the **Fields** tab.

3. Choose the options you want to display in the various text blocks in organization chart shapes, and then click **OK**.

To format the information shown in organization chart shapes

1. On the **Organization Chart** menu, click **Options**.

2. Click the **Text** tab.

3. Choose the text formatting options for the various text fields in organization chart shapes, and then click **OK**.

To change the layout of organization chart shapes

1. Select a top-level shape, such as a manager.

2. On the **Organization Chart** toolbar, click a layout option.

To move a department to a new drawing page and keep it synchronized with the original page

1. Right-click a manager shape, and then click **Create Synchronized Copy** on the shortcut menu.

2. In the **Create Synchronized Copy** dialog box, choose the page you want to move the shapes to, and then click **OK**.

To add a hyperlink from a shape to another page in the same drawing file

1. Select the shape, and then on the **Insert** menu, click **Hyperlinks**.

2. Click **Browse** next to the **Sub-address** box.

3. In the **Page** list, click a page, and then click **OK**.

4. In the **Description** box, type a name for the hyperlink, and then click **OK**.

To use a hyperlink to jump from a shape to another drawing page in the same drawing file

- Right-click the shape that includes the hyperlink, and then click the page name on the shape's shortcut menu.

7　Laying Out Office Spaces

To create an office layout

1. On the **File** menu, point to **New**, point to **Maps and Floor Plans**, and then click **Office Layout**.

2. From the **Walls, Doors and Windows** stencil, drag room or wall shapes onto the drawing page to create the office structure.

3. From the **Walls, Doors and Windows** stencil, drag door and window shapes onto wall shapes on the drawing page.

4. Add furniture and office equipment by dragging shapes from the stencils onto the drawing page.

To change the drawing scale

1. On the **File** menu, click **Page Setup**.

2. On the **Drawing Scale** tab, click options in the **Pre-defined scale** lists, and then click **OK**.

To create walls from Space shapes

1. From the **Walls, Doors and Windows** stencil, drag **Space** shapes onto the drawing page.

2. With the **Space** shapes selected, on the **Plan** menu, click **Convert to Walls**.

3. Select the options you want, and then click **OK**.

To add a door to an office layout

● From the **Walls, Doors and Windows** stencil, drag a **Door** shape onto a wall shape on the drawing page.

To change the size of a door

1. Right-click the door shape, and then click **Properties**.

2. In the **Door Width** list, click a size, and then click **OK**.

To reverse the direction in which a door opens

● Right-click the door shape, and then click **Reverse In/Out Opening**.

To change the direction of the door swing

● Right-click the door shape, and then click **Reverse Left/Right Opening**.

To add a window to an office layout

● From the **Walls, Doors and Windows** stencil, drag a **Window** shape onto a wall shape on the drawing page.

To determine which layers a shape is assigned to

● Select the shape, and then on the **Format** menu, click **Layer**.

To lock the shapes on a layer

1. On the **View** menu, click **Layer Properties**.

2. Click the box in the **Lock** column for the layers you want to lock, and then click **OK**.

To hide the shapes on a layer

1. On the **View** menu, click **Layer Properties**.
2. Click the box in the **Visible** column for the layers you want to hide, and then click **OK**.

To change the color of shapes on a layer

1. On the **View** menu, click **Layer Properties**.
2. Click the box in the **Color** column for a layer.
3. In the **Layer Color** list, click a color, and then click **OK**.

To create a new layer

1. On the **Format** menu, click **Layer**.
2. In the **Layer** dialog box, click **New**.
3. In the **New Layer** dialog box, type the name of the new layer, and then click **OK**.

8   Creating Network Diagrams

To create a network diagram

1. On the **File** menu, point to **New**, point to **Network**, and then click **Basic Network Diagram**.
2. From the **Network and Peripherals** stencil, drag a **Ring network** or **Ethernet** shape onto the drawing page.
3. Drag computer, printer, and other shapes from the stencils onto the drawing page.
4. Drag the control handles on the **Ring network** or **Ethernet** shape to the network equipment shapes to connect them.

To connect network equipment to an Ethernet shape

- Drag a control handle from the **Ethernet** shape to a network equipment shape.

To display the document stencil

- On the Standard toolbar, click the **Shapes** button, and then click **Show Document Stencil**.

To edit a master shape on the document stencil

- In the **Document Stencil**, right-click the master shape, point to **Edit Master**, and then click **Edit Master Shape**.

To create a shape data field for a shape on the document stencil

1. On the **View** menu, click **Shape Data Window**.
2. On the **File** menu, point to **Shapes**, and then click **Show Document Stencil**.
3. Double-click the shape on the document stencil to open the shape editing window.
4. Select the shape in the shape editing window.
5. Right-click the **Shape Data** window, and then click **Define Shape Data**.
6. Click **New**, type a name in the **Label** box, and then click **OK**.
7. In the **Define Shape Data** dialog box, click **OK**.
8. In the shape editing window, click the **Close Window** button. When Visio prompts you to update all instances, click **Yes**.

To create a shape data field for a shape

1. On the **View** menu, click **Shape Data Window**.
2. Select the shape.
3. Right-click the **Shape Data** window, and then click **Define Shape Data**.
4. Click **New**, type a name in the **Label** box, and then click **OK**.
5. In the **Define Shape Data** dialog box, click **OK**.

To run a report

1. On the **Data** menu, click **Reports**.
2. In the **Report** list, click a report, and then click **Run**.
3. Select the format you want, and then click **OK**.

To create a new report definition

1. On the **Data** menu, click **Reports**.
2. Click **New**.
3. Follow the instructions on the wizard pages to create the report definition.
4. In the **Reports** dialog box, click **OK**.

Chapter at a Glance

Get Visio and diagram help

Work within the Visio environment

Start diagrams by using templates

Customize the Visio environment

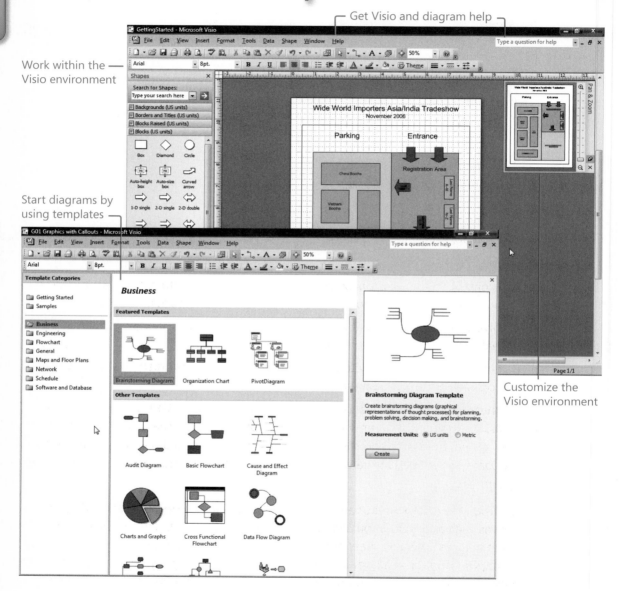

1 Getting Started with Visio 2007

In this chapter, you will learn how to:

- ✔ Start diagrams by using templates.
- ✔ Work within the Visio environment.
- ✔ Customize the Visio environment.
- ✔ Get Visio and diagram help.

Have you ever tried to do any of the following tasks only to find yourself frustrated with the outcome?

- Explain a new team organization or complex inter-departmental process in an e-mail message or a memo only to find that no one quite understood it.

- Give a presentation about critical project milestones, and then watch everyone walk away with a puzzled expression.

- Summarize data and key trends in a spreadsheet for coworkers who just stare at you with blank looks on their faces.

All of these situations are ideal opportunities to use Microsoft Office Visio 2007—the business drawing and diagramming program that helps you visually communicate processes, systems, projects, and resources. *Visually* is the key word. When you can't effectively convey your message verbally—with text, tables, or numbers alone—you need a diagram.

With Visio, you can *show* your audience what you mean by using easy-to-understand diagrams such as organization charts, flowcharts, and project timelines. Whether you need to analyze a new business process, visualize an office space, explore business data, track important data trends, or simply create a map to a company picnic, you can create professional-looking diagrams quickly and easily using Visio—and no artistic talent is required.

1

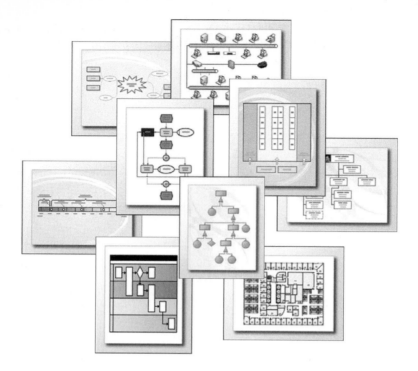

With advanced data connectivity and visualization functionality in Visio Professional 2007, you can even take your diagrams to another level: integrate them with data to track key trends, identify issues, and flag exceptions—all in one diagram that's easy to refresh and share with others across the entire organization. Explore data in hierarchical form using the new PivotDiagram template, identify server issues through data-connected network diagrams, or track resource data in project timelines. Visualize any process, system, project, and resource—in addition to the data behind it—by connecting your diagrams to data and dynamically updating them as the data changes.

This book helps you learn how to use Visio so that you can communicate visually with Visio diagrams. This chapter will first introduce you to Visio drawing and diagram types, and then show you how to start a Visio diagram by using a template. You will learn how to work within and customize the Visio drawing environment. Last, you will practice using Visio online Help so that you can easily find the answers to questions that might arise while you create your Visio diagrams.

See also Do you need a quick refresher on the topics in this chapter? See the Quick Reference entries on pages xxv–xliii.

> **Important** Before you can use the practice files in this chapter, you need to install them from the book's companion CD to their default location. See "Using the Book's CD-ROM" on page xix for more information.

Starting Diagrams by Using Templates

Regardless of your drawing abilities, Visio makes it easy for you to create all types of drawings and diagrams. *Shapes*—pre-drawn symbols included with Visio—are the key to quickly creating effective diagrams. For example, in an organization chart, you might use a Manager shape (a box with a name and job title) to represent a manager in a department, whereas in a flowchart, you might use a Decision shape (a diamond with a label) to indicate a decision someone must make in a process. By simply dragging shapes onto the drawing page, you can assemble a complete diagram.

The best way to start a diagram is by using a *template*—a file that includes all of the tools, formatting, settings, and shapes you need to assemble a particular type of drawing or diagram. For example, if you want to create a flowchart, use the Basic Flowchart template. It includes shapes that represent data, processes, decisions, and so on.

Templates also set up the drawing page and formatting for you. The Basic Flowchart template, for instance, sets up a letter-sized page suitable for printing on a desktop printer, and the shapes are black and white—a style that is often used in flowcharts. In addition, some templates include special-purpose commands or toolbars. For example, the Organization Chart template includes the Organization Chart toolbar, which makes it easy to rearrange employee shapes in a chart that you created with that template. The Brainstorming Diagram template not only includes Brainstorming shapes, a Brainstorming menu, and a Brainstorming toolbar, but also an Outline window that tracks the shapes on the drawing page in outline form.

Brainstorming shapes — Brainstorming menu

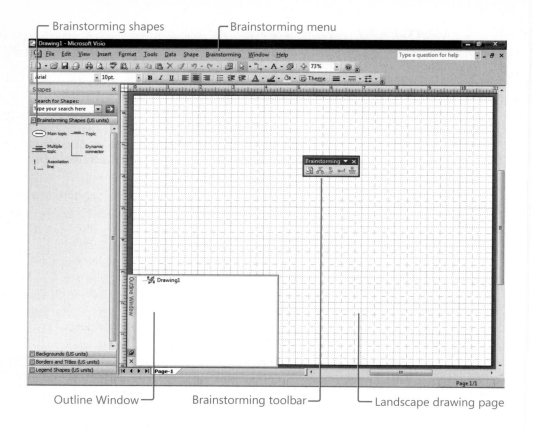

Outline Window — Brainstorming toolbar — Landscape drawing page

Visio makes it easy for you to find the appropriate template by organizing them into simple categories of related diagram types, as shown in the following table. Visio Professional 2007 includes all of the templates available in Visio Standard 2007, in addition to advanced features and special-purpose templates that you can use to create PivotDiagrams, detailed network diagrams, database and software models, engineering schematics, process engineering diagrams, Web diagrams, and extensive building plans.

The following table presents all of the categories and templates available in Visio Professional 2007.

Template Category	Purpose
Business	Diagram business processes such as basic flowcharts, cross-functional flowcharts, data flow diagrams, Information Technology Infrastructure Library (ITIL) diagrams, value stream maps, and workflow diagrams. Show hierarchical structures in organizations. Design charts, graphs, and diagrams for presentations, reports, and marketing documentation. Create brainstorming diagrams that help you formulate plans, solve problems, and make decisions.
Engineering	Create engineering diagrams such as electrical, circuits and logic, fluid power, industrial control systems, piping and instrumentation, process flow, and systems diagrams. Create part and assembly drawings.
Flowchart	Create basic flowcharts, cross-functional flowcharts, work flow diagrams, data flow diagrams, IDEF0 diagrams, and Specification and Description Language (SDL) diagrams.
General	Create basic flowcharts and general-purpose diagrams using geometric shapes.
Maps and Floor Plans	Assemble simple 2-D (two-dimensional) or 3-D (three-dimensional) directional maps. Create home, office, building, and site plans.
Network	Create physical and logical network designs using network and computer equipment shapes, and map Web sites.
Schedule	Track project details in Program Evaluation and Review Technique (PERT) charts, Gantt charts, timelines, and calendars.
Software and Database	Model and design software, databases, and user interfaces.

> **Tip** If you don't want to start your diagrams by using a template with a blank drawing page, visit the Microsoft Office Online Web site at *www.office.microsoft.com* for Visio templates that come with shapes already placed on the drawing page.

Just as templates are organized by categories, related shapes are organized on *stencils*. For example, when you open the Basic Diagram template, all of the geometric shapes included with the template are organized on the Basic Shapes stencil. Likewise, all of the border and title shapes for basic diagrams are organized on the Borders and Titles stencil, and so on. This makes finding shapes quick and easy. After you find the shape you want, just drag it onto the drawing page and you're on your way.

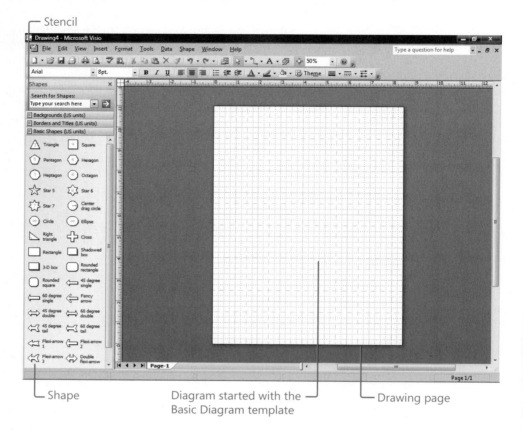

Stencil

Shape

Diagram started with the
Basic Diagram template

Drawing page

In this exercise, you start Visio, and then browse the Visio templates. You open a template, look at the shapes it includes, and then open another template to become acquainted with Visio templates and shapes.

start

1. On the taskbar, click the **Start** button, point to **All Programs**, point to **Microsoft Office**, and then click **Microsoft Office Visio 2007**.

   Visio starts and opens the Getting Started window, which includes the Template Categories, Recent Templates, and Recent Documents lists.

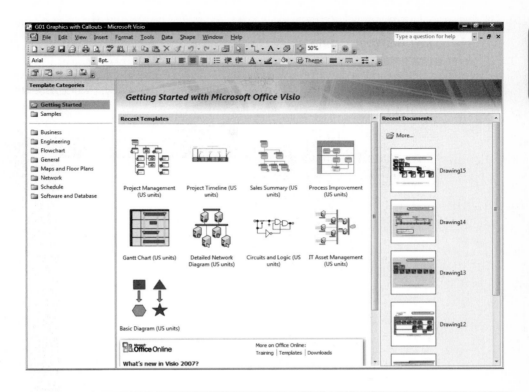

> **Tip** In the Getting Started window, you can also easily access the templates and documents you use often. However, when you start Visio for the fist time, the Recent Templates and Recent Documents lists in the Getting Started window are empty. As you use Visio, templates and documents are added to those lists. If you're using Visio Professional 2007, you can even open a variety of sample diagrams to stimulate ideas for creating your own diagrams. These sample diagrams also show you how you can integrate data with diagrams. You'll learn more about integrating data with diagrams in Chapter 9, "Visualizing Data in Diagrams."

2. On the **Template Categories** list, click **Flowchart**.

   Visio lists all of the templates included in this category and presents those that are featured—the new or popular templates. It also displays a large template preview and description for the selected template in the right area of the Getting Started window.

Tip If none of the templates are exactly what you are looking for, use a template with shapes that closely match what you need. For example, you can use the Basic Diagram template to create a diagram with a variety of geometric shapes. Or, you can use the Basic Flowchart template to diagram any basic process flow. If a template does not include all of the shapes you need, you can search for other shapes while you're creating your diagram. You'll learn more about searching for shapes in Chapter 2, "Adding Shapes to Diagrams."

3. On the **Template Categories** list, click **Cross Functional Flowchart** to display this template's preview and description in the right area of the Getting Started window.

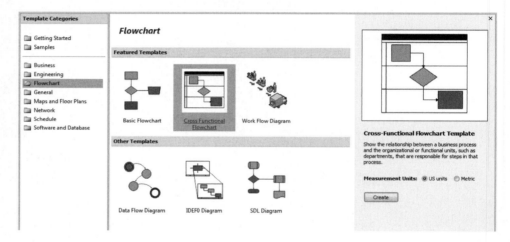

Tip If you see fewer template categories and names than are shown in the images in this book, it's probably because you're using Visio Standard 2007. This book includes images from Visio Professional 2007; however, the same drawing methods apply to both programs. To determine which Visio program you're using, on the Help menu, click About Microsoft Office Visio.

4. On the **Template Categories** list, click **General**.

Visio lists all of the templates included in this category. It also shows a template preview and description for the Basic Diagram template, which is selected by default.

5. Under **All Templates**, double-click **Basic Diagram**.

Visio opens a blank drawing page along with the Basic Shapes, Borders and Titles, and Backgrounds stencils.

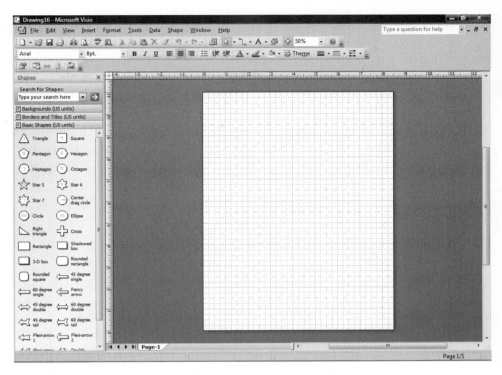

6. On the **File** menu, click **Close** to close the diagram and stencils.

New

7. On the **File** menu, point to **New**, and then click **Getting Started**.

   The Getting Started window appears.

> **Tip** For quick access to Visio templates, on the Standard toolbar, click the New down arrow, point to the template category you want, and then click the name of the template you want to open. Or, on the File menu, point to New, point to the template category you want, and then click the name of the template you want to open.

8. On the **Template Categories** list, click **General**.

9. Under **All Templates**, double-click **Block Diagram**.

   Visio opens a blank drawing page along with the Blocks, Blocks Raised, Borders and Titles, and Backgrounds stencils.

Close Window

10. In the gray area in the upper-right corner of the drawing page window, click the **Close Window** button.

    Visio closes the new diagram without saving changes, but Visio remains open.

> **Troubleshooting** The red Close button on the right side of the Visio window's title bar is directly above the Close Window button on the drawing page window. Don't confuse the two. The red Close button closes the drawing window *and* Visio. The Close Window button closes only the drawing window. In step 10, make sure you click the Close Window button so that Visio remains open.

Close

11. On the right side of the title bar of the Visio window, click the **Close** button.

Visio closes.

Working Within the Visio Environment

When you start a diagram, the Visio window opens. The Visio window contains the Visio menus and toolbars. It also contains the Shapes window, drawing page, pasteboard, and rulers in a drawing window. The stencils that contain the shapes you need are located in the Shapes window to the left of the drawing page. Visio also includes special-purpose windows, menus, and toolbars for creating particular types of diagrams.

The main elements of the Visio environment that most people typically work with are the following:

- **Shapes window** The Shapes window contains the stencils and Search For Shapes box that makes it easy for you to find any shape you need for your drawing.

- **Drawing page** The Visio *drawing page* resembles graph paper with a *grid* that helps you position shapes.

- **Rulers** The horizontal and vertical *rulers* also help you position shapes and show you the size of the drawing page.

- **Menus and toolbars** Above the drawing page are the Visio menus and the Standard and Formatting toolbars (shown by default), which contain the most commonly used tools for creating, modifying, and formatting text, shapes, and diagrams.

- **Toolbar drop-down lists** Many of the buttons on these toolbars have drop-down lists that include options or other tools you can select. To view the list for a specific button, click the down arrow on the button. If you are not familiar with a toolbar button, you can pause the pointer over it to display a *ScreenTip* that tells you which tool or command the button represents.

- **Shortcut menu** Visio also includes easy access to frequently used commands on a *shortcut menu* that appears when you right-click an item. For example, right-click the drawing page, the toolbar area, a page tab, or a shape to view its shortcut menu.

- **Page tabs** Below the drawing page, page tabs help you move between pages in multiple-page drawings, and the status bar displays information about shapes that are selected on the drawing page.

- **Task pane** To the right of the drawing page, you can display *task panes* from which you can quickly access task-specific and diagram-specific information.

- **Pasteboard** The light-blue area surrounding the drawing page is the *pasteboard*, which you can use as a temporary holding area for shapes and other drawing elements. Shapes on the pasteboard aren't printed.

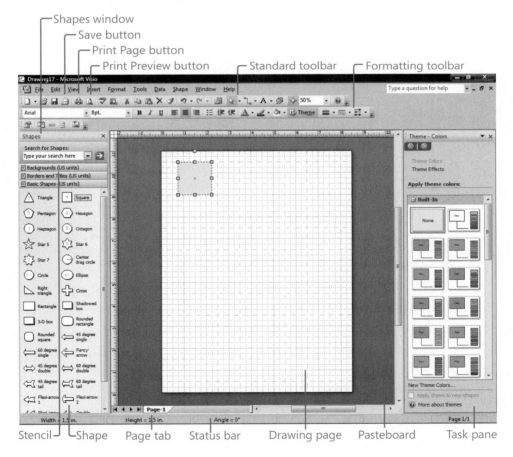

When you start a diagram, Visio displays the entire drawing page. As you add shapes to the diagram, you can *zoom* in to an area for a closer view of that area or zoom out for a broader view of the diagram. Visio includes several ways to zoom in and out, including a toolbar button and keyboard shortcuts. One method isn't necessarily better than another—you can use the one that works best for you. However, when you zoom in using keyboard shortcuts, you can draw a *selection net* around the shapes or area that you want to zoom in on or out of, which gives you greater zooming control.

You can also *pan* large diagrams, which means that you can "grab" the drawing page with the pointer and move the page to see another area of it. Zooming and panning help you move quickly around the drawing page so that you can work efficiently in the Visio environment.

When it's time to print your diagram, you can preview it first to see how it will look when you print it by using the Print Preview command on the File menu. Then, you can print the page shown in the drawing window by clicking the Print Page button on the Standard toolbar. For more printing options, such as printing all of the pages in a diagram or multiple copies of a diagram, you can use the Print command on the File menu.

Print Page
button ─┐   ┌─ Print button   Print preview ─┐

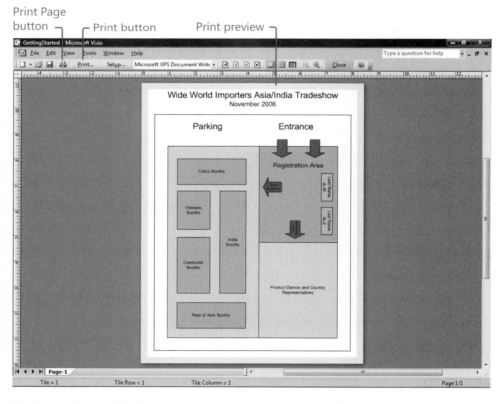

Finally, saving a Visio diagram is just as easy as saving a file in any other program. Just click the Save button on the Standard toolbar or click Save on the File menu. The first time you save a diagram, the Save As dialog box appears so that you can name the file and choose the location where you want to save it. By default, the diagram is saved as a Visio *drawing file* with a *.vsd* file extension.

In this exercise, you explore the fundamental parts of the Visio drawing window. You display stencils in the Shapes window, zoom and pan the drawing page, add a drawing page, view a task pane, and then preview, print, and save your drawing.

1. Start Visio. In the Getting Started window, on the **Template Categories** list, click **General**.

2. Under **All Templates**, double-click **Block Diagram**.

   Visio opens a blank drawing page and four stencils.

3. In the Shapes window, click the title bar of the **Blocks Raised** stencil.

   The Blocks Raised stencil is displayed on top of the other stencils, and the Blocks stencil is minimized at the bottom of the Shapes window.

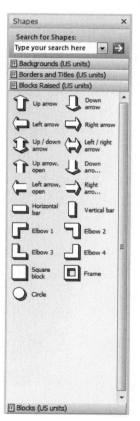

> **Troubleshooting** When you click Blocks Raised, if Visio displays a stencil menu, you clicked the green icon on the stencil's title bar by mistake. Click the stencil name directly to display the stencil. You'll learn more about the stencil menu later in this chapter and in Chapter 12, "Creating Shapes, Stencils, and Templates."

4. Click the title bar of the **Blocks** stencil to display the **Blocks** stencil.

5. Drag the scroll bar on the **Blocks** stencil down to see all of the stencil's shapes.

> **Troubleshooting** Your monitor's resolution and the size of your Visio window determine whether a scroll bar appears on the Blocks stencil. Because of these factors, your screen might not exactly match the images in this book. If you don't see a scroll bar on the stencil, all of the shapes are already visible.

6. Scroll up to the top of the **Blocks** stencil.

7. From the **Blocks** stencil, drag the **Box** shape anywhere on the drawing page. As you drag, watch the status bar at the bottom of the Visio window.

   Visio determines the shape's position on the drawing page by using the horizontal and vertical rulers and displays the position in the status bar. Also, notice that the Box shape snaps to the grid as you move it around the drawing page.

8. Release the mouse button when you've positioned the **Box** shape where you want it.

   The shape remains selected, and the status bar displays its width, height, and angle of rotation.

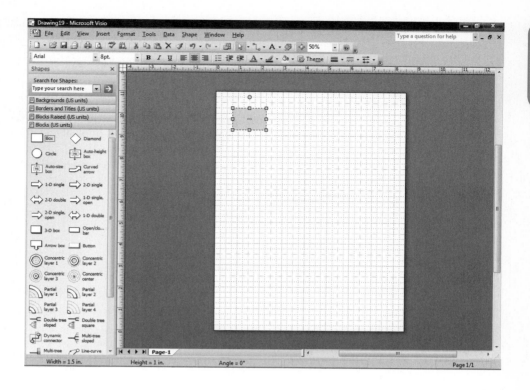

> **Tip** When you pause the pointer over some shapes on the drawing page, Visio displays blue arrows around the shape. These arrows are used to connect the shape to other shapes. You'll learn more about connecting shapes later in Chapter 4, "Connecting Shapes."

9. Right-click the **Box** shape to see its shortcut menu, which gives you quick access to frequently used commands.

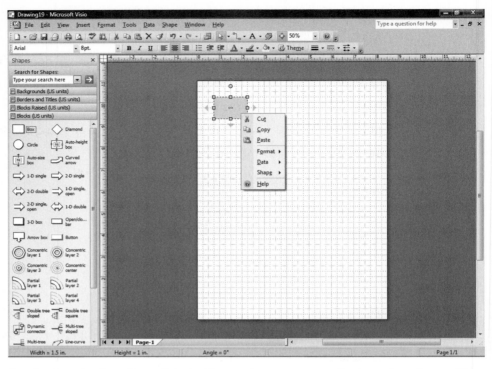

Zoom

10. On the Standard toolbar, click the **Zoom** down arrow to display a list of magnification levels, and then click **100%**.

Visio zooms in to 100 percent.

> **Tip** All Visio toolbar buttons, window buttons, shapes, and even rulers have ScreenTips that explain what you can do with them. If you don't know how to use one of these elements, just pause the pointer over it to view a ScreenTip.

11. Hold down Shift + Ctrl while you right-click once on the drawing page.

Visio zooms out, and the Zoom box displays the current zoom percentage.

12. Hold down Shift + Ctrl while you left-click once to zoom in to 100 percent again.

> **Tip** When you press Shift + Ctrl, the pointer changes to a magnifying glass icon to indicate that left-clicking will zoom in and right-clicking will zoom out.

13. Hold down Shift + Ctrl while you drag a selection net around the **Box** shape on the drawing page, and then release the mouse button.

Visio zooms in to the area you selected.

14. Press Ctrl+W to zoom out to the whole-page view.

15. Hold down Shift+Ctrl while you drag up or down with the right mouse button.

The pointer changes to a hand icon as Visio pans, or moves, the drawing page.

16. Press Ctrl+W to zoom out to the whole-page view.

17. Right-click the **Page-1** page tab at the bottom of the drawing window.

Visio displays a shortcut menu for the page tab.

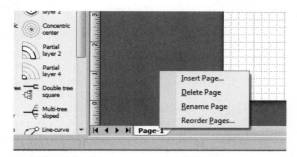

18. On the shortcut menu, click **Insert Page**.

The Page Setup dialog box appears.

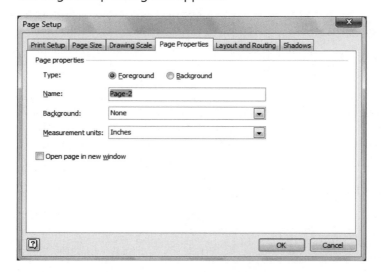

> **Tip** You can change the size of a drawing page and choose the size of your printer paper in the Page Setup dialog box. The Page Setup dialog box includes a preview area that displays the effect of various page settings. Use the preview area in the Page Setup dialog box to verify that the printer paper setting and drawing page match in size and orientation. You can also open the Page Setup dialog box by clicking Page Setup on the File menu.

19. In the **Page Setup** dialog box, click **OK** to add a new drawing page to the diagram that uses the default name, **Page-2**.

20. Click the **Page-1** page tab to go back to the first page of the diagram.

> **Tip** You can easily rename pages in your diagrams. First, double-click the page tab for the page you want to rename. Or, right-click the page tab, and then click Rename Page. Both actions select the page name. Then, simply type the new page name to replace the old one.

21. On the **View** menu, click **Task Pane** to open a task pane.

The Theme - Colors task pane appears to the right of the drawing page. You can use this task pane to change the appearance of your entire document in one click.

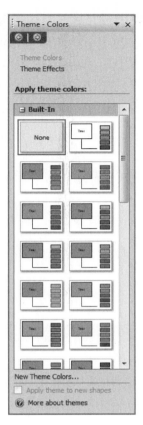

22. In the **Theme - Colors** task pane, pause the pointer over the thumbnail right below the **None** thumbnail.

A ScreenTip appears that contains the name of the theme—Office.

23. Click the **Office** theme.

The color of the box on the drawing page changes to match the new color theme. If your diagram included other shapes, their colors would also change.

24. Click the task pane title bar to see other available task panes.

The task pane currently shown is checked.

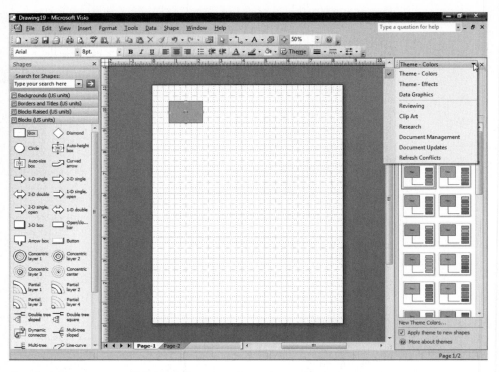

25. On the **View** menu, click **Task Pane** to close the task pane.

26. On the **File** menu, click **Print Preview**.

The Print Preview window opens, displays the Print Preview toolbar, and shows the way your drawing will print.

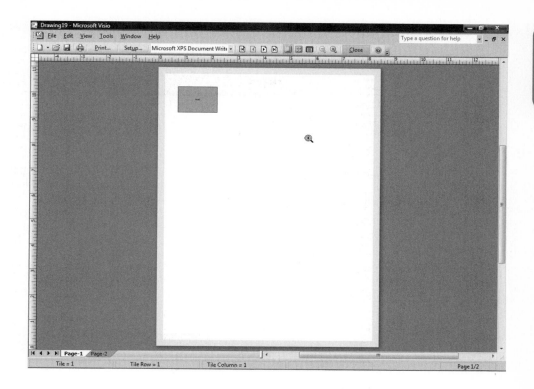

Important You can't modify any of the shapes in the drawing in the Print Preview window. If you want to reposition shapes, on the Print Preview toolbar, click Close to return to the Visio drawing window. However, you can change page settings in the Print Preview window by clicking Setup on the Print Preview toolbar.

Close

27. On the Print Preview toolbar, click **Close**.

The Print Preview window closes and Visio returns to the drawing window.

Print

Tip You can print drawings directly from the Print Preview window by clicking the Print button on the Print Preview toolbar. You can also print by clicking Print on the File menu or the Print button on the Standard toolbar. If you want to print only the page currently shown in the drawing window, you can click the Print Page button on the Standard toolbar.

---

28. On the **File** menu, click **Save**.

The Save As dialog box appears because this is the first time you've saved the drawing.

> **Tip** You can also add file properties to your drawing, such as title, author, company, and so on. On the File menu, click Properties, enter the information you want, and then click OK.

29. In the **File name** box, type BasicSave, and then click **Save**.

By default, Visio saves the drawing as a Visio drawing file with a *.vsd* file extension.

> **Tip** If you want to use a Visio diagram in another program or as an image on the Web, you can save the diagram in the appropriate file format. In the Save As dialog box, in the Save As Type box, scroll the file list to see the available file formats, such as *JPEG File Interchange Format (*.jpg)*. You can also save a Visio 2007 diagram in the Visio 2003 file format so that people with Visio 2003 can work with the diagram.

30. On the **File** menu, click **Exit**.

Visio and the BasicSave diagram closes.

Fixing Page Orientation Problems

The most common problem that people encounter when printing Visio diagrams is a drawing page that is oriented differently than the printer setting. For example, if the drawing page is wider than it is tall (*landscape orientation*), but the printer is set to print in *portrait orientation* (taller than wide), Visio displays a message box that says one or more drawing pages is oriented differently than the printer setting. To correct this problem, click the Page Setup command on the File menu, and then do one of the following:

- Change the drawing page to match the printer's settings. Click the Page Size tab, and then select the Same As Printer Paper Size option.

- Change the printer's settings to match your diagram. Click the Print Setup tab, and then in the Printer Paper area, select the option that matches the preview of the drawing page shown in the preview area of the dialog box.

Customizing the Visio Environment

Most of what you see in the Visio environment can be customized to suit the way that you like to work. For example, you can hide the grid if it makes the drawing page look too cluttered for your taste. You can also hide the rulers, as well as show or hide any toolbars.

> **Tip** To display a list of the Visio toolbars that are available for the template that you have open, right-click the toolbar area to display the toolbar shortcut menu. Then click the name of the toolbar you want to appear. A check mark next to a toolbar's name indicates that it is currently shown.

If you're working with a low-resolution monitor and want more space on the screen, you can move, resize, or close the stencils. If you don't want to have to scroll down a stencil to see all its shapes, you can make the list of shapes more compact by hiding the shape names and showing only the icons. You can also *float*, or detach, windows and stencils from the drawing window, so that you can quickly resize them as you work. After you're done working, you can *dock*, or snap, them back in to their default position.

For quick access to related commands or drawing shortcuts, you can use the tools in various windows, such as the Pan & Zoom and Size & Position windows. The Pan & Zoom window displays a miniature version of your entire diagram that you can use to quickly move to different parts of the drawing page. If you want to enter precise dimensions for the shapes in your diagrams rather than resizing shapes with the pointer, you can do that in the Size & Position window.

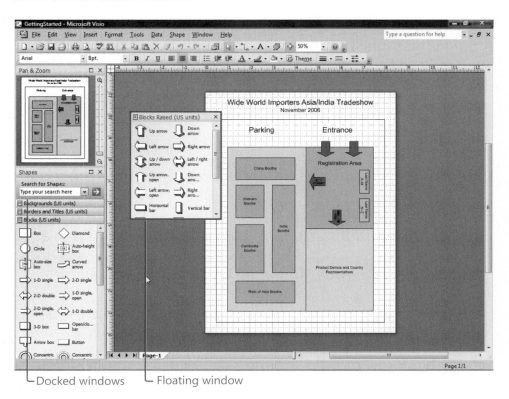

Docked windows   Floating window

Four-headed arrow

Tip By default, the Visio menu bar and toolbars are docked on the Visio window. However, you can float any toolbar or the entire menu bar, or you can dock them in a different location if it's more convenient for you. Position the pointer over the move handle on the menu bar or a toolbar, and when the pointer changes to a four-headed arrow, drag the bar to a new location. If you drag a floating menu bar or toolbar to an edge of the Visio window, Visio docks the item in that location.

In this exercise, you customize the Visio environment. You start by opening a diagram that displays the proposed layout for a tradeshow hosted by Wide World Importers, the fictitious company used throughout this book.

 OPEN the *GettingStarted* file in Documents\Microsoft Press\Visio 2007 SBS\01_Start.

Open

1. Start Visio. On the Standard toolbar, click the **Open** button to display the **Open** dialog box.

2. In the list of files and folder names, double-click the **Microsoft Press** folder, and then double-click the **Visio 2007 SBS** folder.

Troubleshooting By default, Visio opens the Documents folder in the Open dialog box. Also, by default, all of the practice files for this book are installed in the Microsoft Press\Visio 2007 SBS folder in Documents. If you don't see the Visio 2007 SBS folder, go to the Documents\Microsoft Press folder. If you installed the practice files for this book in a different location, you need to go to that location when you use practice files throughout this book.

3. Double-click the **01_Start** folder, and then double-click **GettingStarted**.

Tip If the file extensions on your computer aren't hidden, the file name you will see in the Open dialog box is *GettingStarting.vsd*. The *.vsd* file extension stands for *Visio drawing*.

Visio opens a diagram displaying the layout of a tradeshow and four stencils.

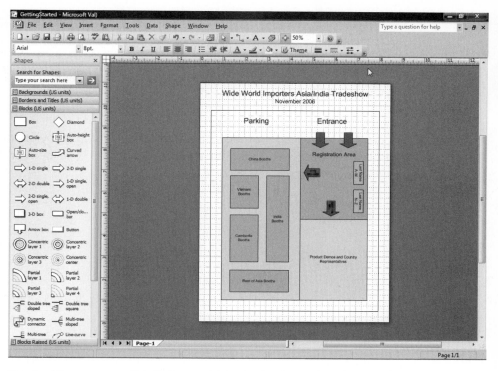

4. On the **View** menu, click **Rulers** to hide the horizontal and vertical rulers.

5. On the **View** menu, click **Grid** to hide the grid on the drawing page.

6. On the **View** menu, click **Pan & Zoom Window**.

   Visio opens the Pan & Zoom window. If you have never opened it before, it is docked in the upper-right corner of the drawing window. If you have opened this window before, the window reappears in the location where it was last displayed.

7. In the **Pan & Zoom** window, drag to draw a selection rectangle around the green area in the upper-right corner of the window.

Visio zooms in to the diagram to show the selected area, which is highlighted with a red rectangle in the Pan & Zoom window. The Zoom box on the Standard toolbar displays the new zoom level.

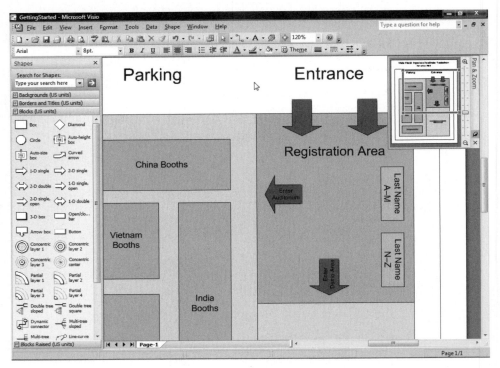

8. In the Pan & Zoom window, drag a corner of the red rectangle out to enlarge the selection area.

   Visio displays the new selected area and changes the level of zoom in the drawing window so that more of the page is visible.

9. On the title bar of the Pan & Zoom window, click the **AutoHide** button, and then move the pointer away from the window.

   Visio slides the window out of sight until only the title bar of the Pan & Zoom window is visible.

10. Point to the title bar of the Pan & Zoom window.

    Visio opens the window. As long as the pointer is over the window, it stays open.

11. Click the **AutoHide** button again.

Visio turns off AutoHide so that the Pan & Zoom window stays open.

Close

12. Click the **Close** button in the lower-right corner of the Pan & Zoom window.

Visio closes the Pan & Zoom window.

13. Press Ctrl+W to zoom out to the whole-page view.

Shapes

14. On the Standard toolbar, click the **Shapes** button.

Visio displays a menu of stencil categories.

15. Point to **Visio Extras**, and then click **Callouts**.

Visio opens the Callouts stencil, which contains annotation shapes, and displays it in the Shapes window on top of the other stencils.

16. On the **Callouts** stencil, click the green stencil icon on the title bar.

Visio displays a menu for the stencil.

17. Point to **View**, and then click **Icons Only**.

Visio displays the shape icons without their names. Notice that Visio also displays the shape icons without their names in the Blocks stencil. The View options on the View menu change the view for all of the stencils.

18. On the **Callouts** stencil, click the green stencil icon on the title bar, point to **View**, and then click **Icons and Names**.

Visio displays both the shape icons and names on all of the stencils.

19. On the **Callouts** stencil, click the green stencil icon on the title bar, and then click **Close**.

Visio closes the stencil.

20. On the **File** menu, click **Exit**.

Visio closes.

Customizing Colors and Other Options

You can customize many other aspects of the Visio environment by using the Options dialog box. For example, if you get tired of the green stencil window or the white drawing page, you can change those colors and others used by Visio. To choose different colors, on the Tools menu, click Options. In the Options dialog box, click the Advanced tab, and then click the Color Settings button. You can even create a new toolbar and add the commands that you use most often to it. On the Tools menu, click Customize to view the options for customizing toolbars.

Keep in mind that the more you customize Visio, the less your screen will match the images shown in this book.

Getting Visio and Diagram Help

Visio offers a variety of ways to get help while you're working, as shown in the following table.

Task	Action
See sample diagrams for several diagram types in Visio Professional 2007 that you can use to generate ideas for creating your own diagrams.	On the File menu, point to New, and then click Getting Started. On the Template Categories list, click Samples. Or, on the Help menu, click Sample Diagrams.
Quickly find answers to your questions by using keywords.	Type a keyword in the Type A Question For Help box on the Visio menu bar, and then press the Enter key. Visio searches through its Help topics to find those related to the keyword. If you're connected to the Internet, Visio also searches Microsoft Office Online for related topics and articles.
Browse the list of Help topics included with Visio as well as updated topics on Microsoft Office Online.	On the Help menu, click Microsoft Office Visio Help to show the Visio Help window. On the toolbar, click the Show Table Of Contents button.
	To see the most recent Visio Help topics, make sure you're connected to the Internet when you use Visio Help. If you're not connected to the Internet, Visio will use the Help topics installed with the Visio program
Find specific information about how to use a template.	Type the name of the template followed by template in the Type A Question For Help box on the Visio menu bar, and then press the ENTER key. For example, type Basic Flowchart template.
Find information on each option in a dialog box.	In a dialog box, click the Help button in the lower-left corner of the dialog box.
Find product tours, templates, sample diagrams, tutorials, tips and tricks, in-depth articles about using Visio, answers to frequently asked questions, and links to Microsoft Knowledge Base articles.	On the Help menu, click Microsoft Office Online.

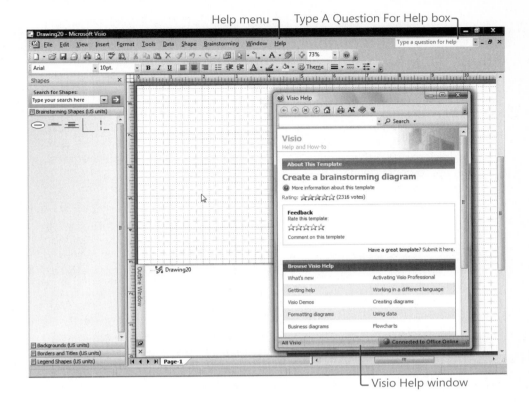

Help menu ⌐   Type A Question For Help box⌐

Visio Help window

In this exercise, you get help using a template and search Visio Help using a keyword.

1. Start Visio. In the Getting Started window, on the **Template Categories** list, click **Business**.

2. Under **Featured Templates**, double-click **Brainstorming Diagram**.

   Visio opens a blank drawing page, four stencils, and other tools used specifically for brainstorming diagrams.

3. On the **Help** menu, click **Microsoft Office Visio Help**.

   The Visio Help window appears.

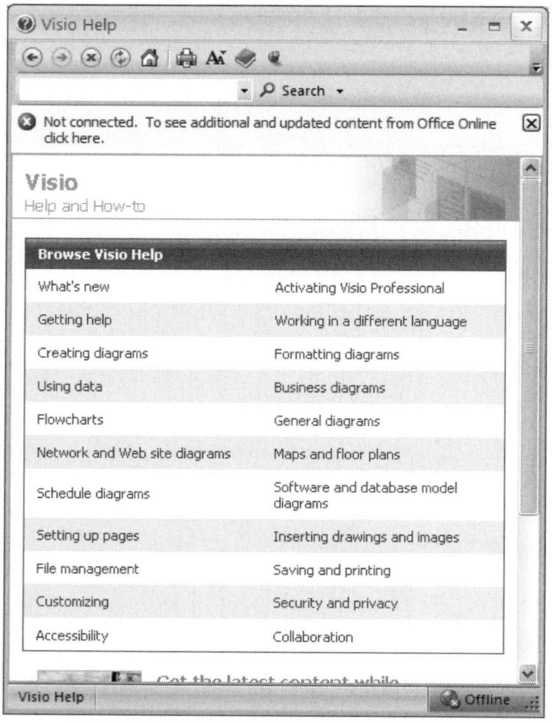

Troubleshooting If you're connected to the Internet while you search Visio Help, the search results you see might be slightly different than the results shown in this book. For example, if you're connected to the Internet when you open Microsoft Office Visio Help in step 3, Visio Help automatically opens the Create a Brainstorming Diagram help topic. If you're not connected to the Internet, you'll see a list of frequently used help topic categories.

4. In the **Search** box, type Brainstorming Diagram template, and then press the Enter key.

   Visio displays the search results.

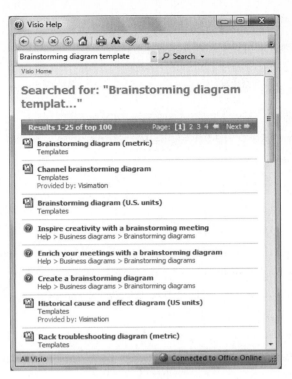

5. In the search results, click **Five great tools for making brainstorming diagrams in Visio**.

    The article opens directly in the Visio Help window.

Close

6. In the upper-right corner of the Visio Help window, click the **Close** button to close the window.

    The Visio Help window closes.

7. On the Visio menu bar, click in the **Type a question for help** box, type pages, and then press the ⌷Enter⌷ key.

    Visio opens the Visio Help window and displays the search results.

8. In the search results, click **Add a new page**.

    The topic opens in the Visio Help window.

9. On the title bar of the Visio Help window, click the **Close** button to close the window.

10. On the **Tools** menu, click **Options**.

    The Options dialog box opens.

Help

11. Click the **Help** button in the lower-left corner of the dialog box.

The Visio Help window opens and displays a Help topic that describes the options in the dialog box.

12. On the title bar of the Help window, click the **Close** button to close the window.

13. In the **Options** dialog box, click **Cancel** to close the dialog box.

14. On the **File** menu, click **Exit**. In the dialog box that appears, click **No** so that you don't save the diagram.

Visio closes.

Key Points

- You can create Visio diagrams by using the templates that come with Visio or templates that you can download from the Microsoft Office Online Web site.

- If none of the templates meet your needs, start your diagram by using a template that closely matches the diagram type.

- You can customize the Visio drawing environment so you can work efficiently.

- If you don't know which command or tool that a toolbar button represents, position the pointer over it to see a ScreenTip.

- You can right-click an item to see its shortcut menu.

- To save Visio diagrams, click the Save button on the Standard toolbar. Or, on the File menu, click Save.

- To check or change any page settings, on the File menu, click Page Setup. When you print your diagrams, make sure the size and orientation of the drawing page matches the printer settings.

- To preview your diagram, on the File menu, click Print Preview.

- To print the drawing page that's currently shown in the drawing window, click the Print Page button on the Standard toolbar.

- Whenever you're stuck and need help, type your question in the Type A Question For Help box.

- If you need help using a particular template, type the template name in the Type A Question For Help box.

- If you need help with the options in a dialog box, click the Help button in the lower-left corner of the dialog box.

Work with groups

Insert pictures into diagrams

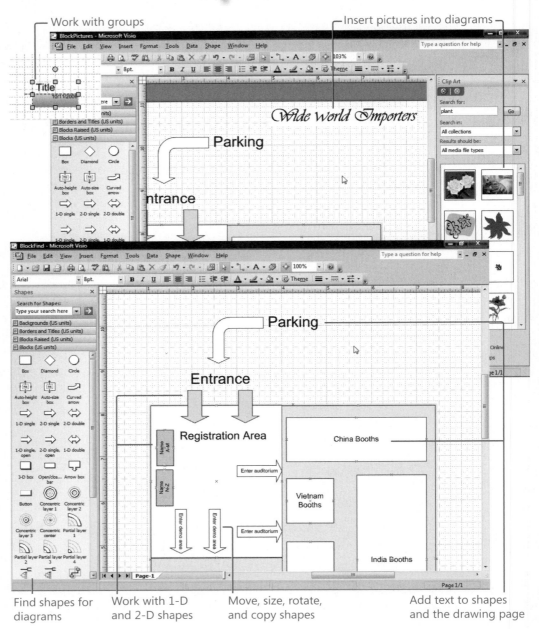

Find shapes for
diagrams

Work with 1-D
and 2-D shapes

Move, size, rotate,
and copy shapes

Add text to shapes
and the drawing page

2 Adding Shapes to Diagrams

In this chapter, you will learn how to:

✔ Work with 1-D and 2-D shapes.

✔ Add text to shapes and the drawing page.

✔ Move, size, rotate, and copy shapes.

✔ Work with groups.

✔ Find shapes for diagrams.

✔ Insert pictures into diagrams.

Microsoft Office Visio includes tens of thousands of shapes that you can use to quickly create diagrams. Shapes in Visio can represent both conceptual graphics and real-world objects, such as office furniture and network equipment. Shapes can be as simple as a rectangle that represents a step in a process flowchart, or they can be as complex as a hub in a network diagram. Because shapes can represent real-world objects, you can interact with them in ways that are similar to the ways you interact with the real-world objects.

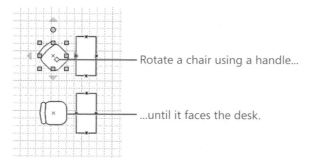

Rotate a chair using a handle...

...until it faces the desk.

All Visio shapes include handles that you can drag to resize the shapes. Visio shapes are *smart*; that's what sets them apart from shapes in other programs and clip art.

As you add shapes to your diagrams, you'll need to arrange them on the drawing page. For instance, in a flowchart, you might move one shape at a time, but in an office layout, you might need to move all the shapes at once.

You can also add titles to your diagrams or labels to your shapes by simply typing the text you want to add. You can customize the appearance of your diagram by modifying the text and shape *attributes*. If you can't find the shape you need on the stencils associated with the template, you can find shapes on other stencils or on the Web. In addition, you can insert a picture, such as a company logo or a piece of clip art, from another program into your Visio diagram.

In this chapter, you'll work with a block diagram—one of the most commonly used diagram types in Visio—that uses simple box and arrow shapes to represent the layout of a tradeshow hosted by Wide World Importers. You'll learn how to work with different types of shapes, add text to shapes, move and size shapes, rotate and copy shapes, and otherwise modify the appearance of shapes. Last, you'll learn how to search for shapes you can use to create diagrams and insert pictures from other programs into your diagrams.

See Also Do you need only a quick refresher on the topics in this chapter? See the Quick Reference entries on pages xxv–xliii.

> **Important** Before you can use the practice files in this chapter, you need to install them from the book's companion CD to their default location. See "Using the Book's CD-ROM" on page xix for more information.

Working with 1-D and 2-D Shapes

Shapes are the building blocks of all Visio diagrams. To work efficiently with any type of shape in any diagram, you need to understand some basic shape behavior, the differences between the types of Visio shapes, and how to interact with Visio shapes.

One of the fundamentals of interacting with shapes is that you drag shapes—one at a time—from stencils onto the drawing page to add them to a diagram. Another is that before you do something to a particular shape, such as move it or change its color, you need to *select* it so that Visio knows you want perform an action on that specific shape. Just place the pointer over the shape you want to select, and when a four-headed arrow appears under the pointer, click the shape to select it. You know that a shape is selected when you see *selection handles* on the shape. To *deselect* a shape, click the pasteboard or a blank area of the drawing page.

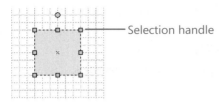

Selection handle

> **Tip** Don't drag shapes back onto stencils to delete them from the drawing page. To delete a shape, select it, and then press the [Del] key.

All Visio shapes behave like *one-dimensional (1-D)* or *two-dimensional (2-D)* shapes. This difference affects the type of selection handles that appear when you select a shape and the way you work with the shape. 1-D shapes behave like lines; 2-D shapes behave like boxes. This information might not seem important now, but as you work with Visio and eventually create your own shapes, knowing how both types of shapes behave will help you use Visio more skillfully.

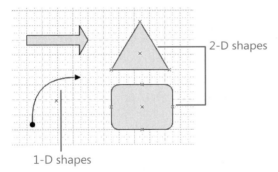

2-D shapes

1-D shapes

When you select a 1-D shape, two selection handles (called *endpoints*) appear that you can drag to resize the shape. The endpoint at the beginning of a 1-D shape is the *begin point* (represented by a × symbol), and the endpoint at the end of the shape is the *end point* (represented by a + symbol).

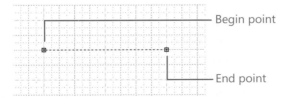

Begin point

End point

When you select a 2-D shape, a rectangular *selection box* appears around the shape. The selection box has eight selection handles: one handle on each of the four corners and one handle on each side of the selection box. One round *rotation handle* also appears above the selection box. You can drag the rotation handle to rotate a shape or any corner selection handle to resize a shape proportionally.

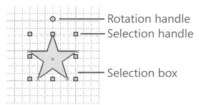

> **Tip** All Visio shapes behave either like 1-D shapes or 2-D shapes. However, some shapes might look 3-D but behave like 2-D shapes, and others might look 2-D but behave like 1-D shapes. You can determine which way a shape will behave by the selection handles that appear when you select it. If, after selecting the shape, you're still confused about a shape's behavior, on the Format menu, click Behavior to see whether the shape will behave like a 1-D or 2-D shape.

In addition to selection handles, some shapes have special handles called *control handles*. When you drag a control handle, it performs an action unique to that shape. For example, the Line-Curve Connector shape has a control handle that adjusts the curvature of the shape's arc, as the ScreenTip explains.

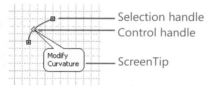

> **Tip** All Visio shape handles—selection, rotation, and control handles—have ScreenTips that explain what you can do with them. If you don't know how to use a particular handle, just pause the pointer over it to display its ScreenTip.

In this short exercise, you practice dragging a few 1-D and 2-D shapes onto the drawing page and selecting them. Then you drag a shape's control handle to change the shape's appearance.

1. Start Visio. In the **Getting Started** window, on the **Template Categories** list, click **General**.

2. Under **All Templates**, double-click **Block Diagram**.

Visio opens a blank drawing page and four stencils.

3. On the **View** menu, make sure that both **Rulers** and **Grid** are checked so that the rulers appear in the Visio drawing window and the grid appears on the drawing page.

4. In the Shapes window, from the **Blocks** stencil, drag the **Box** shape onto the drawing page.

The shape is selected on the drawing page. It's a 2-D shape, so it is surrounded by a selection box with eight selection handles and one round rotation handle.

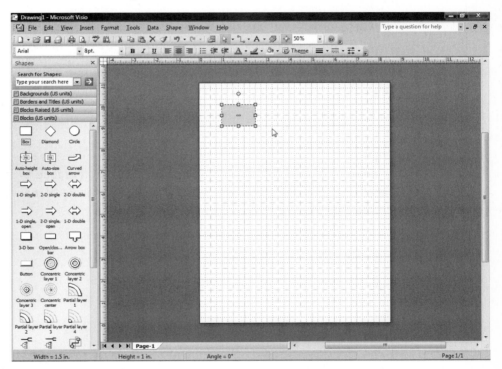

> **Tip** As you drag shapes onto the drawing page, notice how they *snap* to the nearest grid line on the page to help you easily position and align them.

5. Click the pasteboard.

The **Box** shape is no longer selected.

> **Tip** You can also press the Esc key to deselect a shape.

6. Position the pointer over the **Box** shape.

Four-headed
arrow

A four-headed arrow pointer appears, indicating that Visio is ready for you to select the shape.

> **Tip** When you pause the pointer over the shape, blue arrows used for connecting the
> shape to other shapes also appear. You'll learn more about connecting shapes later in
> Chapter 4, "Connecting Shapes."

7. Click the **Box** shape.

The shape is selected again.

8. From the **Blocks** stencil, drag the **1-D Single** shape onto the drawing page.

The shape is selected on the drawing page. This shape is a 1-D shape, so you can
see its begin point and end point. The **Box** shape is no longer selected.

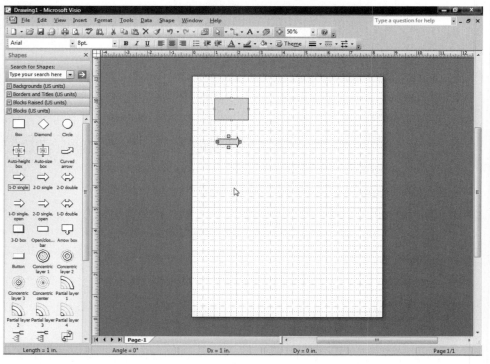

9. From the **Blocks** stencil, drag the **Curved Arrow** shape onto the drawing page.

The shape is selected on the drawing page. It's a 2-D shape, so it is surrounded by a
selection box with eight selection handles and one round rotation handle. You can
also see two yellow control handles on the shape.

10. Pause the pointer over the control handle at the end of the arrowhead.

Four-headed
arrow

A ScreenTip appears that tells you what you can do with the control handle. The pointer changes to a four-headed arrow, indicating that Visio is ready for you to drag the control handle.

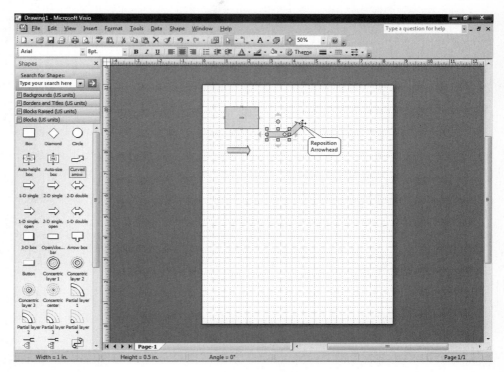

11. Drag the control handle to reposition the arrowhead.

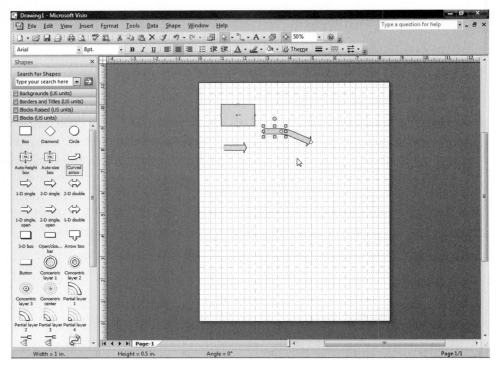

12. On the **File** menu, click **Close**, and then click **No** to close the drawing without saving the changes.

Adding Text to Shapes and the Drawing Page

Most diagrams contain text as well as shapes. By default, most Visio shapes appear either without text or with placeholder text. Adding text or replacing the placeholder text is easy—you simply select the shape and type.

The area in the shape where the text appears is called a *text block*. When you start typing, a blinking cursor appears at the insertion point so that you can keep track of the text placement. Also, the pointer changes to an I-beam when you place it over a text block, indicating that you can click anywhere in the text to insert new text, delete text, or select existing text to replace or format it.

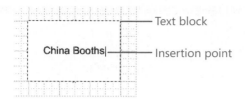

After you add text to a shape, you can format the text using the same methods you would use in any other program in the 2007 Microsoft Office system. You can change the font type, size, color, style, and alignment by using toolbar buttons on the Formatting toolbar. You can also use the Text command on the Format menu. When you want to apply the same text formatting to all the text in a shape, you simply select the shape, and any text changes you make apply to all the text in the shape.

Text Block Tool

> **Tip** You can move, resize, and rotate a text block independently of its shape by using the Text Block tool. For example, you might want to position the text block for an arrow at the end of the arrow rather than over the center of it. Or you might want the orientation of a text block to be different than its shape orientation. To use the Text Block tool, click the Text Tool down arrow, and then click Text Block Tool.

Text Tool

You can also create a *text-only shape*—text that's not associated with a shape—on the drawing page. For example, you can add a title, footer, or bulleted list to a diagram. Just click the Text Tool button on the Standard toolbar, click the location on the drawing page where you want the text to appear, and then type. After you add a text-only shape to a diagram, you can select, move, rotate, and format it just as you would any other shape.

> **Tip** A text-only shape is simply a rectangular shape without a border around it or color inside it.

In this exercise, you work with a diagram that has already been started for you using the Block Diagram template. You drag shapes from a stencil onto the drawing page, add text to shapes, revise the existing text in shapes, add a text-only shape, and then save the diagram.

OPEN the *BlockText* file in Documents\Microsoft Press\Visio 2007 SBS\02_Shapes.

1. From the **Blocks** stencil, drag the **2-D single** arrow shape onto the drawing page and position it directly below the **Enter auditorium** arrow shape.

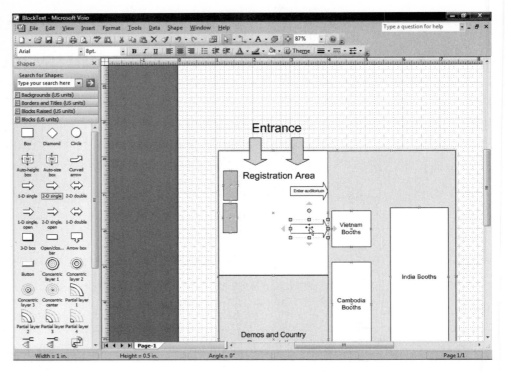

Notice how the shape snaps to the grid, even though the grid is obscured by the white **Registration Area** shape.

2. With the **2-D single** arrow shape selected, type Enter auditorium.

   As soon as you start typing, the text block opens and a blinking cursor appears in the text block. Visio centers the text in the shape.

   > **Tip** Misspelled words are underlined in red. To correct a misspelled word, right-click the word, and then click the correct spelling on the shortcut menu.

3. Click the pasteboard to close the text block and deselect the shape.

   > **Tip** Another way to deselect the shape is to click a blank area of the drawing page. Alternatively, you can press the Esc key to close the text block, but this action will leave the shape selected.

4. Select the top gold rectangle in the left area of the drawing page. Type Name, press the Enter key, and then type A-M.

   As you type, Visio displays the text block horizontally for ease of reading.

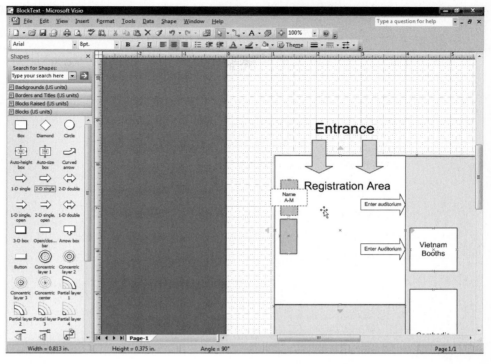

5. Click the pasteboard to close the text block and deselect the shape.

   Visio displays the text vertically in the shape.

6. Repeat steps 4 and 5 for the bottom gold rectangle, but type N-Z (instead of A-M).

   Visio displays the text vertically in the shape.

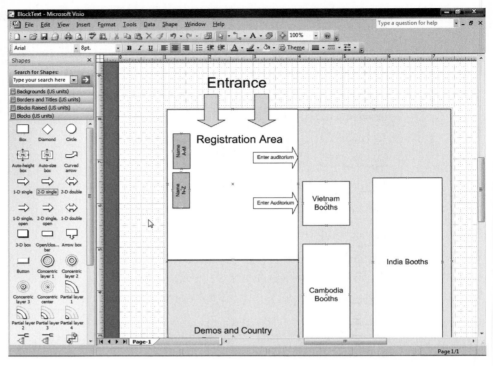

7. From the **Blocks** stencil, drag a **Box** shape onto the drawing page and position it above the **Vietnam Booths** box shape.

8. Align the **Box** shape with the **Vietnam Booths** box shape by snapping the **Box** shape to the grid.

9. With the **Box** shape selected, type China Booths.

   Visio adds and centers the text in the shape.

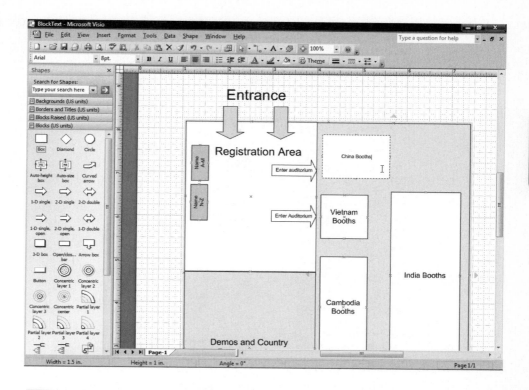

> **Tip** Alternatively, you can open a shape's text block by selecting a shape and pressing the [F2] key.

10. Click the pasteboard to close the text block and deselect the shape.

11. From the **Blocks** stencil, drag the **2-D single** shape onto the drawing page and position it below the **Name N-Z** box.

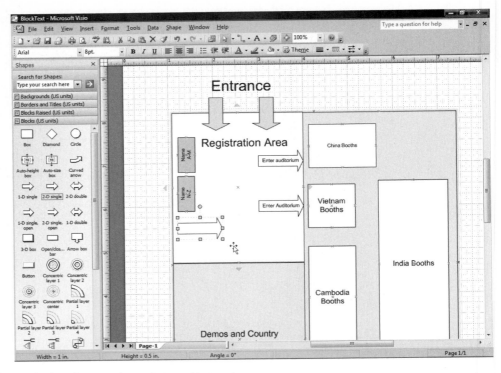

12. With the shape selected, type Enter demo area.

Visio adds and centers the text in the shape.

> **Tip** Visio centers the text in most shapes by default. You can change the alignment of the text in a shape by using the alignment buttons on the Formatting toolbar.

13. Click the pasteboard to close the text block and deselect the shape.

14. If you can't see the **Demos and Country Representatives** shape on the drawing page, drag the vertical scroll bar (on the right side of the drawing window) down until the shape is visible.

Text Tool

15. On the Standard toolbar, click the **Text Tool** button.

The pointer changes to a text box icon.

16. In the **Demos and Country Representatives** shape, click to the left of the letter *D* in *Demos*.

The text block opens and a blinking cursor appears at the insertion point.

17. Type Product, and then press the 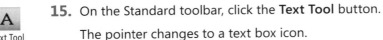 Space .

The new text appears in the shape.

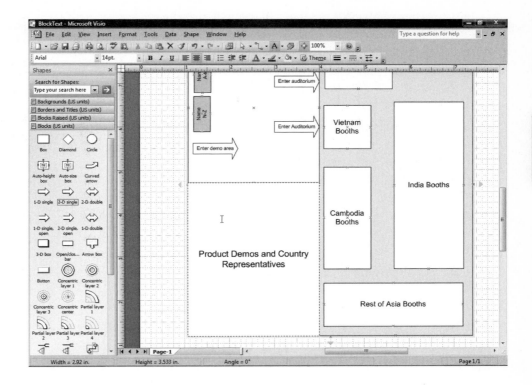

> **Tip** Using the Text Tool button to modify existing text is a good habit because it gives you more control over the text. When you simply select a shape and type, the new text replaces all the existing text. When you click the Text Tool button before you click the text block, however, you can select only the text you want to modify.

18. If you can't see the **China Booths** box shape, drag the vertical scroll bar up until the shape is visible.

Pointer Tool

19. On the Standard toolbar, click the **Pointer Tool** button.

20. Click the **China Booths** shape to select it.

Font Size

21. On the Formatting toolbar, click the **Font Size** down arrow to display a list of font sizes.

22. Click **12 pt.** on the list.

The font size of the text in the selected shape increases to 12 points.

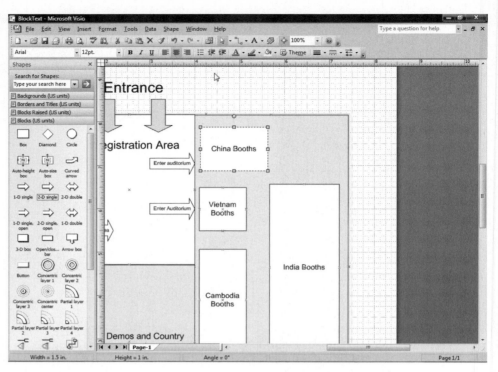

23. If you can't see the top of the drawing page, drag the vertical scroll bar up until it's visible.

24. On the Standard toolbar, click the **Text Tool** button.

25. Approximately one inch above and to the right of the **Entrance** text, click to create a text-only shape.

A text block opens and a blinking cursor appears.

> **Troubleshooting** If you click the wrong location, click the pasteboard or press the Esc key, and then try again.

26. In the text block, type Parking.

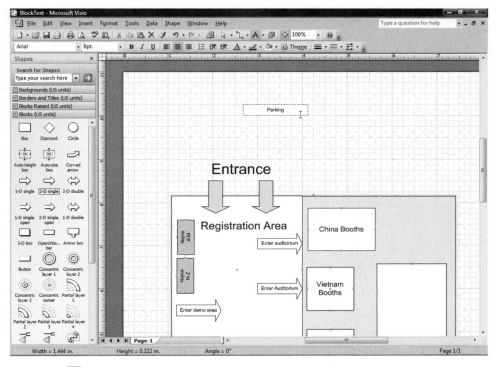

27. Press the ⎋Esc key to close the text block.

    The text-only shape is selected.

28. On the Formatting toolbar, click the **Font Size** down arrow to display a list of font sizes.

29. Click **24 pt.** on the list.

    The font size of the text in the selected shape increases to 24 points.

Save

30. On the Standard toolbar, click the **Save** button to save your changes to the diagram.

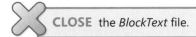
CLOSE the *BlockText* file.

Moving, Sizing, Rotating, and Copying Shapes

As you create your Visio diagrams, you'll need to move shapes around the drawing page, resize shapes, and maybe even rotate and copy them. When you move shapes, you can move one at a time or many shapes at once. Moving one shape is simple—just select the shape and drag it to a new position. Moving multiple shapes at once is as simple as moving one shape. First you select the shapes you want to move, and then you position the pointer over one of the selected shapes. As you drag, all the selected shapes move as one.

One of the most common ways to select multiple shapes is to select one of the shapes and then hold down the Shift key while you select the rest of the shapes. The first shape you select is the *primary shape*. Its selection box turns dark magenta after you click an additional shape while holding down the Shift key. The selection boxes for the other shapes you select, called *secondary shapes*, turn light magenta. Visio also encloses all the selected shapes in a green selection box. Knowing which shape is the primary shape will be useful later when you learn about aligning shapes in Chapter 4 and merging shapes in Chapter 12.

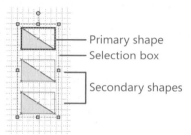

Primary shape
Selection box

Secondary shapes

Visio includes several other methods for selecting multiple shapes. If, for example, all the shapes you want to select are in the same area, as they might be in an office layout, you can use the Pointer tool to drag a selection net around the shapes you want to select. After you release the mouse button, everything within the net is selected. You can also use the selection tools on the Pointer Tool menu (on the Standard toolbar) to select multiple shapes without holding down the Shift key. To see the selection tools on the Pointer Tool menu, click the Pointer Tool down arrow.

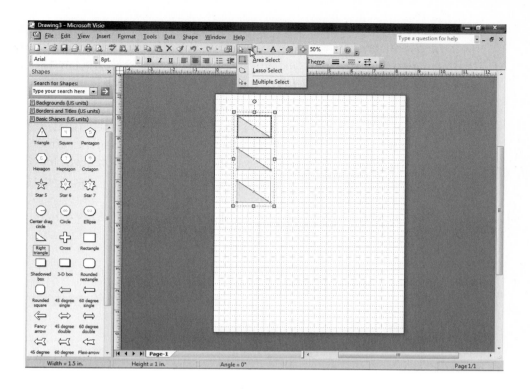

Tip To view Visio Help topics that tell you how to use the selection tools on the Pointer Tool menu, type **select shapes** in the "Type A Question For Help" box, and then press the Enter key.

The way you resize a shape depends on whether the shape is 1-D or 2-D. You can drag a 1-D shape's endpoints in any direction to lengthen the shape. When you're working with a 2-D shape, you can change the height or width of the shape by dragging a side, top, or bottom handle. You can also resize the entire shape proportionally by dragging a corner selection handle. To rotate a shape, you can simply drag the shape's rotation handle in the direction you want.

Tip You can resize more than one shape at a time by selecting all the shapes you want to resize and then dragging a selection handle on the green selection box that encloses the selected shapes.

Copying a shape is also a simple procedure. Select a shape, and on the Edit menu, click Copy. Then, on the Edit menu, click Paste. With Visio, you can go a step further by copying a shape and positioning it in the same action. To do so, instead of working with commands on menus, hold down the Ctrl key while you drag a shape. This action copies the shape and positions it in the location where you release the mouse button. When you're done creating the copy, make sure you release the mouse button *before* you release the Ctrl key. Otherwise, Visio moves the shape instead of copying it.

In this exercise, you continue working with the block diagram that you updated in the previous exercise. You resize, move, rotate, and copy shapes in the diagram.

OPEN the *BlockMove* file in Documents\Microsoft Press\Visio 2007 SBS\02_Shapes.

1. Click the **China Booths** shape to select it.

2. Position the pointer over the middle selection handle on the right side of the shape.

Two-headed arrow

The pointer turns to a two-headed arrow and displays a ScreenTip.

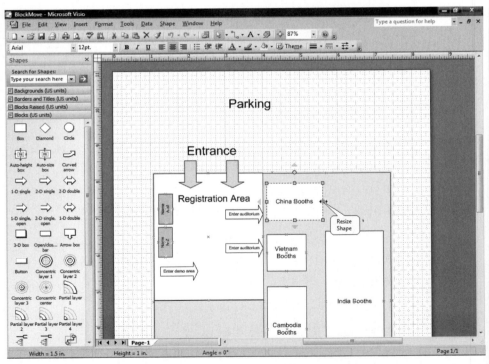

3. Drag the section handle until the right side of the box is aligned with the right side of the **India Booths** shape.

4. To get a closer look, position the pointer over the center of the **China Booths** shape, and hold down Shift + Ctrl while you left-click.

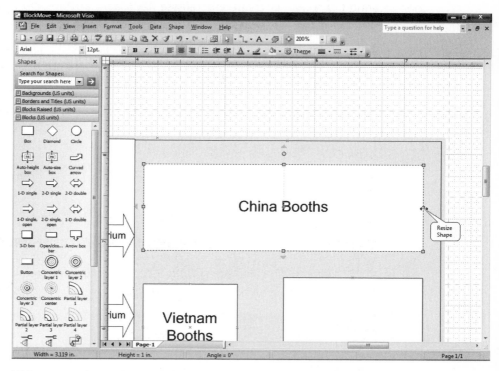

Visio zooms in, and the **Zoom** box on the Standard toolbar displays the current level of zoom.

5. If you need to adjust the size of the box, drag the selection handle again.

6. Hold down Shift + Ctrl, and then right-click to zoom out.

7. Click the pasteboard to deselect the **China Booths** shape.

8. Position the pointer over the **Enter demo area** shape.

A four-headed arrow pointer appears, indicating that you can select the shape.

Four-headed
arrow

9. Click the shape to select it.

10. Position the pointer over the **Enter demo area** shape.

When a four-headed arrow appears, Visio is ready for you to move the shape.

Four-headed
arrow

11. Drag the shape to move it down a little, and then click the pasteboard or a blank area of the drawing page to deselect the shape.

> **Important** If you resize a shape accidentally instead of moving it, you can immediately undo your mistake by clicking Undo on the Edit menu; the keyboard shortcut for this command is ⌈Ctrl⌉+⌈Z⌉. To avoid making this mistake, don't place the pointer over a selection handle when you want to move a shape. Place the pointer over the middle of the shape, and make sure the pointer changes to a four-headed arrow before you move the shape.

12. Position the pointer over the top **Enter auditorium** shape.

A four-headed arrow pointer appears, so you know you can select the shape.

13. Click the top **Enter auditorium** shape to select it.

14. Hold down the ⌈Shift⌉ key, and then click the bottom **Enter auditorium** shape.

Visio selects both shapes and encloses the two selected shapes in a green selection box. The selection box for the first shape you select (the primary shape) changes to a dark magenta line. The selection box for the second shape you select (the secondary shape) changes to a light magenta line.

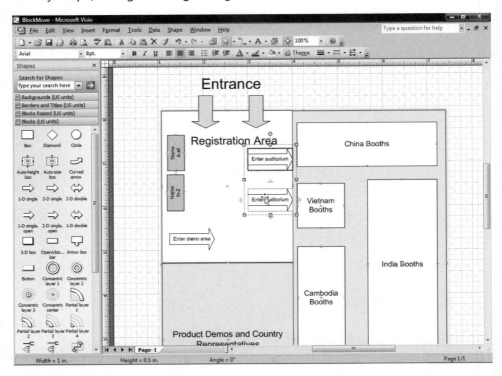

> **Troubleshooting** If you select a shape by mistake, simply undo your mistake by clicking Undo on the Edit menu. Then, begin selecting the shapes again. Or, hold down the ⎣ Shift ⎦ key, and then click a *selected* shape to deselect it.

15. Point to the top **Enter auditorium** shape.

When a four-headed arrow appears, you can move the selected shapes.

16. Drag the top shape down approximately one inch.

As you drag, notice that all the selected shapes move at once. Also notice the tick marks that appear on the horizontal ruler to show the shape's position.

> **Tip** To constrain the direction of shape movement horizontally or vertically, press the ⎣ Shift ⎦ key while you drag one or more shapes. To nudge one or more selected shapes just a little, use the arrow keys on your keyboard.

17. Click the pasteboard or a blank area of the drawing page to deselect both shapes.

18. Click the top **Enter auditorium** shape to select it. Press the ⎣ Shift ⎦ key and drag the shape back up approximately one inch.

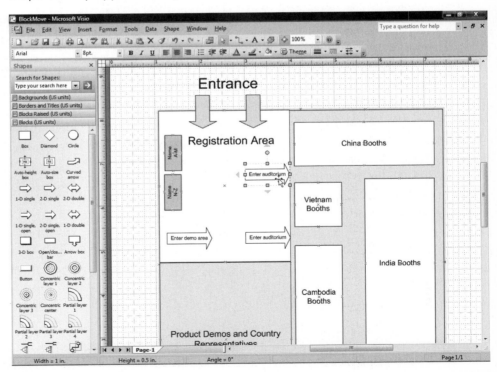

19. Select the **Enter demo area** shape, and then position the pointer over the rotation handle on the shape.

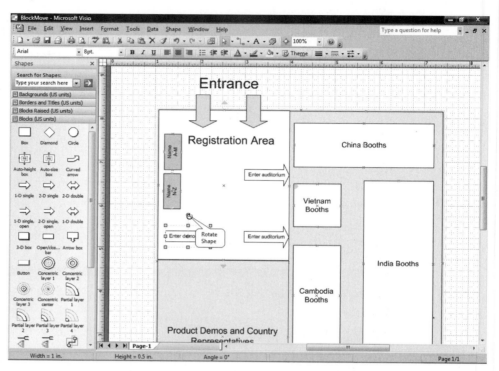

Circular arrow

The pointer changes to a circular arrow, indicating that Visio is ready to rotate the shape.

20. Drag the rotation handle to the right until the shape points downward or is rotated clockwise 90 degrees. As you drag the rotation handle, watch the status bar, which shows the angle of rotation for the selected shape.

The shape is rotated clockwise 90 degrees and remains selected.

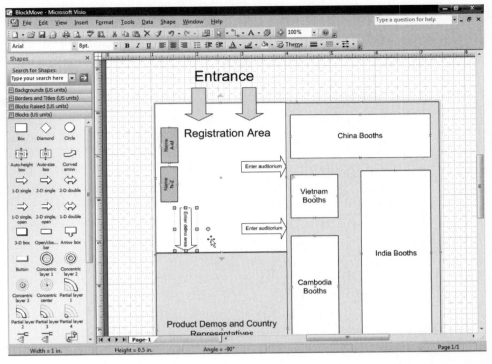

21. Position the pointer over the selected **Enter demo area** shape, and then hold down the [Ctrl] key.

When a plus sign pointer appears, Visio is ready for you to copy the selected shape.

Plus sign pointer

22. Drag the **Enter demo area** shape to the right to create a copy of the shape, release the mouse button, and then release the [Ctrl] key.

A copy of the **Enter demo area** shape appears to the right of the original shape.

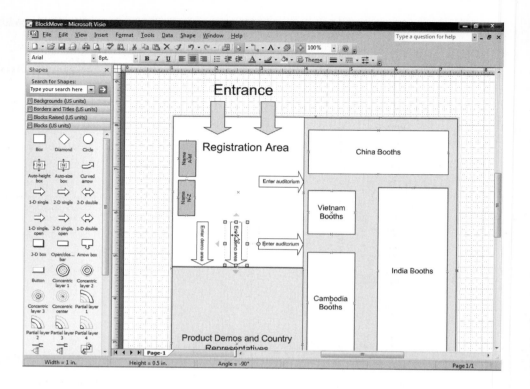

> **Troubleshooting** If you moved the shape instead of copying it, you released the
> [Ctrl] key before you released the mouse button. You must release the mouse button
> first. Press [Ctrl]+[Z] to undo your action, and try again.

23. Click the pasteboard or a blank area of the drawing page to deselect the shape.

24. If you can't see the **Parking** label at the top of the diagram, drag the vertical scroll
bar up until the label is visible.

25. From the **Blocks** stencil, drag the **Curved Arrow** shape onto the drawing page, and
position it to the left of the **Parking** label.

26. On the **Shape** menu, point to **Rotate or Flip**, and then click **Flip Horizontal**.

The shape is flipped horizontally.

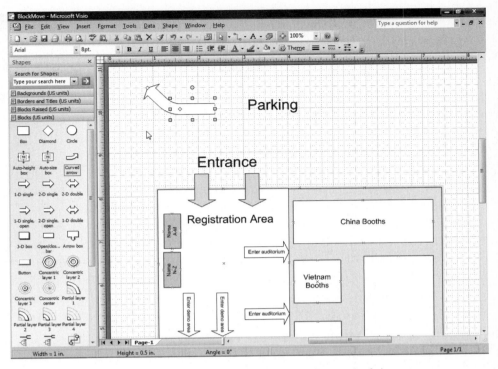

27. Pause the pointer over the yellow control handle at the end of the arrow.

Visio displays a ScreenTip.

28. Drag the control handle down until the shape points toward the **Entrance** label.

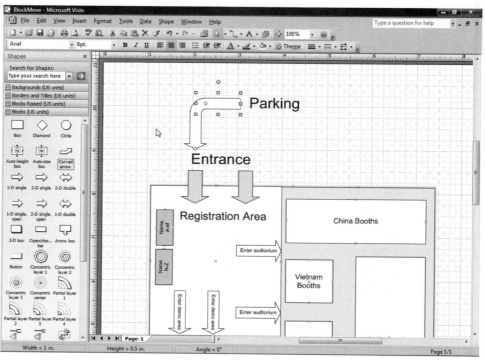

29. If you need to align some of the shapes in your diagram more precisely, select them, and then nudge them using the arrow keys on your keyboard.

30. On the Standard toolbar, click **Save** to save your changes to the diagram.

Save

✕ **CLOSE** the *BlockMove* file.

Working with Groups

Up to this point in the book, you've worked with simple individual shapes, such as rectangles, circles, and lines. However, many Visio shapes are made up of several shapes. This type of Visio shape is called a *group*—two or more shapes that function as a unit. For instance, the title block shapes on the Borders and Titles stencil are groups composed of boxes, lines, circles, text, and so on. Instead of dragging each individual piece of a title block onto the drawing page, you can drag the group onto the page. Instead of moving or resizing each piece on the drawing page, you can resize or move the group. You can even rotate a group by using the rotation handle that appears on the group when you select it.

──────── Group

──────── Individual shapes within the group

Even though the shapes in a group function as a unit, you can still work with the shapes individually. However, the shapes within groups are often *locked*—protected against particular types of changes—to prevent you from deleting or inadvertently moving them individually when you intended to move the whole group. In other words, you can work with the individual shapes in groups, but your actions are limited depending on the group.

When you *subselect* a shape you want to work with in the group, if that shape is locked, its selection handles are gray instead of green. To subselect a shape within a group, se-lect the group, and then select the individual shape. For example, you can subselect the text in a title block group to replace the placeholder text with your own title and change the text attributes, but you can't delete or move the locked text-only shape.

──────── Subselected shape within a group
──────── Gray handles signify that the
           shape is locked

In this short exercise, you practice selecting, moving, and resizing groups. Then you sub-select a shape within a group to work with it individually.

1. On the **File** menu, point to **New**, point to **General**, and then click **Block Diagram**.

   Visio opens a blank drawing page and four stencils.

2. Click the title bar of the **Borders and Titles** stencil to display the shapes on the stencil.

3. From the **Borders and Titles** stencil, drag the **Title block compass** shape onto the drawing page. You might need to zoom in on the shape to see it better.

   The shape is selected on the drawing page. Because groups are 2-D shapes, the se-lection box includes eight selection handles and one round rotation handle.

4. Click the **Title** placeholder text.

   Visio subselects the text-only shape within the group.

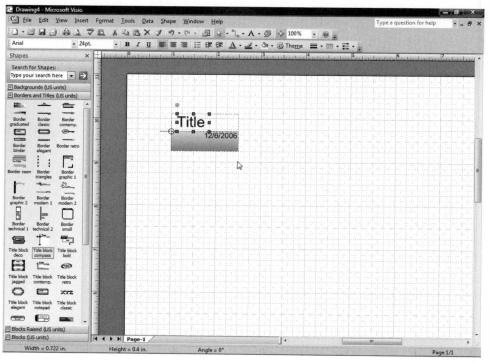

5. Type Tradeshow.

   Visio opens the shape's text block, replaces the placeholder text with the new text, and resizes the title block to accommodate the text.

6. Click the gray box below the title to subselect it.

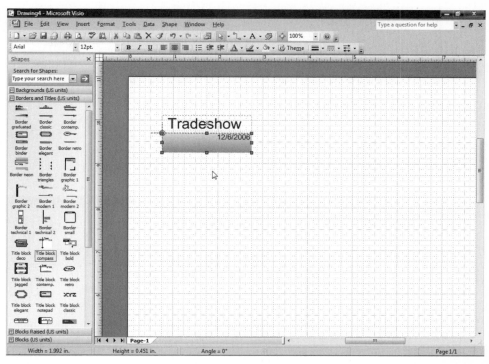

Fill Color

7. On the Formatting toolbar, click the **Fill Color** down arrow, and then under **Theme Colors**, click the top red color (**Accent 1**) on the palette.

Visio changes the color of the box to red. The rest of the shapes in the group are unaffected.

8. On the **File** menu, click **Close**, and then click **No** to close the drawing without saving the changes.

Finding Shapes for Diagrams

Visio templates open stencils that contain the shapes used most often for a particular diagram type. However, you might want to add shapes to your diagram that aren't on any of the template's stencils. For example, in a brainstorming diagram, you might want to include a text callout shape to highlight a topic, but how do you find the shape you need?

It's easy. In the Shapes window, use the Search For Shapes box to quickly search for shapes on your computer and on the Web. Using this method, you don't need to open and browse additional Visio stencils—although you could do that if you wanted to familiarize yourself with shapes on different stencils.

> **Tip** To open a stencil, on the File menu, point to Shapes, point to a category, and then click the name of the stencil you want to open.

To search for shapes quickly by using keywords, type the keyword for the shape you want to find in the Search For Shapes box. For example, to find furniture shapes, you might type **desk** or **chair**. To find callout or annotation shapes, you might type **callout**, **text**, **label**, or **annotation**. Then when you click the arrow next to the Search For Shapes box, Visio searches your computer and the Microsoft Office Online Web site for the shapes that match the keyword.

> **Tip** In the Search For Shapes box, you can type more than one keyword and separate them with spaces, commas, or semicolons.

In this exercise, you continue working with the block diagram that you updated in a preceding exercise. You search for shapes that aren't on the stencils opened by the Block Diagram template, and then you drag the shapes you find onto the drawing page.

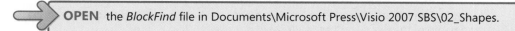

OPEN the *BlockFind* file in Documents\Microsoft Press\Visio 2007 SBS\02_Shapes.

1. In the Shapes window, in the **Search for Shapes** box, type Plants.

2. Click the arrow to the right of the **Search for Shapes** box, or press the ⌨Enter key.

   Visio searches for shapes with *plants* in the name or keyword stored with the shape.

   > **Tip** By default, Visio searches for shapes on your computer and on the Microsoft Office Online Web site. To change the search options, on the Tools menu, click Options, and then click the Shape Search tab.

3. Do any combination of the following:

   ❑ If a dialog box appears asking you if you want to enable the Indexing Service, click **Yes** to perform faster future searches.

   ❑ If a dialog box appears telling you that Visio can't establish an Internet connection, click **OK** to view the results.

   ❑ If a dialog box appears telling you that the search results are greater than the specified maximum, click **Yes** to view the results.

   Visio completes its search and creates a **plants** stencil that contains all the shapes it found.

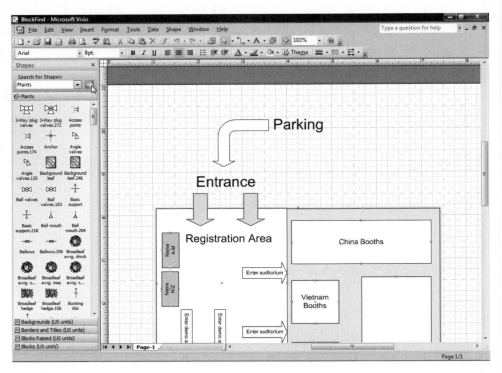

4. From the **plants** stencil in the Shapes window, drag the **Potted plant 2** shape onto the drawing page and position it to the right of the of the word, **Entrance**.

> **Tip** You might need to scroll the **plants** stencil to find the **Potted plant 2** shape.

5. Drag another **Potted plant 2** shape onto the drawing page and position it to the right of the other plant you just added to the drawing page.

Notice that both of the plant shapes you dragged onto the drawing page are groups because they are composed of two or more shapes that function as a unit.

> **Tip** To find shapes that are similar to ones that are already in your drawing, right-click a shape on the drawing page, point to Shape, and then click Find Similar Shapes.

6. On the title bar of the **plants** stencil, click the stencil icon to the left of the title **Plants**, and then click **Close** on the stencil menu.

The **plants** stencil closes.

> **Tip** You can save the plants stencil so that you can use it again to add plants to your diagrams. To do so, click the stencil icon to the left of the stencil's title, click Save, and then in the Save As dialog box, click the Save button. To open the stencil later, on the File menu, point to Shapes, point to My Shapes, and then click plants.

Save

7. On the Standard toolbar, click the **Save** button to save your changes to the diagram.

 CLOSE the *BlockFind* file.

Inserting Pictures into Diagrams

Although Visio includes most of the shapes you need for your diagrams, sometimes you need an image that was created in a different program. You can insert a *picture*—a graphic file—into Visio whether or not the program that created the image is currently installed on your computer.

When you want to add a picture to your diagram, you can use the Picture command on the Insert menu or the Clip Art task pane. To display the Clip Art task pane, on the View menu, click Task Pane. Then click the down arrow on the task pane's title bar, and click Clip Art. Adding clip art from the Clip Art task pane to your diagram is as simple as adding a Visio shape from a stencil—you simply drag it onto the drawing page.

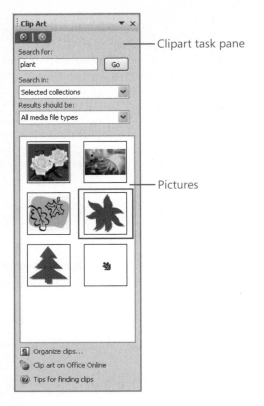

— Clipart task pane

— Pictures

You can insert pictures into Visio diagrams that have been saved in the file formats shown in the following table.

File Format	File Extension
Compressed Enhanced Metafile	.emz
Enhanced Metafile	.emf
Graphics Interchange Format	.gif
Joint Photographic Experts Group File Interchange Format	.jpg
Portable Network Graphics	.png
Scalable Vector Graphics	.svg and .svgz
Tag Image File Format	.tif and .tiff
Windows Bitmap	.bmp and .dib
Windows Metafile	.wmf

After you insert a picture, you can size, position, and *crop* it, which means cut out portions you don't want to appear. You can also format a picture's properties to change its brightness, sharpness, transparency, and other qualities that affect appearance. Visio includes a Picture command on the Format menu that even previews your changes before you apply them.

> **Tip** If you insert a lot of pictures into your diagrams, you can display the Picture toolbar, which includes the Insert Picture button, for quick access to picture formatting commands. Right-click the toolbar area, and then click Picture on the shortcut menu to display the Picture toolbar. This toolbar is usually displayed only when you select a picture on the drawing page. However, if you choose the toolbar from the toolbar shortcut menu, the toolbar will appear at all times; Visio won't hide it when a picture isn't selected.

In this exercise, you insert a logo and a piece of clip art into the block diagram from the preceding exercise, and then you resize the pictures. Last, you will you make the logo transparent.

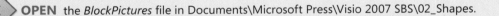

OPEN the *BlockPictures* file in Documents\Microsoft Press\Visio 2007 SBS\02_Shapes.

1. On the **Insert** menu, point to **Picture**, and then click **From File**.

   > **Tip** Using the Picture command, you can also insert clip art, charts, equations, and photographs from a scanner or digital camera.

2. In the **Look in** box, go to the **02_Shapes** folder.

3. Double-click the **Logo.png** file.

   Visio inserts the logo on the drawing page, selects it, and displays the Picture toolbar.

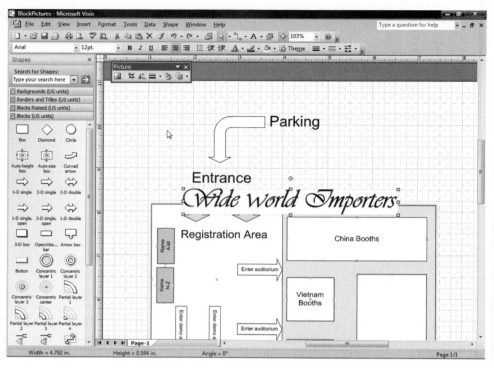

4. Drag the logo to the upper-right corner of the drawing page.

5. Drag one of the corner selection handles to make the logo a little smaller.

6. On the **Picture** toolbar, click the **Transparency** down arrow, and then click **60%**.

   Visio makes the logo 60 percent transparent so that the grid shows through.

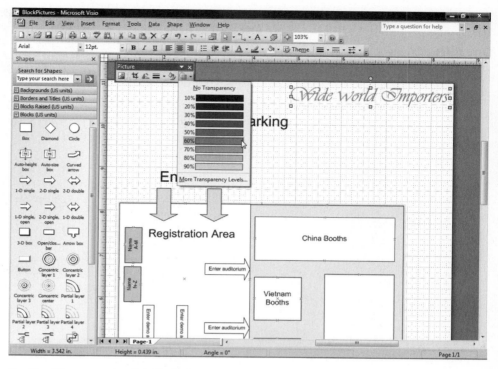

7. On the **View** menu, click **Task Pane**.

   Visio displays a task pane to the right of the drawing page.

8. Click the down arrow on the task pane's title bar, and then click **Clip Art**.

   Visio displays the **Clip Art** task pane.

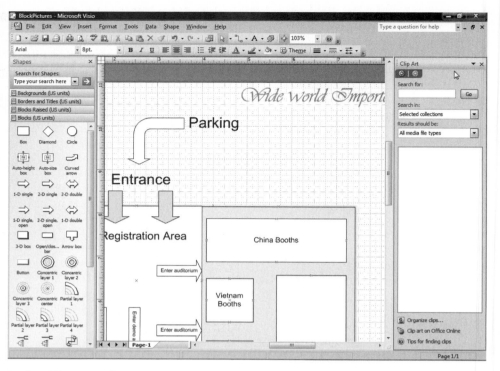

9. In the **Clip Art** task pane, in the **Search for** box, type **plant**. To the right of the **Search for** box, click the **Go** button.

10. If you see a dialog box asking you if you want to search Microsoft Office Online, click **Yes** to find clip art on Office Online.

    Visio searches your computer and Office Online for all available clip art that match-es the keyword and displays the results in the task pane.

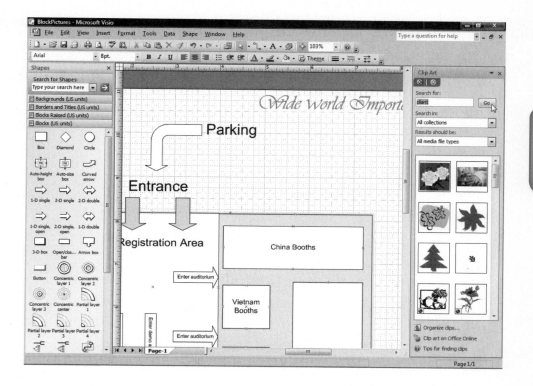

> **Important** The clip art you see on your computer might differ from the images shown in this book, depending on the clip art you have installed.

11. Pause the pointer over the **Plant** clip art.

A ScreenTip appears that tells you the name, dimensions, file size, and file type of the piece of clip art.

12. Drag the **Plant** clip art onto the drawing page, and position it to the right of the entrance.

13. Drag a corner selection handle on the shape to decrease the size of the shape and move the shape into position.

14. While you hold down the Ctrl key, drag the **Plant** clip art directly to the right to copy a new piece of art and position it all at once.

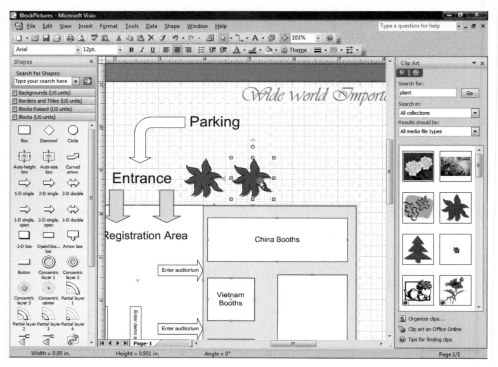

15. On the **File** menu, click **Close**, and then click **No** to close the drawing without saving the changes.

Key Points

- All Visio shapes behave like 1-D or 2-D shapes. 1-D shapes, such as lines, have endpoints that you can use to shorten or lengthen them. 2-D shapes, such as rectangles, circles, diamonds, and triangles, have selection handles that you can use to increase their height or width.

- You can drag a corner selection handle on a 2-D shape to resize it proportionally. Drag the rotation handle on a 2-D shape to rotate it.

- When the pointer changes to a four-headed arrow pointer, you can move the shape. When the pointer changes to a two-headed arrow pointer, you can resize the shape.

- To copy and position a shape in a single action, drag it while holding down the Ctrl key. Be sure to release the mouse button before the Ctrl key; otherwise, you'll move the shape.

- To add text to a shape, select it, and then type your text. To add independent text to a diagram, use the Text tool.
- To work with an individual shape in a group, subselect the shape within the group.
- To find additional shapes for your diagrams, type keywords in the Search for Shapes box.
- To insert pictures created in other programs into your diagrams, use the Picture command on the Format menu or the Clip Art task pane.Chapter Title

Add decorative elements to diagrams

Apply themes to entire diagrams

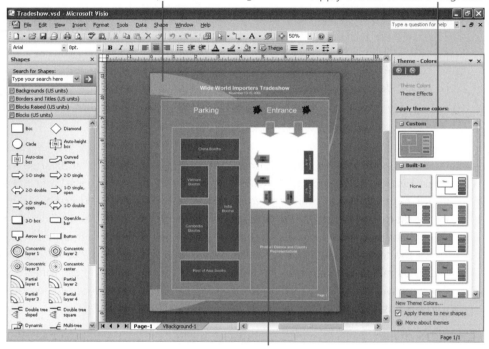

Format individual shapes

3 Formatting Shapes and Diagrams

In this chapter, you will learn how to:

✔ Format individual shapes.

✔ Add decorative elements to diagrams.

✔ Apply themes to entire diagrams.

You can create effective, professional-looking diagrams simply by dragging Microsoft Office Visio shapes onto the drawing page. However, to ensure that a flowchart, for example, captures the attention of your colleagues, you can spend just a few more minutes on the diagram to make it look great. For example, add colors to individual shapes to make them stand out, insert a background image to add interest, and increase the font size of the text to make it easier to see. You can also customize the appearance of the shapes to meet your organization's design specifications, and apply themes to entire diagrams with just a single click. With Visio, formatting individual shapes and entire diagrams is easy.

In this chapter you'll learn the quickest methods of formatting individual shapes and adding finishing touches to entire diagrams. You'll learn how to add decorative elements, such as ornamental borders and attractive title shapes, to your diagrams. Last, you will apply themes to entire diagrams.

See Also Do you need only a quick refresher on the topics in this chapter? See the Quick Reference entries on pages xxv–xliii.

Important Before you can use the practice files in this chapter, you need to install them from the book's companion CD to their default location. See "Using the Book's CD-ROM" on page xix for more information.

Formatting Individual Shapes

The right *formatting*—a combination of attributes that makes up the appearance of a shape, diagram, or text—can add emphasis and interest to your diagrams and help you communicate more effectively. For example, you can draw attention to important steps in a process by adding high-contrast colors to individual shapes, or refine the overall look of your diagram by adding something as simple as a shadow to a shape. Every shape in Visio has attributes that you can format:

- The *weight* (thickness), color, pattern, and transparency of the border around a 2-D shape; and the weight, color, pattern, and transparency of a 1-D shape. Use the Line command on the Format menu to change these attributes.

- The color, pattern, and transparency of a 2-D shape's interior, called its *fill*. Use the Fill command on the Format menu to change these attributes.

- The color, pattern, and transparency of a shape's shadow. Use the Fill command on the Format menu to change these attributes.

- The *line ends* on a 1-D shape. Some examples of line ends are arrowheads, diamonds, and circles. Use the Line command on the Format menu to change these attributes.

- The *line caps* (round or square) on a 1-D shape and the corners on a 2-D shape. Use the Line command on the Format menu to change these attributes.

- The text size, style, color, and so on. Use the Text command on the Format menu to change these attributes.

When you drag any shape from a stencil onto the drawing page, it appears with the shape's default formatting. For example, the Box shape on the Blocks stencil has a gray fill color and a solid black border. Text that you type in this shape is black, the font size is 8 points, and the font name is Arial. By formatting a shape's attributes, you can change the look of a shape or an entire diagram to better convey your message.

Gray fill color   Solid black border

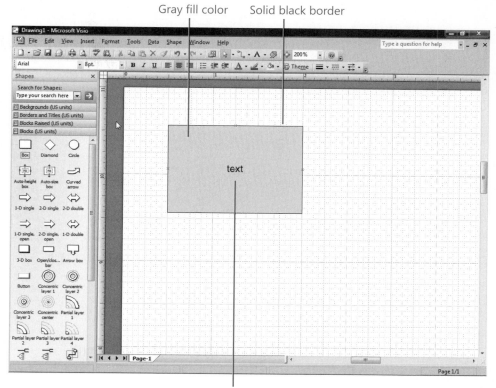

Black, 8-point, Arial text

Visio makes it easy to change the default formatting of any shape by using the Text, Line, and Fill commands on the Format menu, or the buttons on the Formatting toolbar. Most of these buttons have drop-down lists with options that you can select. To view the options for a specific button, click the down arrow on the button. For example, to change a shape's fill color, select the shape, click the Fill Color down arrow, and then click the color you want from the palette of colors that appears.

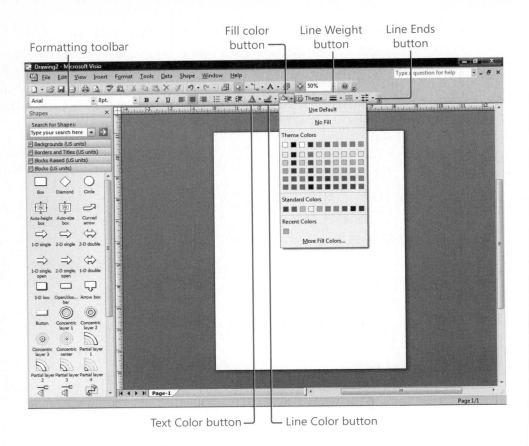

Formatting toolbar

Fill color button

Line Weight button

Line Ends button

Text Color button

Line Color button

> **Tip** Pause the pointer over any toolbar button to display a ScreenTip that tells you the button's function.

In a diagram that includes many shapes, you can save time by formatting multiple shapes at the same time. Do this by clicking Select All on the Edit menu, and then specifying the attributes you want to apply. Visio applies the changes to all the selected shapes. If you want to apply the same formatting to only some of the shapes in a diagram, hold down the Shift key while selecting the shapes you want to format, and then specify the attributes you want to apply.

> **Tip** If you want to format an entire diagram with pre-defined, coordinated colors that Visio provides for you, use the methods covered in the "Applying Themes to Entire Diagrams" section later in this chapter.

If you want to apply the formatting of one shape to other shapes, you can copy the formatting from that shape and apply it to the others. The Format Painter tool copies the fill, line, and text attributes of one shape and applies them to another shape. When you click the Format Painter button on the Formatting toolbar, the format of the selected shape is copied. You then click the shape you want to format. If you double-click the Format Painter button, you can format multiple shapes on the drawing page.

In this exercise, you refine an unfinished diagram of the conference hall layout for a tradeshow hosted by Wide World Importers. Using the buttons on the Formatting toolbar, you apply a new fill color and line weight to a shape. Then you use the Format Painter tool to copy the formatting from one shape to another. Finally, you change the font size and color of some shapes.

OPEN the *FormatShapes* file in Documents\Microsoft Press\Visio 2007 SBS\03_Format.

1. Click the **China Booths** shape on the drawing page to select it.

Fill Color

2. On the Formatting toolbar, click the **Fill Color** down arrow.

   A color palette appears.

3. Pause the pointer over a color in the palette to see a ScreenTip that identifies the color.

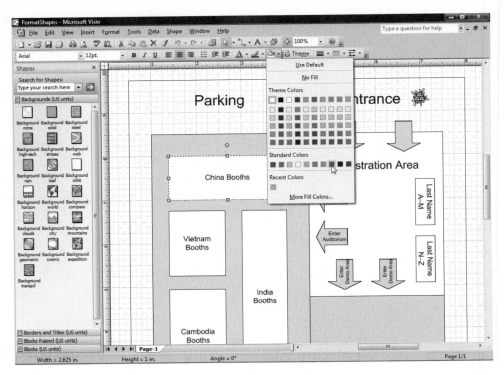

4. Under **Standard Colors**, click the blue color.

Visio fills the interior of the shape with the blue color. The shape remains selected.

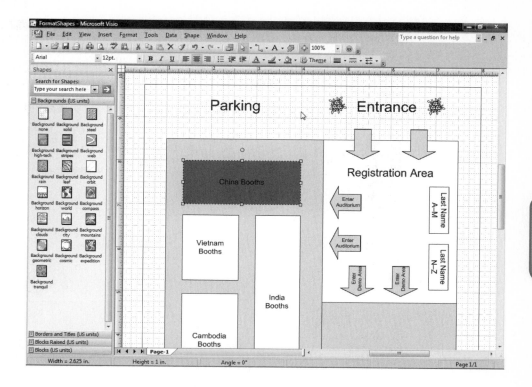

Tip After you choose a color from the color palette, you don't need to view the color palette each time you want to apply that color to a shape. Clicking the Fill Color button will apply the last color you selected from the palate to the shape.

Line Weight

5. On the **Formatting** toolbar, click the **Line Weight** down arrow to display a list of line weights.

6. Pause the pointer over a weight in the list to see a ScreenTip that describes the weight.

7. Click the line weight that displays the **Line Weight 9** ScreenTip.

   Visio applies a thicker border to the shape. The shape remains selected.

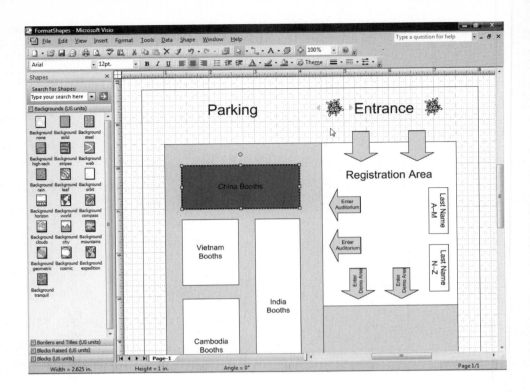

Format Painter

8. On the Standard toolbar, *double-click* the **Format Painter** button.

The pointer changes to a black color and a paintbrush appears next to it, indicating that the Format Painter tool is selected and you can now copy the formatting from one shape to another one.

Format Painter

9. One shape at a time, click the **Vietnam Booths** shape, the **Cambodia Booths** shape, the **India Booths** shape, the **Rest of Asia Booths** shape, the **Name A-M** shape, and the **Name N-Z** shape.

Visio copies the formatting from the China Booths shape to the selected shapes, changing their fill color to blue and line weight to 9.

> **Troubleshooting** If you can copy the formatting from the China Booths shape to only the Vietnam Booths shape, you didn't double-click the Format Painter button. You must double-click the button to copy the formatting to more than one shape. Select the China Booths shape again, double-click the Format Painter button, and then copy the formatting to the rest of the shapes.

10. Press the Esc key to switch back to the Pointer tool.

The pointer changes back to the Pointer tool icon.

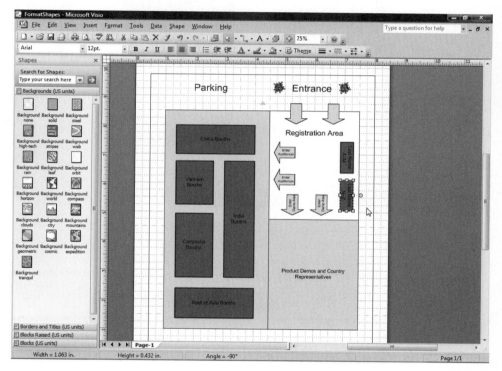

11. Position the pointer above and to the right of the **Name A-M** shape, and outside the large, white, rectangular shape.

> **Troubleshooting** You might need to zoom out of the drawing to see all the shapes on the drawing page.

12. Drag a selection box around the **Name A-M** and **Name N-Z** shapes.

As you drag, Visio draws the selection box. When you release the mouse button, the two shapes within the box are selected.

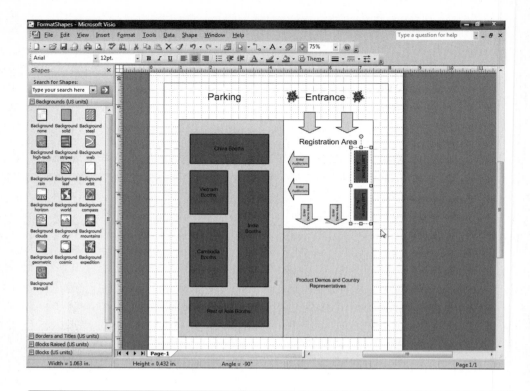

> **Troubleshooting** If you move the large, white, rectangular shape instead of select-ing the two shapes, you didn't position the pointer correctly. Press `Ctrl`+`Z` to undo your action and try again. Make sure you position the pointer outside the large shape and over a blank area of the drawing page where you can see the grid, and then drag to select the two shapes within the selection box.

Font Size

13. On the Formatting toolbar, click the **Font Size** down arrow, and then click **10 pt.** in the list.

Visio decreases the text size for both of the selected shapes.

> **Tip** You can also type a number in the Font Size box to change the text size rather than clicking a size in the list.

14. Click the top **Enter auditorium** shape.

15. While holding down the `Shift` key, click the bottom **Enter auditorium** shape and the two **Enter Demo Area** shapes.

The first shape you select (the primary shape) has a dark magenta selection box; the other shapes (secondary shapes) have light magenta selection boxes.

Text Color

16. On the Formatting toolbar, click the **Text Color** down arrow to display the color palette.

17. Pause the pointer over a color in the palette to see a ScreenTip that identifies the color.

18. Under **Standard Colors**, click the dark blue color.

Visio changes the text in the four selected arrows to dark blue.

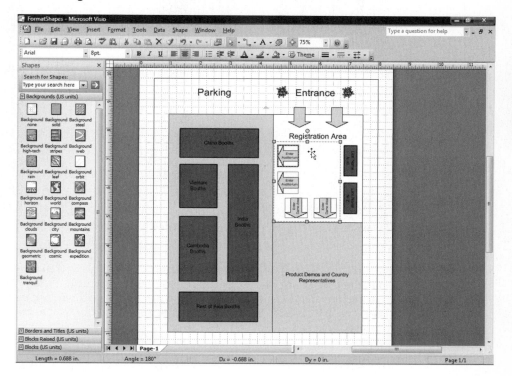

> **Tip** For quick access to all the commands on the Format menu, you can right-click a shape to display its shortcut menu, point to Format, and then click the appropriate command.

19. Click the pasteboard to deselect the shapes.

20. Hold down the [Shift] key while you select both **Potted Plant** shapes to the left and right of the word, **Entrance**.

21. On the Standard toolbar, click the **Fill Color** button, and then under **Standard Colors**, click the green color.

Save

22. On the Standard toolbar, click **Save** to save your changes to the diagram.

CLOSE the *FormatShapes* file.

Adding Decorative Elements to Diagrams

In addition to formatting individual shapes, you can add decorative elements, such as borders, title blocks, and *backgrounds*, to diagrams:

- **Border** A border is a design that appears around all or part of the drawing page.
- **Title block** A title block is a formatted title that can include information such as the date created.
- **Background** A background is a pattern that appears behind a diagram, much like the background of a Microsoft Office PowerPoint slide.

Borders, title blocks, and backgrounds are all special types of shapes that can add a professional look to your diagram. You'll find many of these shapes on the Backgrounds stencil and the Borders and Titles stencil that opens with many of the business-oriented templates in Visio, including the Block Diagram template. You can add a border, title, or background at any time, but these shapes are usually added as finishing touches just before you print or distribute your diagram.

A border shape that includes a title and date

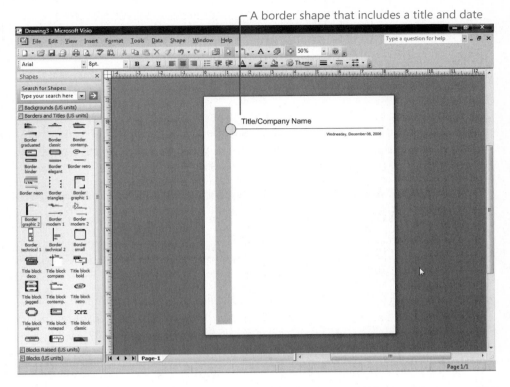

Visio includes dozens of border, title block, and background shapes. You can add them to a diagram the same way you would add any other shape—by dragging. When you drag a border onto the drawing page, Visio sizes it to fit the drawing page. Most borders include text, such as a title and page number. Visio adds the page number and generic text as a title placeholder, which you can replace with the real title. Some borders and title blocks display the date as well; like page numbers, dates are added by default.

When you add background shapes to your diagrams, Visio sizes them to fit the drawing page. However, they are different from borders in that when you drag a background shape onto the drawing page, Visio first creates a new *background page* named *Vbackground*. The background shape is placed on the new background page so it doesn't get in the way as you move and format the shapes in your diagram. Although it is on a separate page, the background shape on the background page appears on the drawing page and is printed with the diagram.

In this exercise, you fine-tune the appearance of the tradeshow layout by adding a border, title block, and background shape to the diagram.

> **OPEN** the *FormatDecorate* file in Documents\Microsoft Press\Visio 2007 SBS\03_Format.

1. Click the **Borders and Titles** stencil to display the shapes on the stencil.

2. From the **Borders and Titles** stencil, drag the **Border Classic** shape onto the drawing page.

   Visio centers and snaps the border shape into place. The shape includes generic title placeholder text, the date at the top of the page, and the page number at the bottom of the page.

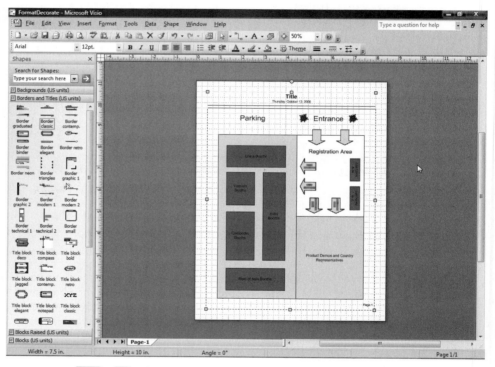

3. Hold down ⌈Shift⌋+⌈Ctrl⌋, and then drag a selection box around the generic title placeholder text to zoom in on it.

   Visio zooms in on the text.

4. Press the ⌈F2⌋ key to open the shape's text block and select the shape's text.

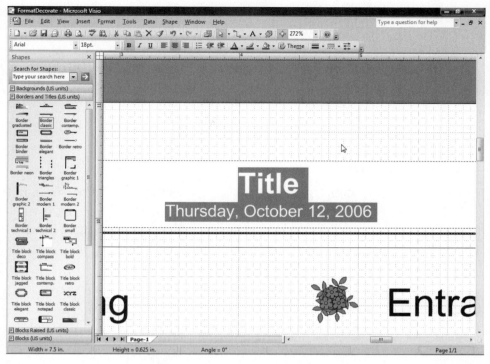

5. Double-click the word **Title** in the text block to select just that word, and then type
Tradeshow to replace the placeholder text.

Visio replaces the placeholder text with the new text.

> **Troubleshooting** If you select a title block shape and type, you can inadvertently
> replace the automatic date text as well as the title. If this happens, immediately press
> Ctrl + Z, and then try again. Make sure you select only the word *Title*, and then type.

6. Click the date to select it.

7. Type November 10–15, 2006.

Visio replaces the old date with the new date.

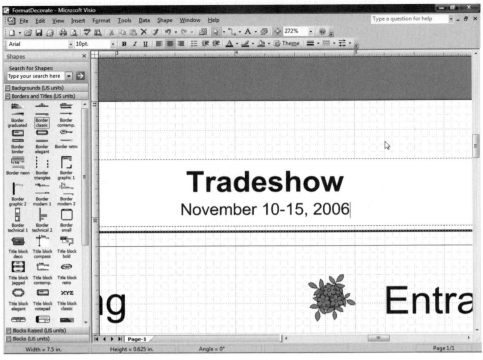

8. Press [Ctrl]+[W] to zoom out and view the whole drawing page.

9. Click the **Backgrounds** stencil to display the shapes on the stencil.

10. From the **Backgrounds** stencil, drag the **Background web** shape to the drawing page.

    Visio inserts a new page named *Vbackground-1* and adds the Background web shape, which appears behind the drawing page, to the background page. Notice the new *Vbackground-1* page tab at the bottom of the drawing window.

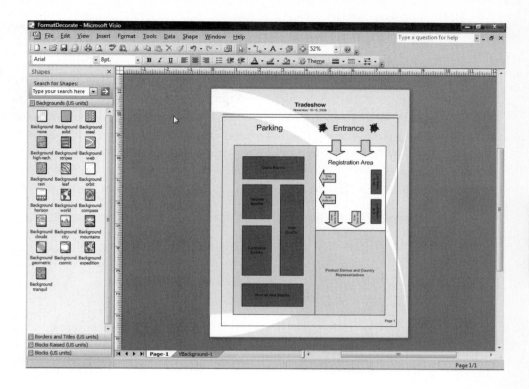

> **Tip** If you add a background shape to your diagram that you don't like, you can immediately undo your action by pressing [Ctrl]+[Z].

Save

11. On the Standard toolbar, click **Save** to save your changes to the diagram.

CLOSE the *FormatDecorate* file.

Using Shapes that Include Dates

Many of the title block and border shapes display a date when you add them to the drawing page. This special type of text is called a *field*—a type of text that Visio updates with the current date, for example, based on your computer's date and time settings. A date field can display the date in several formats, which are predetermined by the shape you select. However, you can edit date fields to display the date in a different format. Fields can contain other information, such as page numbers, document information, and custom formulas. To insert a field into a shape, select a shape, and then on the Insert menu, click Field.

Applying Themes to Entire Diagrams

The quickest way to add polish to a diagram is to use a *theme*—a set of coordinated colors and effects that Visio applies to all the shapes and text in a diagram, including backgrounds and borders. *Effect themes* include font, fill, pattern, shadow, and line formatting. *Color themes* include fill formatting for shapes. You can combine color and effect themes in a diagram. After you choose from any of the themes in the Theme – Colors or Theme – Effects task pane, Visio applies the theme immediately; if you don't like the result, you can simply choose a different theme. If you decide against applying a theme to your diagram, you simply click the color or effect theme named None.

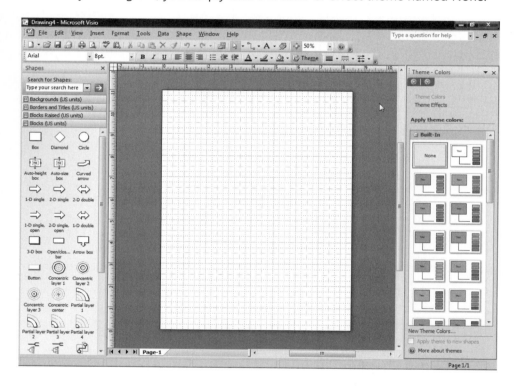

> **Tip** Effect themes also include formatting for connectors. You'll learn more about connectors and connecting shapes in Chapter 4, "Connecting Shapes."

If you already formatted some of the shapes in your diagram, you can apply themes to your diagram without changing the existing formatting of the pre-formatted shapes. You can also create, modify, and duplicate your own color and effect themes. For example, you can create themes that reflect your company's corporate color schemes.

> **Tip** The theme colors in Visio match the theme colors available in other Microsoft Office applications, such as PowerPoint and Word.

In this exercise, you add pizzazz to the layout of the tradeshow hosted by Wide World Importers by applying themes to the entire diagram, except for two plant shapes that you want to retain their custom formatting.

> **OPEN** the *FormatTheme* file in Documents\Microsoft Press\Visio 2007 SBS\03_Format.

1. On the **View** menu, click **Connection Points** to uncheck and turn them off so you can see your diagram better when zoomed out.

2. On the **Format** menu, click **Theme**.

   Visio opens the Theme – Colors task pane to the right of the drawing page.

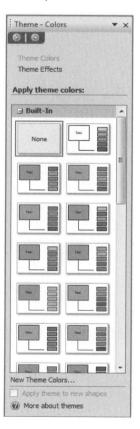

> **Tip** To create your own custom color theme, at the bottom of the task pane, click New Theme Colors.

3. Hold down the SHIFT key while you click both **Potted Plant** shapes next to the word, **Entrance**.

4. Right-click the shapes, point to **Format**, and then click **Allow Themes** to uncheck the command. Press the ⎋Esc key to deselect the shapes.

When you uncheck the Allow Themes command, Visio won't change the formatting of the selected shapes when you apply a theme to your diagram.

5. In the **Theme – Colors** task pane, pause the pointer over a theme button to see a ScreenTip that displays the name of the theme.

6. Click the **Median – Dark** theme.

Visio applies a coordinated set of colors to the entire diagram.

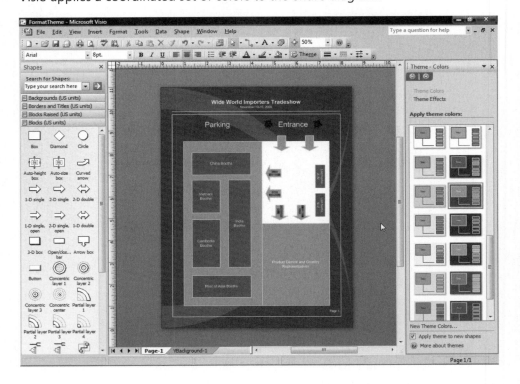

> **Important** Notice that when you apply a theme, Visio changes the color of the background, but not the color of the Potted Plant shapes and the clip art in the diagram. Visio does not apply the theme to Potted Plant shape because, in a previous step, you chose not to allow themes for these shapes, so Visio preserves their custom formatting. And, themes don't apply to clip art. If you decide you don't like a theme and you want to return to the original formatting in your diagram, you can press Ctrl + Z to undo the action.

7. Click the task pane title bar, and then click **Theme – Effects**.

Visio opens the Theme – Effects task pane.

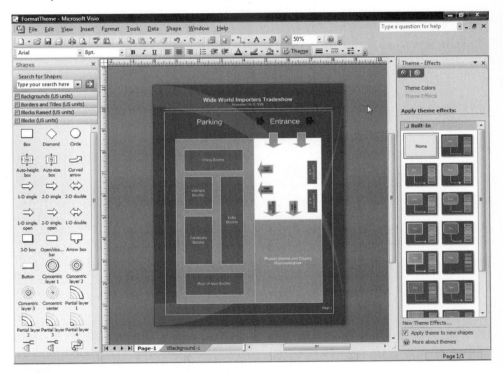

> **Tip** To create your own custom effect theme, at the bottom of the task pane, click New Theme Effects.

8. In the **Theme – Effects** task pane, pause the pointer over a theme button to see a ScreenTip that displays the name of the theme.

9. Click the **Mesh** theme.

Notice how Visio rounds the box corners of the shapes, adds a mesh fill pattern to shapes, makes the shapes slightly transparent, and changes the text type, color, and size.

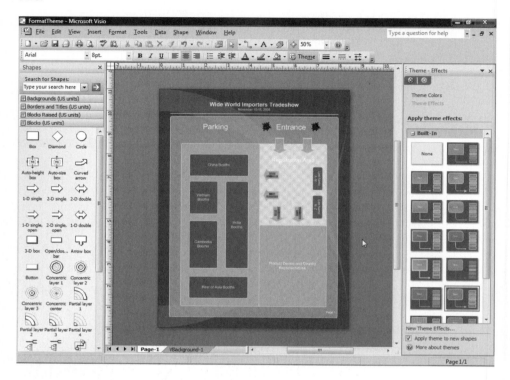

> **Tip** To apply a theme to all the pages in your drawing, right-click a theme, and then on the shortcut menu that appears, click Apply To All Pages.

10. At the bottom of the **Theme – Effects** task pane, click **New Theme Effects**.

Visio opens the New Theme Effect dialog box, which you use to create your own theme effects. Visio populates the dialog box with all the effect formatting from the drawing page.

11. In the **New Theme Effects** dialog box, in the **Name** box, type Wide World Importers.

12. Click the **Text** tab, and then in the **Font** box, make sure **Arial** is selected. Click **OK**.

Visio adds the new effect theme to the list in a new Custom area directly above the Built-in themes.

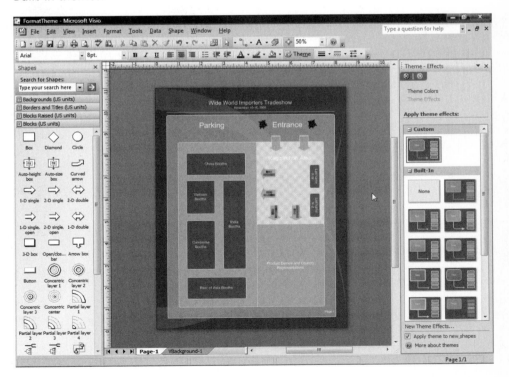

> **Troubleshooting** You might need to scroll up to the top of the theme effects to see the new theme.

13. Pause the pointer over the thumbnail preview to see the name of the custom theme, **Wide World Importers**.

14. Click the **Wide World Importers** custom theme to apply it to your diagram.

Notice the font in your diagram change to Arial.

> **Tip** You can edit, duplicate, or delete a custom theme by right-clicking it to see the theme's shortcut menu. You might want to duplicate a theme when, for example, you want to create several themes that are all slightly different. Start with a theme that includes the majority of formatting you want, and then modify each duplicate theme to fit your purpose.

15. At the top of the task pane, click **Theme Colors** to switch to the **Theme – Colors** task pane.

16. At the bottom of the **Theme – Colors** task pane, click **New Theme Colors**.

Visio opens the New Theme Colors dialog box, which you use to create your own theme colors. Visio populates the dialog box with all the color formatting from the drawing page.

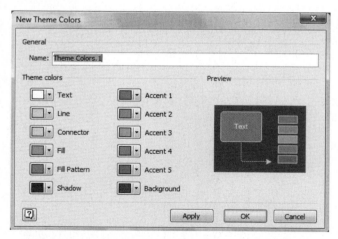

17. In the **New Theme Colors** dialog box, in the **Name** box, type Wide World Importers Colors.

18. Click the arrow next to the box that shows the **Background** color.

Visio displays a list of colors you can apply to the background.

19. Click **Tint 10%** to make the background a little lighter.

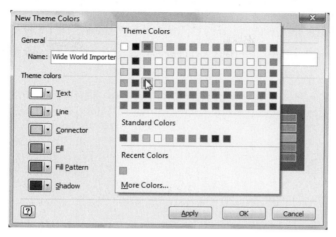

20. Click **OK**.

Visio adds the new color theme to the list in a new Custom area directly above the Built-in themes.

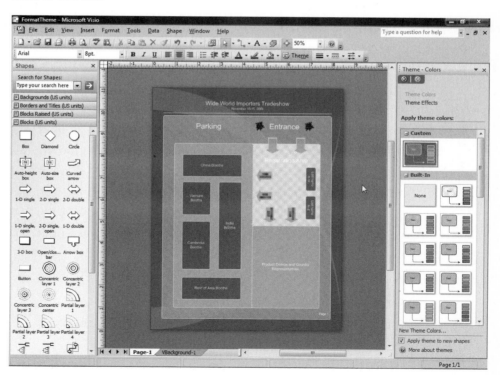

21. Pause the pointer over the thumbnail preview to see the name of the custom theme, **Wide World Importers Colors**.

22. Click the **Wide World Importers Colors** custom theme to apply it to your diagram.

    Notice the background change to a lighter shade of brown.

> **Tip** You can copy a custom theme from one drawing to another. In the drawing that has the custom theme, copy one of the shapes that has the theme applied. Open the other drawing and paste the shape into the drawing (on the pasteboard if you don't want to include the shape in your drawing). Open the appropriate task pane (Theme – Colors for a color theme or Theme – Effects for an effect theme) and you'll see the custom theme in the Custom list above the Built-in list. Apply the theme to the drawing, and then save the drawing. You can delete the shape you pasted from the other drawing. You cannot copy a custom theme from one 2007 Microsoft Office system program to another.

Save

23. On the Standard toolbar, click **Save** to save your changes to the diagram.

 CLOSE the *FormatTheme* file.

Key Points

- To format individual shapes, use the commands on the Format menu or the buttons on the Formatting toolbar.

- To quickly copy all the formatting from one shape to another shape, use the Format Painter tool. Double-click the tool to copy the formatting from one shape to multiple shapes.

- To add borders, backgrounds, or titles to your diagrams, drag a shape from the Borders and Titles stencil or the Backgrounds stencil onto the drawing page.

- To apply a color or effect theme to your entire diagram, use the Theme – Colors and Theme – Effects task panes. On the Format menu, click Theme.

- An effect theme includes formatting for fonts, fills, shadows, and lines.
- Create a new color theme by clicking New Theme Colors in the Theme – Colors task pane.
- Create a new effect theme by clicking New Theme Effects in the Theme – Effects task pane.
- Copy a custom theme from one drawing to another by copying a shape from the drawing with the custom theme to the other drawing. You can delete the shape from the second drawing if you don't need it.

Chapter at a Glance

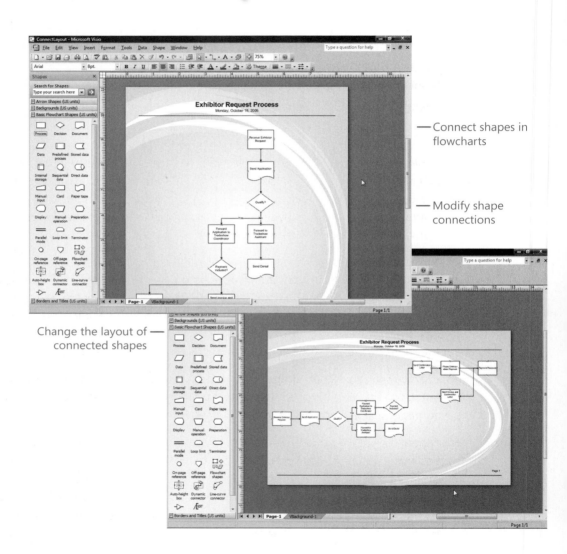

Connect shapes in flowcharts

Modify shape connections

Change the layout of connected shapes

4 Connecting Shapes

In this chapter, you will learn how to:

✔ Connect shapes in flowcharts.

✔ Modify shape connections.

✔ Change the layout of connected shapes.

Many types of Microsoft Office Visio diagrams depict related ideas, relationships, or sequences by showing shapes that are connected with lines. For example, a flowchart shows each of the steps in a process as a series of shapes connected by lines. Organization charts show employee relationships as a hierarchy of shapes connected by lines. Network diagrams use lines to show equipment connected to hubs.

Visio makes it easy to connect the shapes in these diagrams by using *connectors*—1-D shapes (usually lines or arrows) that connect 2-D shapes, such as the process shapes in a flowchart. If you rearrange the connected 2-D shapes, the connectors stay attached to the shapes and reroute for you, so you don't waste time redrawing lines. In some diagrams, such as flowcharts, you can even drag a 2-D shape between two connected shapes, and Visio reroutes the connector and connects all three shapes.

Visio 2007 makes connecting shapes even easier by adding a new feature: AutoConnect. With AutoConnect, Visio does all the connection work for you. Just drag shapes onto the drawing page, and Visio connects, aligns, and evenly distributes the shapes for you.

This chapter shows you how to connect shapes and work with connectors in a flowchart. However, the techniques that you use to connect flowchart shapes apply to other types of diagrams as well. As you modify shape connections and arrange connected shapes, you can take advantage of several layout tools that help you evenly distribute, align, and position shapes. You can even change the orientation of all the connected shapes in a diagram; for example, you can change the layout in a flowchart from top to bottom and from left to right.

See Also Do you need only a quick refresher on the topics in this chapter? See the Quick Reference entries on pages xxv–xliii.

> **Important** Before you can use the practice files in this chapter, you need to install them from the book's companion CD to their default location. See "Using the Book's CD-ROM" on page xix for more information.

Connecting Shapes in Flowcharts

Flowcharts are the ideal diagrams for visually representing business processes. For example, if you need to show the flow of a custom-order process through various departments within your organization, you can use a flowchart. Visio includes several different flowchart templates; however, the most common type of flowchart uses simple shapes to represent the basic elements in a business process, as shown in the following table.

Shape Name	Shape	What It Represents
Process		Steps in a business process
Decision		Decisions in a business process
Document		Steps that result in or require documentation
Data		Steps that require data

> **Tip** As you drag a flowchart shape onto the drawing page, a *dynamic grid* appears as a dotted line through the shape to show you how to align it with respect to the shapes already on the page.

You add connectors between these flowchart shapes to show relationships between them and the sequence of steps in a process. Flowchart connectors are usually lines with arrowheads that can include text to clarify the process being depicted. When Visio adds a connector (or you add one yourself), the endpoints of the connector *glue* to the shapes it connects—that is, Visio creates a bond that won't break unless you move a connector endpoint or delete the connector. When you select a connector that is glued to a shape, the connector's endpoints turn red, indicating that the connector will be rerouted when you move the connected shapes.

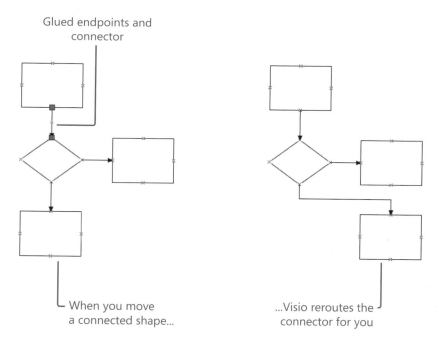

Glued endpoints and connector

When you move a connected shape...

...Visio reroutes the connector for you

The method you use to connect shapes in a flowchart determines how the connectors reroute and how much control you have over where connectors are attached to shapes. If you simply connect one shape to another without specifying a point of connection, you don't have any control over how the connectors reroute, which is preferable for many diagram types. However, when you need total control over your shape connections, you can connect shapes using *connection points*—specific points on a shape represented by a blue × symbol. That way, the connector stays connected to those specific points, regardless of where you move the shapes.

Visio provides several methods for connecting shapes. Each method offers different levels of control, and some are more suited for particular drawing types, as shown in the following table. When you work with Visio, you typically use a combination of these methods when creating your diagrams.

Connection Method	How To Use It	When To Use It
AutoConnect shapes by dragging a shape onto the drawing page	Drag a shape onto another shape on the drawing page, and when blue arrows appear around the shape on the drawing page, position the shape over one of the arrows.	Use this method when you want Visio to connect, align, and evenly distributes the shapes for you—all in one step. Example diagram types: Any diagram that shows relationships, such as basic flowcharts, cross-functional flowcharts, or audit diagrams. Level of control: When you don't care exactly where two shapes connect to each other, how the connectors reroute, and the exact position of the connected shapes.
AutoConnect shapes by clicking a shape on a stencil	Click a shape on a stencil, and then position the pointer over a shape on the drawing page. When blue arrows appear around the shape on the drawing page, click one of them.	Use this method when you want Visio to automatically connect shapes for you and you want to rapidly connect multiple shapes. Example diagram types: Any diagram that shows relationships, such as basic flowcharts, cross-functional flowcharts, or audit diagrams. Level of control: When you don't care exactly where two shapes connect to each other, how the connectors reroute, and the exact position of the connected shapes.

Connection Method	How To Use It	When To Use It
AutoConnect neighboring shapes that are already on the drawing page	Pause the pointer over a shape on the drawing page, and when blue arrows appear around the shape, move the pointer over the blue arrow closest to the neighboring shape to which you want to connect. The blue arrow turns dark blue, a red box appears around the neighboring shape to which you can connect, and a Connect to Neighboring Shape ScreenTip appears. Click the blue arrow to connect the two shapes.	Use this method when you want to connect neighboring shapes that are already on the drawing page. Example diagram types: Any diagram that shows relationships, such as basic flowcharts, cross-functional flowcharts, or audit diagrams. Level of control: When you don't care exactly how the connectors reroute.
Connect shapes as you drag them onto the page using the Connector tool	Click the Connector tool, and then drag shapes onto the drawing page. Each new shape is connected to the selected shape on the drawing page.	Use this method when you want to connect new shapes to the selected shape on the drawing page. Example diagram types: Any diagram that shows relationships, such as basic flowcharts, cross-functional flowcharts, or audit diagrams. Level of control: When you don't care exactly where two shapes connect to each other and how the connectors reroute, but you do want to precisely position the connected shapes.

Connection Method	How To Use It	When To Use It
Connect shapes already on the drawing page using the Connector tool	Position the pointer over a shape on the drawing page, and then drag to another shape to draw a connector between the two shapes. Or, position the pointer over a shape's connection point, and then drag to another shape's connection point to draw a connector between two shapes.	Use this method when you want to connect shapes that are already on the drawing page. Example diagram types: Basic flowcharts and data flow diagrams. Level of control: This method gives you control over the precise point of connection between two shapes, if you connect the shapes using their connection points.
Connect shapes that are already on the drawing page using the Connect Shapes command	Hold down the Shift key, select all the shapes you want to connect, in the order you want to connect them, and then on the Shape menu, click Connect Shapes.	Use this method when you want to connect shapes that are already on the drawing page in a specific order. Example diagram types: Any diagram that shows relationships, such as basic flowcharts, cross-functional flowcharts, audit diagrams, fault-tree analysis diagrams, and work flow diagrams. Level of control: When you don't care exactly where two shapes connect to each other or how the connectors reroute.

Connection Method	How To Use It	When To Use It
Connect shapes already on the drawing page by using a connector from a stencil	Drag a connector from a stencil onto the drawing page, position one endpoint on a connection point on one shape, and then position the other endpoint on the connection point on the other shape.	Use this method in diagrams that use specific types of connectors—for example, a 3-D arrow in block or ITIL diagram and network equipment in racks.
		Example diagram types: Basic, block, brainstorming, cause and effect, charts and graphs, ITIL, network diagrams, and value stream maps.
		Level of control: This method gives you control over the precise point of connection between two shapes.

> **Important** The next section of this chapter covers different types of connections, connection points, and how to reroute connectors in more detail.

In this exercise, you start a new diagram based on the Basic Flowchart template. You use AutoConnect and the Connector tool so that Visio draws connectors and connects the shapes in your flowchart for you. You add text to the shapes and connectors to indicate a *yes* or *no* decision.

1. Start Visio. On the **Template Categories** list, click **Flowchart**.

2. Under **Featured Templates**, double-click **Basic Flowchart**.

   The Basic Flowchart template opens a blank drawing page and the Basic Flowchart Shapes, Backgrounds, Arrow Shapes, and Borders and Titles stencils.

3. From the **Basic Flowchart Shapes** stencil, drag a **Process** shape onto the drawing page and position it near the top of the page.

4. From the **Basic Flowchart Shapes** stencil, drag a **Document** shape onto the drawing page, position it over the **Process** shape, position it over the bottom blue arrow that appears below the **Process** shape, and then release the mouse.

   Visio draws a connector between the shapes, and aligns and distributes them.

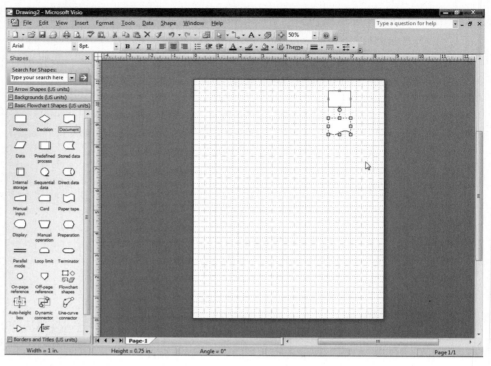

5. On the **Basic Flowchart Shapes** stencil, click the **Decision** shape.

6. Pause the pointer over the **Document** shape on the drawing page until blue arrows appear around the shape, and then click the bottom blue arrow.

   Visio adds a Decision shape below the Document shape and draws a connector between the shapes.

7. On the **Basic Flowchart Shapes** stencil, click the **Document** shape.

8. Pause the pointer over the **Decision** shape on the drawing page until blue arrows appear around the shape, and then click the bottom blue arrow.

   Visio adds a Document shape below the Decision shape and draws a connector between the shapes.

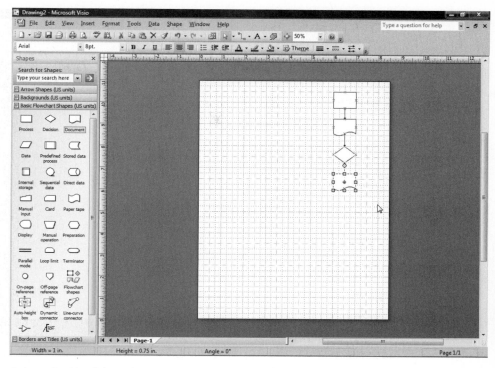

9. Select the **Decision** shape on the drawing page.

Connector Tool

10. On the Standard toolbar, click the **Connector Tool** button.

   The pointer displays a connector icon.

11. From the **Basic Flowchart Shapes** stencil, drag another **Process** shape onto the drawing page and position it to the left of the bottom **Document** shape.

   Visio draws a connector between the Decision and Process shapes.

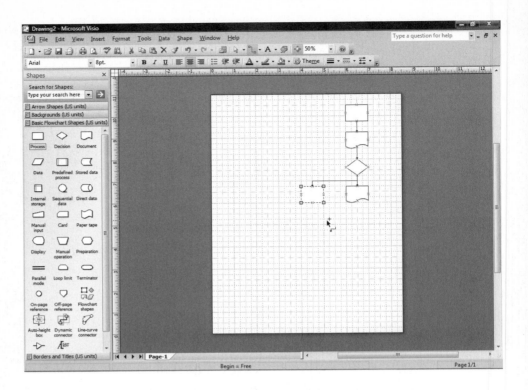

> **Tip** Visio can number the shapes in your flowchart for you. To specify the numbering settings, on the Tools menu, point to Add-Ons, point to Visio Extras, and then click Number Shapes.

12. From the **Basic Flowchart Shapes** stencil, drag a **Decision** shape onto the drawing page and position it below the **Process** shape you just added to the drawing page.

Visio draws a connector between the Decision and Process shapes.

13. From the **Basic Flowchart Shapes** stencil, drag a **Document** shape onto the drawing page and position it to the below the **Decision** shape you just added to the drawing page.

Visio draws a connector between the Decision and Document shapes.

Pointer Tool

14. On the Standard toolbar, click the **Pointer Tool** button.

15. From the **Basic Flowchart Shapes** stencil, drag a **Document** shape onto the drawing page and position it to the left of the **Document** shape you just added to the drawing page.

> **Tip** You can use the dynamic grid to align the two shapes.

16. On the Standard toolbar, click the **Connector Tool** button.

17. Pause the pointer over the last **Decision** shape you added to the drawing page until a red box encloses the shape.

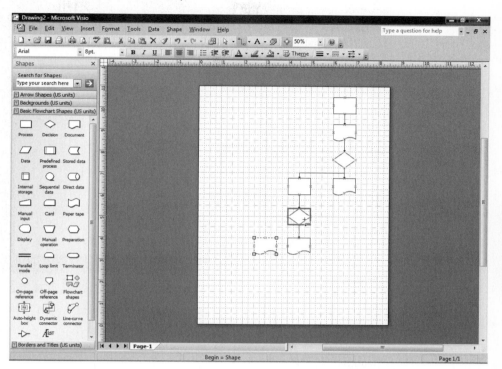

18. Drag to the last **Document** shape you added to the drawing page until a red box encloses that shape, and then release the mouse.

Visio draws a connector between the Decision and Document shapes.

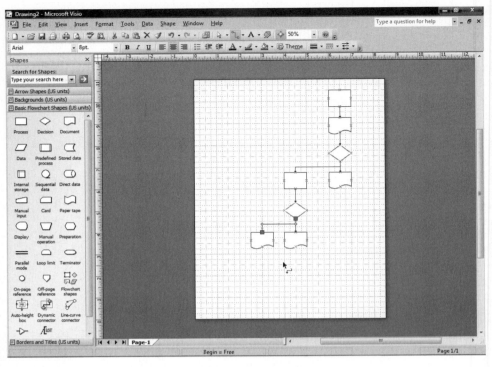

19. On the Standard toolbar, click the **Pointer Tool** button.

20. Click the top **Process** shape to select it.

21. Hold down ⌈Shift⌉+⌈Ctrl⌉ and left-click the top **Process** shape to zoom in on it.

22. With the top **Process** shape selected, type Receive Exhibitor Request.

    The text is added to the shape.

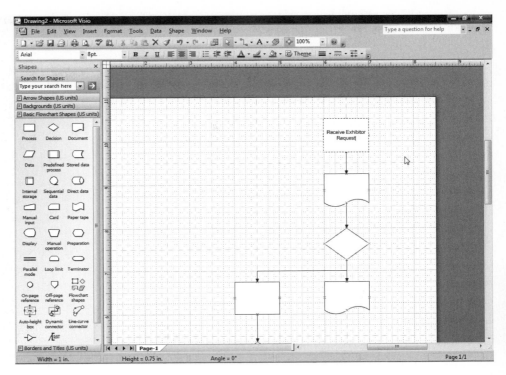

23. Select the next **Document** shape, and type Send Application.

24. Select the next **Decision** shape, and type Qualify?.

25. Select the next **Document** shape that's below the **Decision** shape, and type Send Denial.

26. Select the **Document** shape that's to the left of the previous **Document** shape, and type Forward Application to Tradeshow Coordinator.

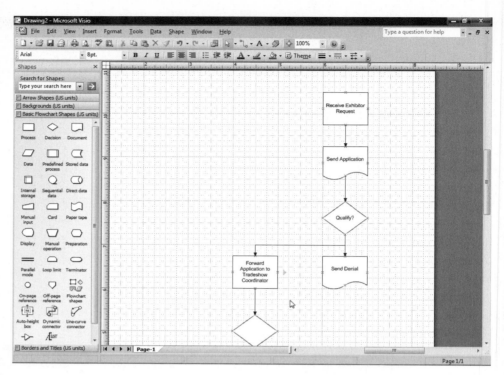

27. Select the connector that connects the previous **Qualify?** shape to the **Forward Application to Tradeshow Coordinator** shape.

The connector's endpoints turn red, indicating that the connector is glued to the shapes and will be rerouted when you move the connected shapes.

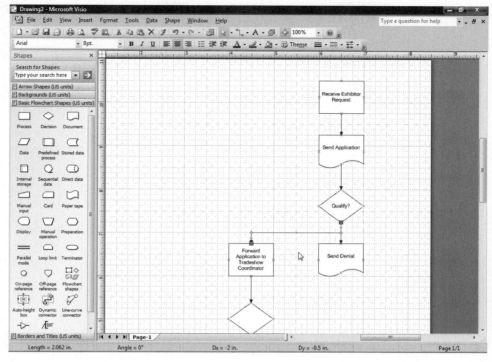

28. Type Yes.

    The text is added to the connector.

29. Select the connector that connects the previous **Qualify?** shape to the **Send Denial** shape, and then type No.

    The text is added to the connector.

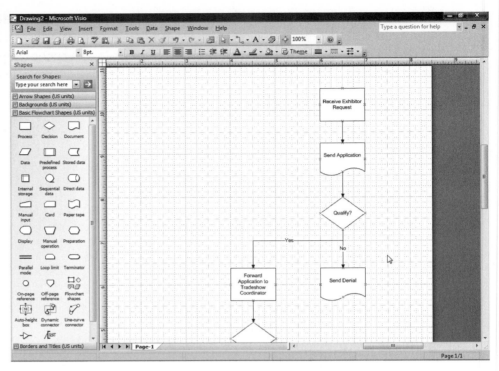

30. Click the pasteboard to deselect the connector.

31. On the **File** menu, click **Save As** to open the **Save As** dialog box.

32. In the **File name** box, type **ConnectFlowchart**, and then click the **Save** button to save the flowchart.

CLOSE the *ConnectFlowchart* file.

Modifying Shape Connections

Not only does Visio make it easy to create connections in diagrams, it also makes it easy to modify those connections. Perhaps you need to add a missing step to a flowchart or adjust a series of steps to make a process more efficient. Maybe you need some of the connectors in a flowchart to be rerouted in a specific way. With Visio, you can insert shapes between shapes that are already connected and move shapes around while the connections stay intact, which makes modifying a flowchart painless.

In the previous exercise, you connected shapes with a *shape-to-shape connection*; that is, you connected shapes without specifying a point of connection. When you move

shapes connected by a shape-to-shape connection, the connector reroutes and connects the shapes between the two closest points on the shapes. When you insert a shape
between two shapes that are connected by a shape-to-shape connection, Visio connects
all three shapes. For most types of flowcharts, shape-to-shape connections are sufficient
because you don't usually need to control the exact point of connection on each shape.
When you select the connector between two shapes with a shape-to-shape connection,
the glued connector endpoints are large, light red, and have no begin point or end point
symbols.

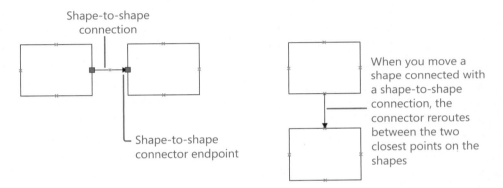

Shape-to-shape
connection

Shape-to-shape
connector endpoint

When you move a
shape connected with
a shape-to-shape
connection, the
connector reroutes
between the two
closest points on the
shapes

There might be times when you're working within design constraints that, for example,
require all Yes connectors to flow from the right side of the shapes and all No connectors
to flow downward in a flowchart. When you need total control over your shape connections, you can connect shapes with a *point-to-point connection*, which connects specific
points on the shapes. When you move shapes connected by a point-to-point connection,
the connector stays connected to those specific points, regardless of where you move
the shapes. When you add a shape between two shapes already connected by a point-
to-point connection, Visio connects all three shapes at specific connection points. When
you select the connector between shapes connected by a point-to-point connection, the
glued endpoints on the connector are small, dark red, and include begin and end point
symbols.

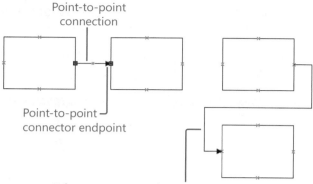

Point-to-point
connection

Point-to-point
connector endpoint

When you move a shape connected with a point-
to-point connection, the connector reroutes and
stays connected to the same points on the shapes

To create a point-to-point connection, instead of positioning the Connector tool over the
shape, you position it over a connection point—a specific point, represented by a blue ×
symbol.

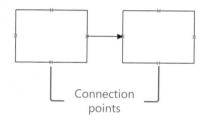

Connection
points

When you place the Connector tool over a connection point on a shape, a small red box
appears. Then you drag the connector to the small red box around the connection point
on the shape to which you are connecting.

> **Tip** You can use both shape-to-shape connections and point-to-point connections in a
> flowchart. You can also create your own connection points. For information about creating
> connection points and the different types of connection points, type **connection points** in
> the Type A Question For Help box.

In this exercise, you move a flowchart shape to a new position and see how the connector moves with the shape. You also insert a flowchart shape between two shapes that are
already connected. Then you create a point-to-point connection between a couple of
shapes using the Connector tool. Finally, you modify a connector segment and attach a
connector endpoint to a different shape.

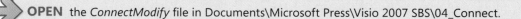

OPEN the *ConnectModify* file in Documents\Microsoft Press\Visio 2007 SBS\04_Connect.

1. Drag the **Send Denial** shape down approximately one inch.

The connector is resized but stays connected to the shape.

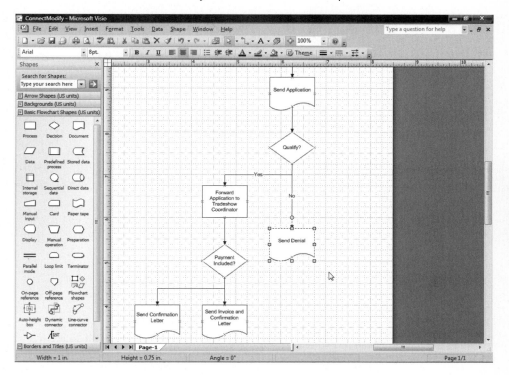

Tip You might need to zoom in to see the shapes better. Also, you can use the dynamic grid to precisely position the shape or hold down the [Shift] key to restrict its movement.

2. From the **Basic Flowchart Shapes** stencil, drag a **Process** shape onto the drawing page and position it on the connector between the **Qualify?** shape and the **Send Denial** shape.

As you hold the Process shape over the connector, the pointer changes to a scissors icon, indicating that you can cut, or split, the existing connection and reconnect all three shapes in the series.

Scissors icon

3. Release the mouse button.

Visio connects all three shapes in the series.

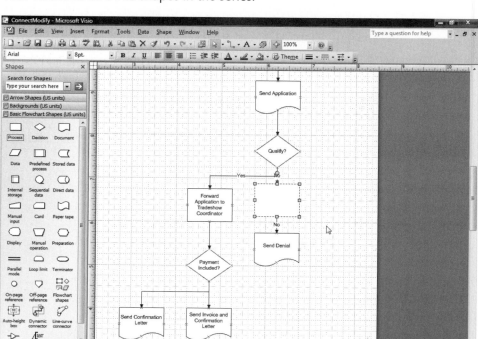

> **Important** Not all templates and connectors support connector-splitting behavior. To determine whether a template and connector support this behavior, drag a shape onto a connector between two shapes. If the connector is rerouted around the shape rather than attaching to it, the template, connector, or both don't support this behavior. To determine whether a particular connector supports splitting behavior, right-click the connector, point to Format on the shortcut menu, and then click Behavior to see the Connector splitting settings.

4. With the **Process** shape selected, type Forward to Tradeshow Assistant.

   Visio zooms in so that you can easily read the text as you type.

5. Click the connector between the **Forward to Tradeshow Assistant** shape and the **Send Denial** shape.

6. Press the F2 key to enter the text mode, and then press the Del key to delete the text from the connector.

> **Tip** To delete a connector, select it, and then press the Del key.

7. Click the pasteboard to deselect the shape.

8. Select the connector between the **Payment Included?** shape and the **Send Invoice and Confirmation Letter** shape.

The endpoints on the connector are large and light red, indicating that the shapes are connected with a shape-to-shape connection.

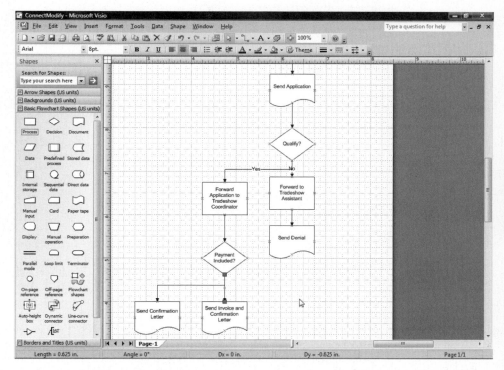

9. Drag the **Send Confirmation Letter** shape to the left a little, and use the dynamic grid to align the shape with the **Send Invoice and Confirmation Letter** shape.

The connector is rerouted and connects the shapes between the two closest points.

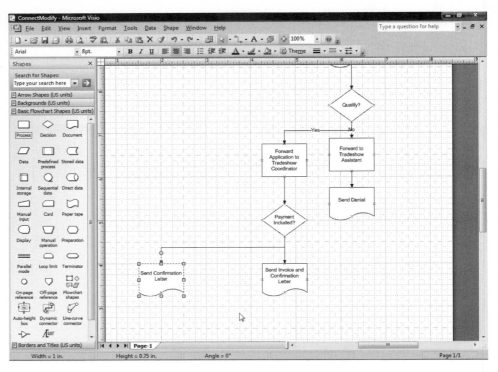

10. Select some of the other connectors in the flowchart—one by one—and notice that all the shapes in the flowchart are connected with shape-to-shape connections.

11. From the **Basic Flowchart Shapes** stencil, drag a **Process** shape onto the drawing page and position it below the **Send Confirmation Letter** shape.

12. With the **Process** shape selected, type Phone Exhibitor about Payment.

13. Click the pasteboard to deselect the shape.

Connector Tool

14. On the Standard toolbar, click the **Connector Tool** button.

15. Position the pointer over the bottom connection point on the **Send Confirmation Letter** shape.

A small, dark-red box encloses the connection point, indicating that you can draw a connector starting from that connection point.

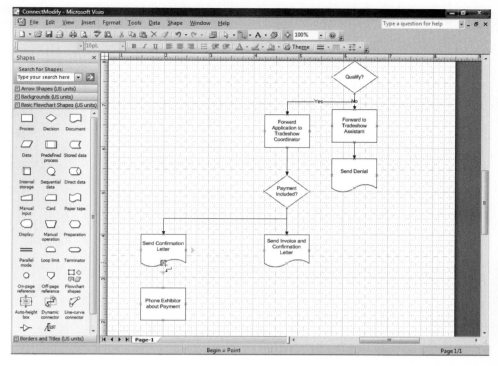

16. Drag the pointer to the top connection point on the **Phone Exhibitor about Payment** shape.

A red box encloses the connection point on the Phone Exhibitor about Payment shape.

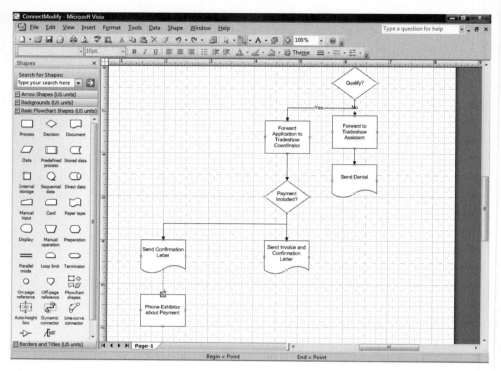

17. Release the mouse button.

Visio draws the connector and connects the two shapes using a point-to-point connection. Notice the small, dark-red endpoints on the connector, which indicate a point-to-point connection.

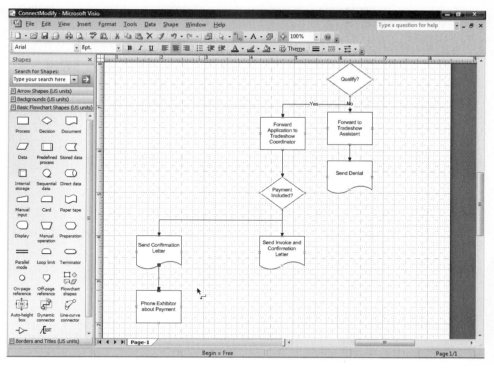

18. Click the **Phone Exhibitor about Payment** shape to select it.

19. From the **Basic Flowchart Shapes** stencil, drag a **Process** shape onto the drawing page and position it below the **Phone Exhibitor about Payment** shape.

Visio automatically connects the two shapes.

20. With the **Process** shape selected, type Payment Received, and then press the `Esc` key to exit the text mode.

21. Position the pointer over the right connection point on the **Payment Received** shape.

A small, dark-red box encloses the connection point, indicating that you can draw a connector starting from that connection point.

22. Drag the pointer to the left connection point on the **Send Invoice and Confirmation Letter** shape.

A red box encloses the connection point on the Send Invoice and Confirmation Letter shape.

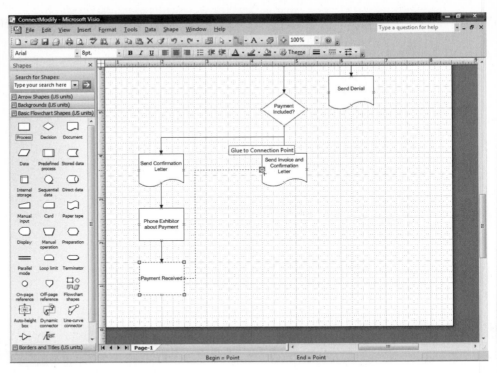

23. Release the mouse button.

Visio draws the connector and connects the two shapes using a point-to-point connection. Notice the small, dark-red endpoints on the connector, which indicate a point-to-point connection.

Pointer Tool

24. On the Standard toolbar, click the **Pointer Tool** button.

25. Position the pointer over the midpoint on the left segment of the connector you just drew.

A ScreenTip appears.

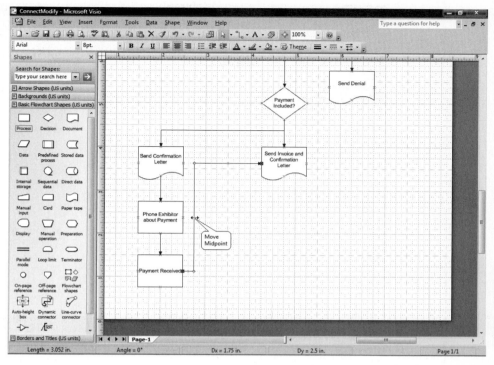

26. Drag the midpoint a little to the right to move that segment of the connector.

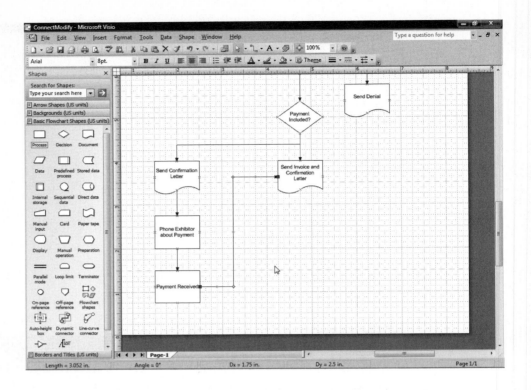

> **Tip** Connectors have a shortcut menu just as other shapes do. You can use the commands on a connector's shortcut menu to access commands that are unique to connectors, such as the Right-Angle Connector, Straight Connector, and Curved Connector commands. Right-click a connector to display its shortcut menu.

27. Move the **Payment Received** shape up and to the right to position it below the **Send Invoice and Confirmation Letter** shape.

The connector stays attached to both connection points on the shapes.

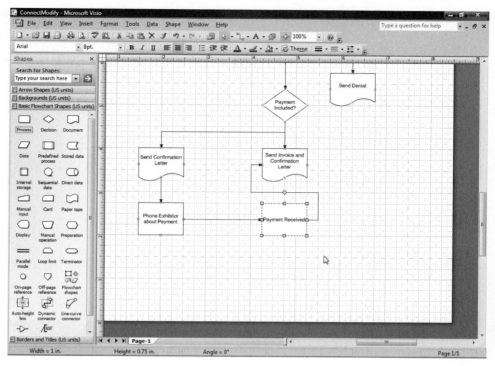

28. Select the connector between the **Payment Received** shape and the **Send Invoice and Confirmation Letter** shape.

29. Place the pointer over the red connector endpoint on the **Send Invoice and Confirmation Letter** shape.

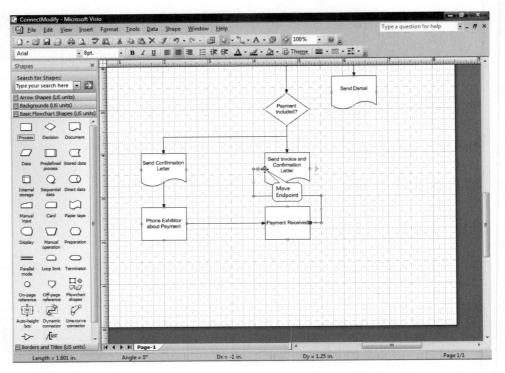

30. Drag the endpoint to the bottom connection point on the **Send Invoice and Confirmation Letter** shape.

Visio glues the endpoint to the connection point on the Send Invoice and Confirmation Letter shape and creates a new point-to-point connection.

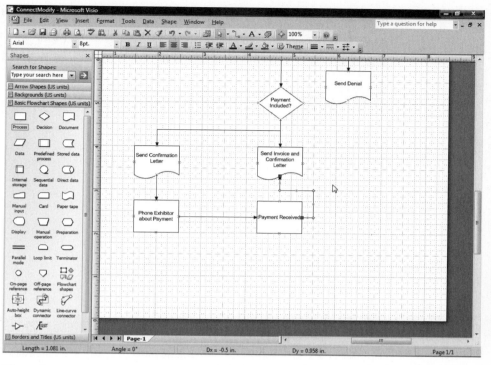

31. Place the pointer over the red connector endpoint on the **Payment Received** shape.

32. Drag the endpoint to the top connection point on the **Payment Received** shape.

Visio glues the endpoint to the connection point on the Payment Received shape and creates a new point-to-point connection.

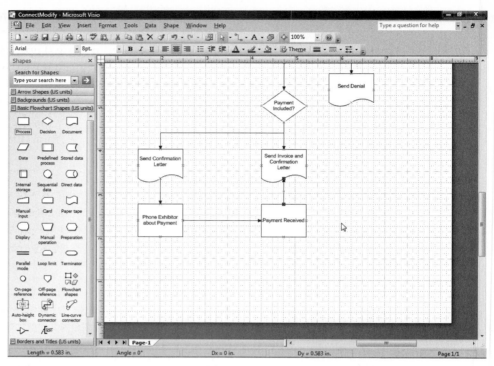

Save

33. On the Standard toolbar, click **Save** to save your changes to the diagram.

CLOSE the *ConnectModify* file.

Changing the Layout of Connected Shapes

Although flowchart layouts often flow from top to bottom, you can connect shapes from left to right, right to left, or even in a circular fashion. You can change the direction of the connected shapes in a diagram by using the Configure Layout command on the Shape menu. As long as you've created shape-to-shape connections throughout a diagram, you can change the entire layout and reroute connectors.

In addition, if you need to update a large flowchart to include a new process, you can use the Configure Layout command to realign the diagram. For example, you can add a new shape to an existing flowchart. After you connect the new shape, you can use the Configure Layout command to adjust the layout and realign all the shapes.

> **Troubleshooting** When you change the layout of a diagram, you might find that it no longer fits on the drawing page. In this case, you can change the page size or orientation by clicking Page Setup on the File menu. Then click the Page Setup tab, and select a different page size or orientation.

You can also adjust the spacing between three or more shapes at a time by using the Distribute Shapes command on the Shape menu. When you distribute shapes vertically, the spacing is defined by the top and bottom shapes in the selection. When you distribute shapes horizontally, the spacing is defined by the leftmost and rightmost shapes in the selection.

> **Tip** When you distribute shapes, the order in which you select the shapes is not important.

You can use the Align Shapes command on the Shape menu to align two or more shapes. When you align shapes, the order in which you select the shapes *is* important. The secondary shapes you select align with the first selected shape (the primary shape). The primary shape is indicated by its dark-magenta selection box.

In this exercise, you use the Configure Layout command to change a top-to-bottom flowchart to a left-to-right flowchart. You distribute several shapes so that they are evenly spaced, and then you align some shapes.

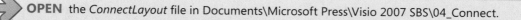 **OPEN** the *ConnectLayout* file in Documents\Microsoft Press\Visio 2007 SBS\04_Connect.

1. On the **Shape** menu, click **Configure Layout** to open the **Configure Layout** dialog box.

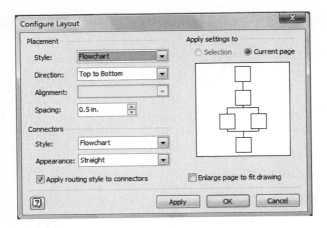

> **Tip** You can also change the layout of selected shapes in a diagram. To do this, first select the shapes whose layout you want to change, and then on the Shape menu, click Configure Layout.

2. In the **Placement** area, click the down arrow in the **Direction** box, and then click **Left to Right.**

A preview of the new layout appears in the preview area.

3. Click **OK**.

Visio changes the flowchart layout to left to right, but some shapes extend beyond the drawing page onto the pasteboard.

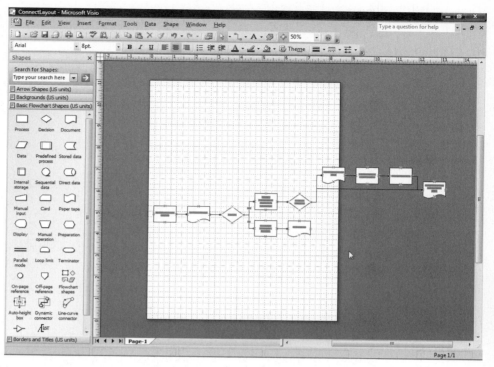

4. On the **File** menu, click **Page Setup** to open the **Page Setup** dialog box.

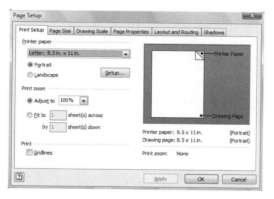

5. Click the **Page Size** tab, and then in the **Page size** area, click **Pre-defined size**. On the page size list, click **Folio: 8.5 in. x 13 in**.

6. In the **Page orientation** area, click **Landscape**.

A preview of the new page orientation appears in the preview area.

7. Click **OK**.

The drawing page is now set to a landscape orientation (wider than it is tall); however, the flowchart is slightly off center.

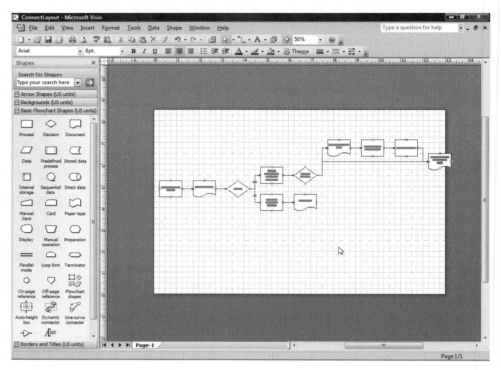

8. On the **Shape** menu, click **Center Drawing**.

    Visio centers the flowchart on the drawing page.

9. If you can't see the shapes on the right side of the flowchart, drag the horizontal scroll bar until you can see the **Send Invoice and Confirmation Letter** shape.

10. Select the **Payment Received** shape, and move it up and to the right a little.

11. Select the **Payment Received** shape, hold down the [Shift] key, and select the **Phone Exhibitor about Payment** shape and the **Send Confirmation Letter** shape.

    Visio selects all three shapes.

> **Important** Make sure you select shapes in this order because the order is important later in the procedure when you align the shapes.

12. On the **Shape** menu, click **Distribute Shapes** to open the **Distribute Shapes** dialog box.

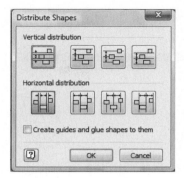

13. In the **Horizontal distribution** area, click the leftmost button, and then click **OK**.

Visio positions the shapes so the horizontal spacing between them is even.

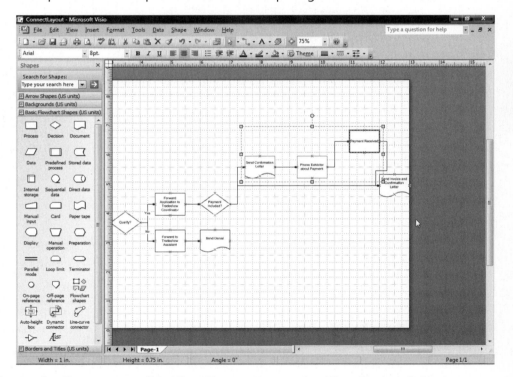

14. On the **Shape** menu, click **Align Shapes** to open the **Align Shapes** dialog box.

15. In the **Vertical alignment** area, click the leftmost button, and then click **OK**.

Visio aligns the top of the secondary shapes you selected with the top of the primary shape—the first shape you selected.

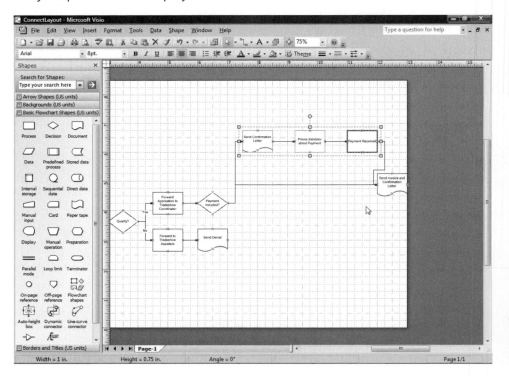

> **Tip** For quick access to the Distribute Shapes and Align Shapes commands, use the Distribute Shapes and Align Shapes buttons on the Action toolbar. To display this toolbar, right-click the toolbar area, and then click Action on the shortcut menu.

16. Select the **Phone Exhibitor about Payment** shape, hold down the [Shift] key, and then select the **Send Invoice and Confirmation Letter** shape.

Visio selects both shapes.

17. On the **Shape** menu, click **Align Shapes** to open the **Align Shapes** dialog box.

18. In the **Horizontal alignment** area, click the middle button, and then click **OK**.

Visio aligns the center of the Send Invoice and Confirmation Letter shape with the center of the Phone Exhibitor about Payment shape—the first shape you selected.

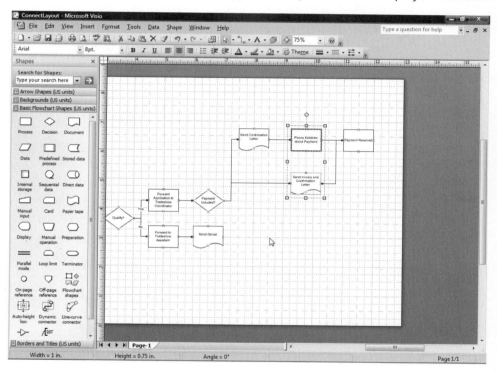

19. On the Standard toolbar, click **Save** to save your changes to the diagram.

Save

✕ **CLOSE** the *ConnectLayout* file.

Key Points

- Diagrams, such as flowcharts, organization charts, and network diagrams, include connectors that represent process sequences, employee relationships and hierarchies, and physical relationships among pieces of equipment.

- Visio 2007 makes connecting shapes even easier by adding a new feature: AutoConnect. With AutoConnect, Visio does all the connection work for you. Just drag shapes onto the drawing page, and Visio connects, aligns, and evenly distributes the shapes for you.

- You can use AutoConnect or the Connector tool to create connections in flowcharts. Connectors are 1-D shapes that connect 2-D shapes. In flowcharts, connectors are usually lines or arrows.

- Connectors can be glued to the shapes that they connect. You can break the bond by moving a connector endpoint or deleting the connector. Connectors that are glued to shapes are represented with a red endpoint.

- You can create two types of connections in Visio diagrams: shape-to-shape connections and point-to-point connections. Shape-to-shape connections connect shapes at the two closest points. Point-to-point connections connect shapes at specific connection points. When you move a shape connected by a point-to-point connection, the connector stays attached to the connection point.

- You can add text to a connector the same way you would any other shape—by selecting the connector and typing. Each connector also has a shortcut menu; right-click the connector to display it.

- You can reroute connectors by dragging an endpoint to a new shape or connection point, or by dragging a midpoint on a connector segment. Delete a connector by selecting it and pressing the Delete key.

- You can change the layout of all the shapes in your flowchart by clicking Configure Layout on the Shape menu.

- You can distribute three or more shapes evenly by using the Distribute Shapes command on the Shape menu.

- You can align two or more shapes by using the Align Shapes command on the Shape menu. Visio aligns the secondary shapes with the primary shape.

Chapter at a Glance

Create timelines to view
projects at a glance

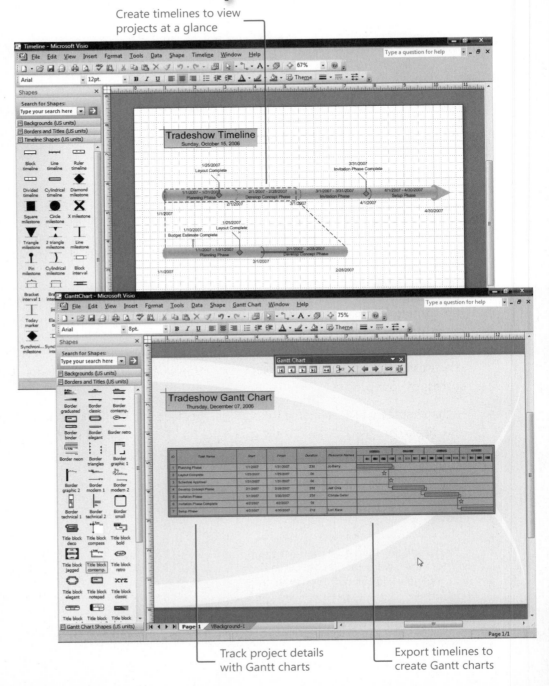

Track project details
with Gantt charts

Export timelines to
create Gantt charts

5 Creating Project Schedules

In this chapter, you will learn how to:

✔ Create timelines to view projects at a glance.

✔ Export timelines to create Gantt charts.

✔ Track project details with Gantt charts.

Effective project schedules are vital to a successful project. Project schedules help you track project dates, milestones, phases, and tasks. Although there are many ways to create project schedules, the finished product should make it easy to see the progress of the project from the big picture down to the details.

In Microsoft Office Visio, you can use *timelines* to visualize your overall project plan and present this information to executives and others who need to grasp it quickly. For project managers or team members who need more detail, you can create *Gantt charts* that display project specifics in a visual form that's easy to comprehend. Timelines and Gantt charts can help you keep your project on track, and they ultimately contribute to the success of your project.

In this chapter, you'll learn how to use Visio timelines and Gantt charts to track projects and display progress visually. You'll learn how to create a timeline to view the project schedule at a glance, export the timeline data to create a Gantt chart, and track project details with the Gantt chart.

See Also Do you need only a quick refresher on the topics in this chapter? See the Quick Reference entries on pages xxv–xlii.

> **Important** Before you can use the practice files in this chapter, you need to install them from the book's companion CD to their default location. See "Using the Book's CD-ROM" on page xix for more information.

Creating Timelines to View Projects at a Glance

When you're planning a project, timelines help you visualize the big picture and identify the project's scope. They come in handy when you want to present high-level project information to those who need to view this information at a glance. You can begin creating your timelines during brainstorming sessions and modify them as your project plans develop.

A timeline is a graphic that represents a specific period of time and the events that occur during that period. Timelines are particularly good at showing an overview of a project—project status, history of events, and what's to come. They also usually include milestones and interval markers.

Your project-schedule diagrams can include one or more timelines on a drawing page, and the timelines can be synchronized. For example, you can use an *expanded timeline* to represent a segment of the *primary timeline*, and then work with the expanded timeline individually to show more detail. You can add milestones or intervals to the expanded timeline just as you would to the primary timeline. The items you add to the expanded timeline don't appear on the primary timeline. However, any shape you add to the primary timeline also appears on the expanded timeline and is synchronized with the shape on the primary timeline. Think of the primary timeline as the complete high-level view of events, and the expanded timeline as a more detailed glimpse into a particular portion of that time period. You can use this synchronized timeline method to display various levels of information for one project—all on one page—in easy-to-understand form.

Milestones represent significant events or dates in a schedule, such as the date the building phase of a project is complete. They can highlight dates when you want to evaluate the progress of your project and make necessary decisions or adjustments. *Interval markers* specify a length of time. Use them to represent the beginning and end of a process or phase. For example, you could use an interval marker to represent the time period of a building phase in a project. You can even show the percentage of the interval that's complete as a line on the interval marker.

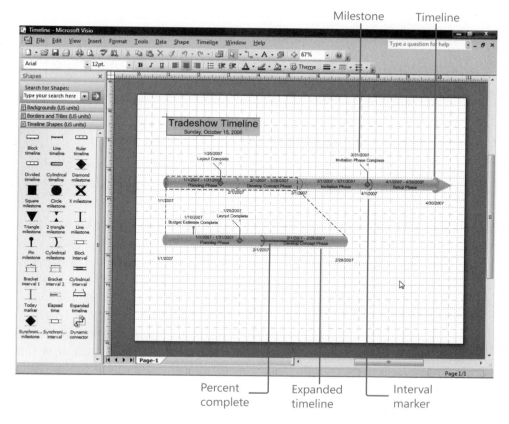

Milestone   Timeline

Percent complete   Expanded timeline   Interval marker

Create timelines with the Timeline template by adding shapes that represent milestones and interval markers to a timeline. After you add shapes to the timeline, you can reposition the shapes by dragging them. Visio updates a shape's date according to its position on the timeline. You can also right-click a shape and reconfigure it by clicking the appropriate command on the shape's shortcut menu. Visio repositions the shape on the timeline according to the shape's date.

In this exercise, you create a primary timeline and an expanded timeline. You add interval markers and milestones to both timelines, and then add a title and background to the diagram.

1. Start Visio. In the **Template Categories** list, click **Schedule**.

2. Under **All Templates**, double-click **Timeline**.

   Visio opens the Timeline template, which opens a blank drawing page and the Timeline Shapes, Borders and Titles, and Backgrounds stencils. Opening the Timeline template also inserts a Timeline menu on the Visio menu bar.

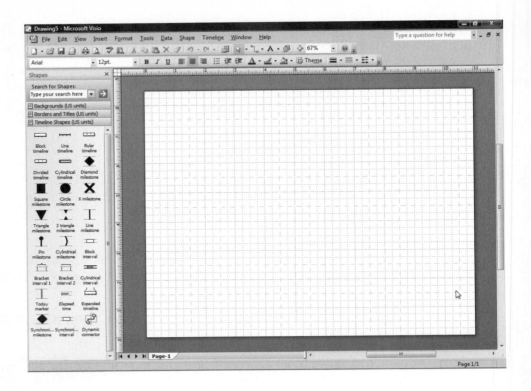

> **Tip** If you already have project data in a Microsoft Project, Microsoft Excel, or text file format, you can import it into Visio by using the Import Timeline Wizard. After you open the Timeline template, drag a timeline onto the drawing page and configure it. Then on the Timeline menu, click Import Timeline Data. Follow the steps in the wizard to import the project data.

3. From the **Timeline Shapes** stencil, drag a **Cylindrical timeline** shape onto the drawing page.

The Configure Timeline dialog box appears.

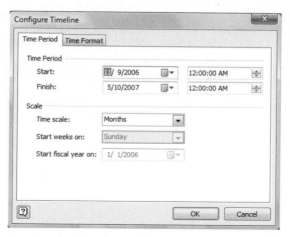

4. In the **Start** box, click the down arrow to display a monthly calendar. In the calendar, click the left or right arrow to display the month of January, and then select the start date for the timeline by clicking **1**.

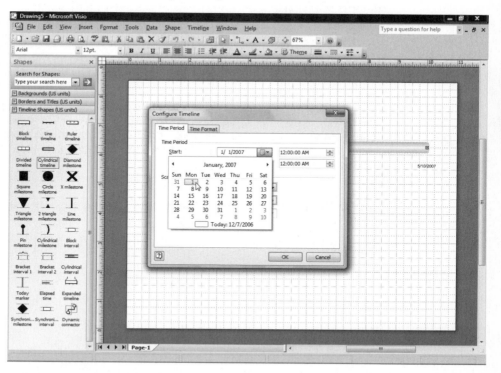

5. In the **Finish** box, click the down arrow to display a monthly calendar. In the calendar, click the left or right arrow to display the month of April, select the finish date for the timeline by clicking **30**, and then click **OK**.

Visio positions the timeline on the drawing page and adds dates to it.

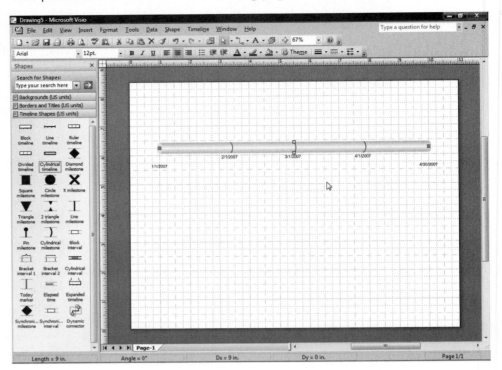

> **Tip** To reconfigure the timeline, right-click it, and then click Configure Timeline on the shortcut menu. Notice the shortcut menu also includes commands for changing the timeline type and date and time formats.

6. On the **Format** menu, click **Theme**.

   Visio opens the **Theme – Colors** task pane.

7. In the **Apply theme colors** list, scroll the theme color list until you see the green **Metro** theme, and then click it.

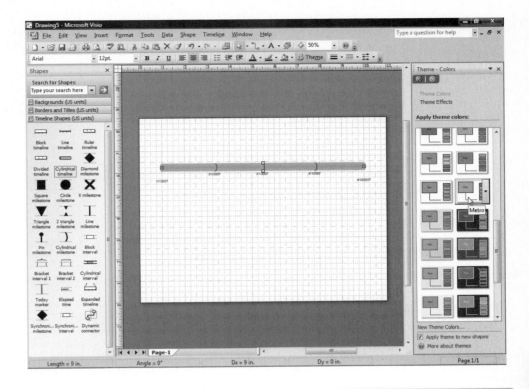

> **Tip** When you pause the pointer over a theme preview, Visio displays its name.

8. To add an arrowhead to the right end of the timeline, right-click the timeline, and then click **Show Finish Arrowhead**.

Visio adds an arrowhead to the right end of the timeline.

> **Tip** To change the orientation of a timeline, select the timeline, and then on the Shape menu, point to Rotate or Flip, and click the appropriate command.

9. From the **Timeline Shapes** stencil, drag a **Cylindrical interval** shape onto the left area of the timeline.

The Configure Interval dialog box appears.

10. In the **Start date** box, click the down arrow to display a monthly calendar. In the calendar, click the left or right arrow to display the month of January, and select the start date for the interval by clicking **1**.

11. In the **Finish date** box, click the down arrow to display a monthly calendar. In the calendar, click the left or right arrow to display the month of January, and select the finish date for the interval by clicking **31**.

12. In the **Description** box, select the placeholder text, and replace it by typing Planning Phase.

13. Click **OK**.

Visio positions the interval shape in the correct position on the timeline.

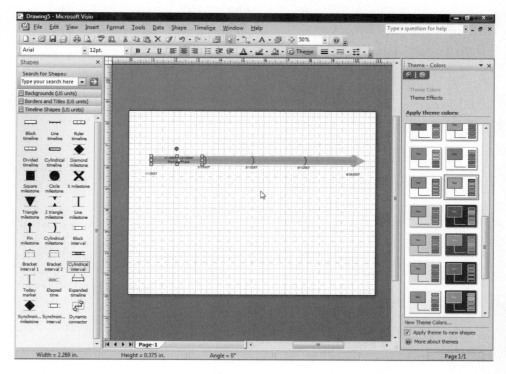

> **Tip** To reconfigure the interval, right-click it, and click Configure Interval on the shortcut menu. To quickly modify the interval description, select the shape, press the F2 key to open the shape's text block, and type a new description. Notice the short-cut menu also includes commands for changing the interval type and showing the percentage of the interval that's complete.

14. From the **Timeline Shapes** stencil, drag three more **Cylindrical interval** shapes onto the timeline and configure them with the information shown in the following table.

Start Date	Finish Date	Label
February 1	February 28	Develop Concept Phase
March 1	March 31	Invitation Phase
April 1	April 30	Setup Phase

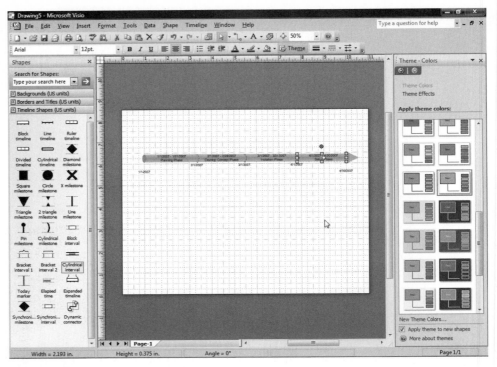

15. From the **Timeline Shapes** stencil, drag a **Diamond milestone** shape anywhere on the timeline.

    The Configure Milestone dialog box appears.

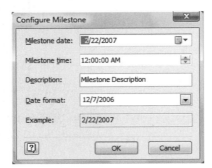

16. In the **Milestone date** box, click the down arrow to display a monthly calendar. In the calendar, click the left or right arrow to display the month of March, and select the milestone date by clicking **31**.

17. In the **Description** box, select the placeholder text, and replace it by typing Invitation Phase Complete.

18. Click **OK**.

Visio positions the milestone shape on the timeline.

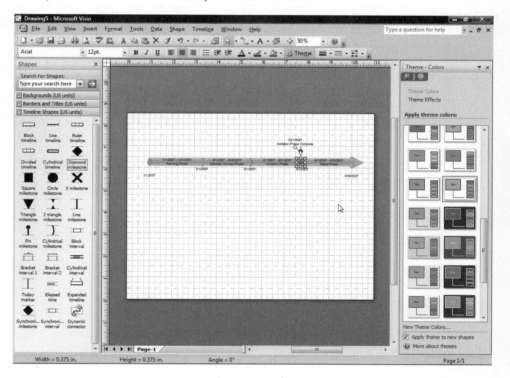

> **Tip** To reconfigure the milestone, right-click it, and click Configure Milestone on the shortcut menu. Notice the shortcut menu also includes commands for changing the milestone type. To quickly modify the milestone description, select the shape, press the F2 key to open the shape's text block, and type a new description.

19. From the **Timeline Shapes** stencil, drag an **Expanded timeline** shape onto the drawing page and position it below and left-aligned with the primary timeline.

The Configure Timeline dialog box appears.

20. In the **Start** box, click the down arrow to display a monthly calendar. In the calendar, click the left or right arrow to display the month of January, and select the start date for the timeline by clicking **1**.

21. In the **Finish** box, click the down arrow to display a monthly calendar. In the calendar, click the left or right arrow to display the month of February, and select the finish date for the timeline by clicking **28**.

22. Click **OK**.

Visio adds an expanded timeline for January and February to the drawing page. On the expanded timeline, Visio adds intervals that are synchronized with the intervals on the primary timeline. Gray dashed lines associate the two timelines and indicate the section of the primary timeline that the expanded timeline represents.

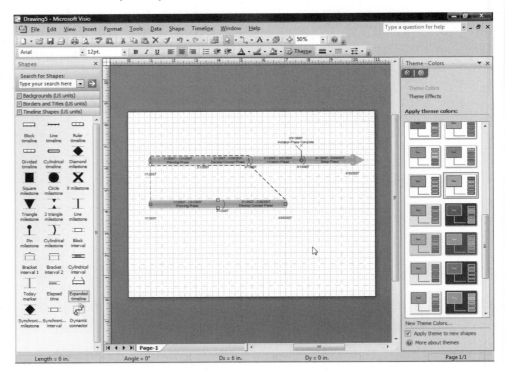

23. From the **Timeline Shapes** stencil, drag a **Pin milestone** shape onto the expanded timeline.

The Configure Milestone dialog box appears.

24. In the **Milestone date** box, click the down arrow to display a monthly calendar. In the calendar, click the left or right arrow to display the month of January, and select the milestone date by clicking **10**.

25. In the **Description** box, select the placeholder text, and replace it by typing Budget Estimate Complete.

26. Click **OK**.

Visio positions the milestone shape on the expanded timeline. Notice that the milestone doesn't appear on the primary timeline.

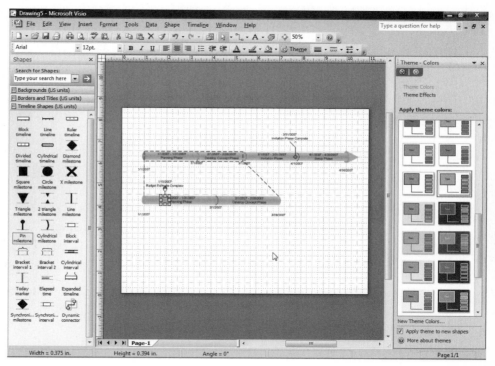

27. From the **Timeline Shapes** stencil, drag a **Diamond milestone** shape onto the primary timeline.

The Configure Milestone dialog box appears.

28. In the **Milestone date** box, click the down arrow to display a monthly calendar. In the calendar, click the left or right arrow to display the month of January, and select the milestone date by clicking **20**.

29. In the **Description** box, select the placeholder text, and replace it by typing Layout Complete.

30. Click **OK**.

Visio positions the milestone shape on the primary timeline. Notice that the milestone also appears on the expanded timeline.

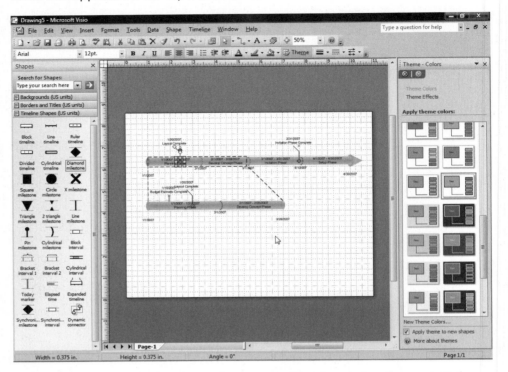

31. Right-click the **Layout Complete** milestone on the primary timeline, and click **Configure Milestone** on the shortcut menu.

32. In the **Milestone date** box, click the down arrow to display a monthly calendar. In the calendar, select the milestone date by clicking **25**, and then click **OK**.

Visio repositions the milestone shape on both timelines.

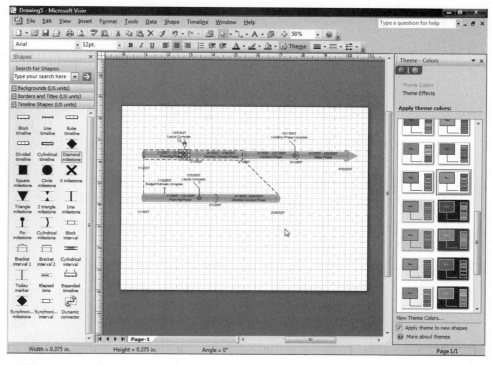

33. Right-click the **Develop Concept Phase** interval marker on the expanded timeline, and click **Set Percent Complete** on the shortcut menu.

34. In the **Percent Complete** box, type 50, and then click **OK**.

35. Right-click the **Develop Concept Phase** interval marker on the expanded timeline, and click **Show Percent Complete** on the shortcut menu.

    Visio shows the percent complete with a line on the interval marker. Notice the line appears on the expanded timeline, but not on the primary timeline.

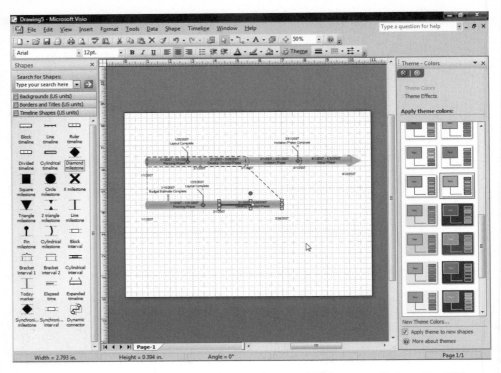

36. To add a title to the diagram, click the **Borders and Titles** stencil, drag the **Title block contemp.** shape onto the drawing page, and position it in the upper-left corner of the page.

The Title block contemp. shape includes title placeholder text and the current date.

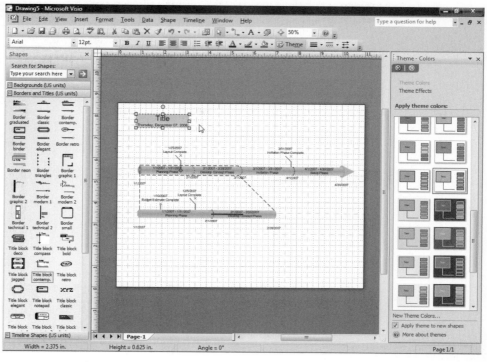

37. With the **Title block contemp.** shape selected, press the F2 key.

38. Highlight the word *Title*, and type Tradeshow Timeline.

  The shape expands to fit your title.

39. Click the pasteboard to close the text block and deselect the title shape.

40. Click the title shape, and drag it to align it with the left edge of the timeline.

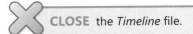

41. On the **File** menu, click **Save As** to open the **Save As** dialog box.

42. In the **File name** box, type Timeline, and then click the **Save** button to save the diagram.

CLOSE the *Timeline* file.

> **Tip** For more information about creating timelines, type Timeline in the Type A Question For Help box in the upper-right corner of the Visio window.

Exporting Timelines to Create Gantt Charts

When you use Visio diagrams to schedule your projects, you usually start by visualizing the big picture with timelines, and then you create Gantt charts to display project details. Instead of creating a Gantt chart from scratch, you can export your timeline data to the Microsoft Office Project file format with the Export Timeline Data command. You can use this data to create a Visio Gantt chart by using the Import Project Data Wizard, which is available on the Gantt Chart menu in a diagram started using the Gantt Chart template.

> **Tip** As you revise your Gantt charts, you'll no doubt make changes to the overall schedule as well. Just as you can export timeline data to create Gantt charts, you can also export Gantt chart data to create new timelines by using the Export Project Data Wizard, which you can start by clicking the Export command on the Gantt Chart menu.

In this exercise, you open an existing timeline, and use the Export Timeline Data command to export the timeline data. Then you use the Import Project Data Wizard to create a Gantt chart from that data.

> **Important** To complete this exercise, you need Microsoft Office Project (version 2000 or later) installed on your computer. If you don't have Project installed, the Export Timeline Data command doesn't appear on the Timeline menu.

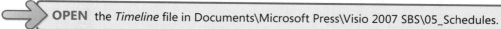 **OPEN** the *Timeline* file in Documents\Microsoft Press\Visio 2007 SBS\05_Schedules.

1. Select the primary timeline on the drawing page.

> **Troubleshooting** You must select a timeline on the drawing page before you can export timeline data. To quickly select a timeline, click either edge of the timeline.

2. On the **Timeline** menu, click **Export Timeline Data**.

3. A message appears that asks you if you'd like to export all markers on the timeline's expanded child timelines. Click **No**.

   The Export Timeline Data dialog box appears.

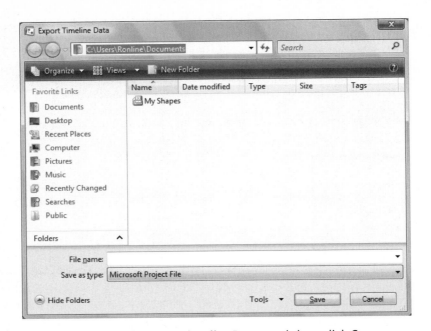

4. In the **File name** box, type TimelineData, and then click **Save**.

   Visio saves the timeline data in Microsoft Project File (*.*mpp*) file format and in the Documents folder by default.

   > **Tip** You can open the exported timeline data in Project to plan your projects in more detail and incorporate them into other enterprise schedules.

5. When you see a message stating that the project has been successfully exported, click **OK**.

6. On the **File** menu, point to **New**, point to **Schedule**, and then click **Gantt Chart**.

   Visio opens the Gantt Chart template and three stencils, and the Gantt Chart Options dialog box appears. When you open the Gantt Chart template, a Gantt Chart menu and toolbar also appear.

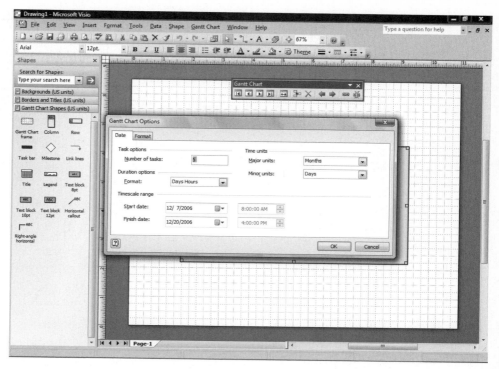

7. In the **Gantt Chart Options** dialog box, click **Cancel**.

   Visio deletes the Gantt chart frame from the drawing page and closes the Gantt Chart Options dialog box.

8. On the **Gantt Chart** menu, click **Import**.

   The first page of the Import Project Data Wizard appears.

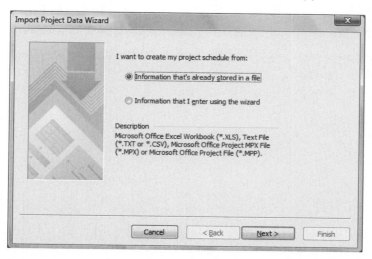

9. On the first page of the **Import Project Data Wizard**, select the **Information that's already stored in a file** option, and then click **Next**.

10. On the second page of the **Import Project Data Wizard**, click **Microsoft Office Project File**, and then click **Next**.

11. On the third page of the **Import Project Data Wizard**, click **Browse**, navigate to the Documents folder, double-click **TimelineData**, and then click **Next**.

12. On the fourth page of the **Import Project Data Wizard**, click **Next**.

    The wizard populates the pages with information used most often in Gantt charts, so you don't need to make any changes and can accept the default information.

13. On the fifth page of the **Import Project Data Wizard**, click **Next**.

    By default, Visio includes all tasks from the data in the Gantt chart.

14. On the last page of the **Import Project Data Wizard**, click **Finish**.

    Visio creates the Gantt chart from the timeline data.

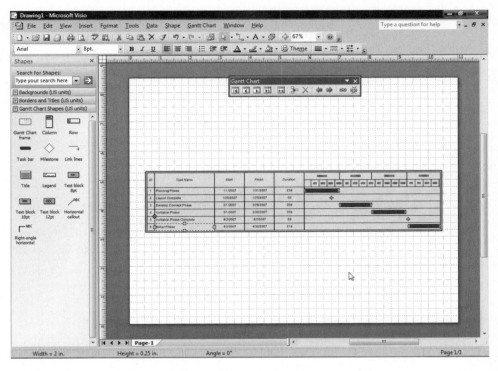

15. On the **File** menu, click **Save As** to open the **Save As** dialog box.

16. In the **File name** box, type **NewGantt**, and then click the **Save** button to save the drawing.

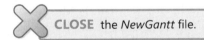

CLOSE the *NewGantt* file.

Tracking Project Details with Gantt Charts

Just as you use Visio timelines to view your project at a glance, you use Gantt charts to manage the project details. With Gantt charts, you can track the details of each project task, create task dependencies, see how changes to one task affect another, and quickly identify task owners and status. A Gantt chart includes a list of project tasks and details about the tasks, *Gantt bars* that represent the duration of each task, and a timescale. With Gantt charts, you can track the specifics that project managers and project members need to complete their tasks and keep the project on schedule.

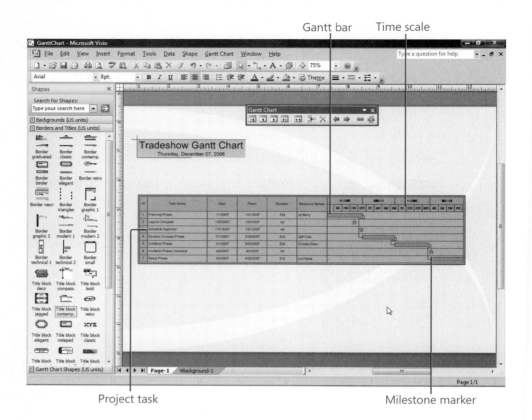

Gantt bar   Time scale

Project task   Milestone marker

You can create Gantt charts from existing timeline data by using the Import Project Data Wizard or from scratch by using the Gantt Chart template. To create a Gantt chart from scratch, on the File menu, point to New, point to Project Schedule, and then click Gantt Chart. Then use the Gantt Chart Options dialog box to configure and format your Gantt chart.

After you create a Gantt chart from existing data or from scratch, you add rows and columns to the chart. Each row represents a task, and each Gantt bar in a row represents the duration of the task. Each column represents project data you want to track, such as start date, end date, percentage complete, resource name, and task notes.

You can also show that one task can't start until another ends by creating task dependencies. To create task dependencies, you select the Gantt bar for the task that starts first, select the bar for the next task, and then link the bars. Visio draws arrows between the linked tasks.

In this exercise, you open the Gantt chart you created in the previous exercise and track task details by creating task dependencies, inserting columns, and creating new tasks. For visual appeal, you also add a title and background to the diagram.

OPEN the *NewGantt* file in Documents\Microsoft Press\Visio 2007 SBS\05_Schedules.

1. Select the first blue Gantt bar in the chart.

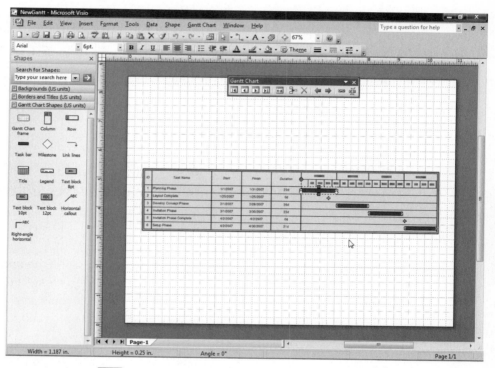

2. Hold down the [Shift] key while you select the three other Gantt bars, from top to bottom.

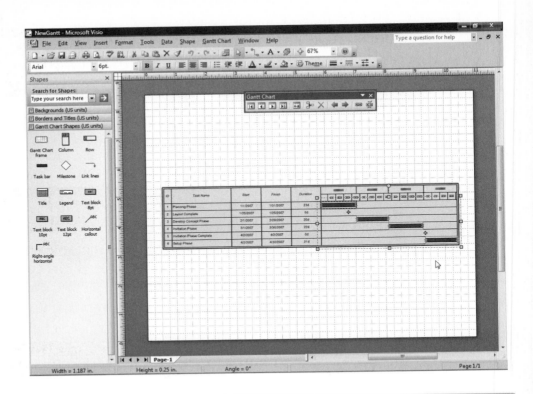

> **Important** The order in which you select and link the tasks is important. Select the Gantt bar for the task that starts first, the bar for the task that can't start until the other ends, and so on. The bar you select first (the primary shape) is enclosed by a dark magenta selection box. The selection boxes for the other bars (secondary shapes) are light magenta, and the selection box for all the shapes is green.

3. To create task dependencies, on the **Gantt Chart** menu, click **Link Tasks**.

Visio links the selected tasks with lines that show the dependences between tasks.

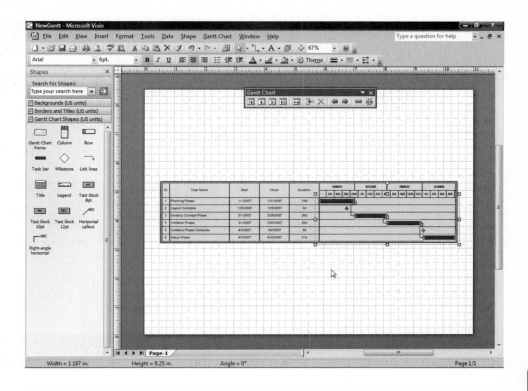

> **Tip** Alternatively, you could right-click one of the selected tasks, and click Link Tasks on the shortcut menu. To unlink tasks, select the tasks you want to unlink, right-click one of the selected tasks, and then click Unlink Tasks on the shortcut menu.

4. Press the `Esc` key to deselect everything.

5. To track more task details, right-click the **Duration** column, and click **Insert Column**.

The Insert Column dialog box appears.

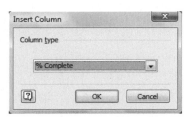

6. To add columns with which you can track each task owner, click the down arrow, click **Resource Names** in the list, and then click **OK**.

Visio inserts the Resource Names column after the Duration column.

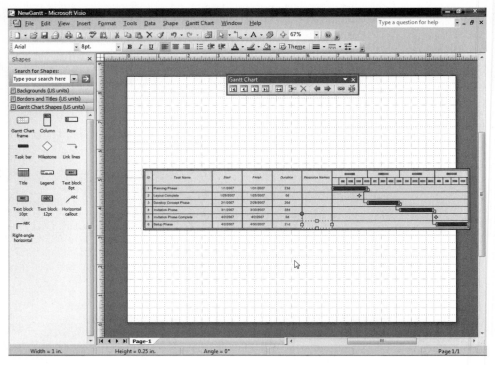

7. On the **Shape** menu, click **Center Drawing**.

   Visio centers the Gantt chart on the drawing page.

8. Select the first cell in the **Resource Names** column, and type Jo Berry.

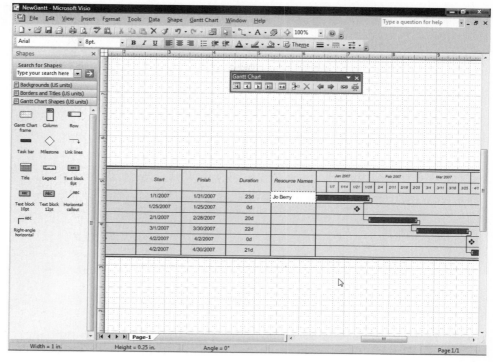

9. Skip the second cell, select the third cell in the **Resource Names** column, and type Jeff Chia.

10. Select the fourth cell in the **Resource Names** column, and type Christa Geller.

11. Skip the fifth cell, select the last cell in the **Resource Names** column, and type Lori Kane.

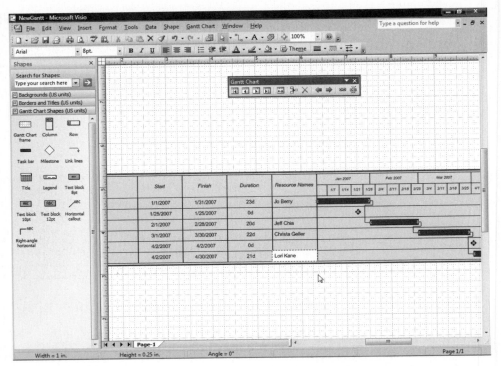

12. To add one more milestone to the Gantt chart, in the **ID** column, right-click **3** (the third row), and then click **New Task** on the shortcut menu.

Visio inserts a row before the Develop Concept Phase task row and selects the Task Name cell in the new row.

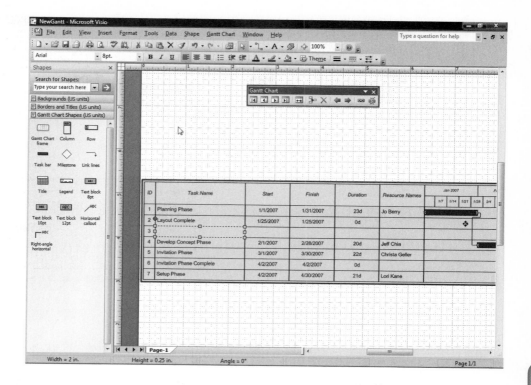

> **Tip** You can add more tasks to the end of your Gantt chart by selecting the Gantt chart frame and dragging it down. You can delete tasks at the end of the chart by dragging the Gantt chart frame back up.

13. With the **Task Name** cell for the new milestone selected, type Schedule Approval.

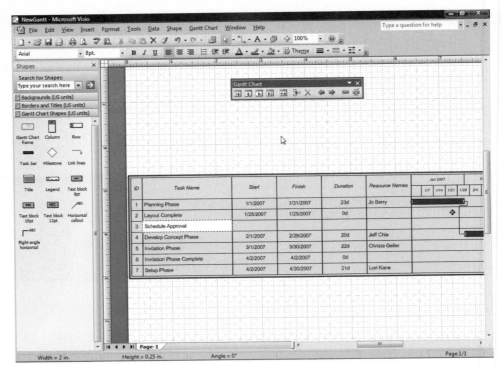

14. Select the **Start** cell for the new milestone.

    Visio inserts default task information for you.

15. Type 1/31/07, and click the drawing page outside the Gantt chart.

    Visio inserts the start date (including the year) and changes the finish date to match the start date of the milestone.

16. To make this task a milestone, select the **Duration** cell for the task, type 0 because milestones don't have duration, and then click the drawing page outside the Gantt chart.

    Visio changes the Gantt bar to a diamond.

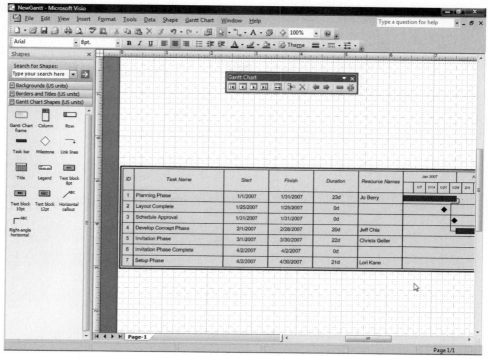

17. To change the milestone shape to a star for all the milestones in the Gantt chart, on the **Gantt Chart** menu, click **Options**.

    The Gantt Chart Options dialog box appears.

18. Click the **Format** tab, and in the **Shape** drop-down list, click **Star**.

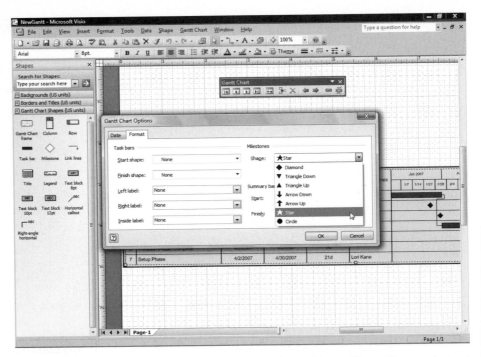

19. Click **OK**. The milestone shapes in the Gantt chart change from diamonds to stars.

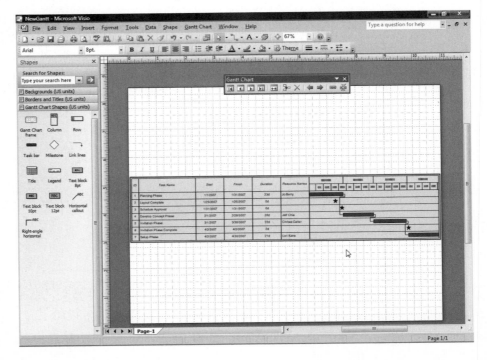

20. To change the drawing page size so the Gantt chart fits on the page, on the **File** menu, click **Page Setup**.

The Page Setup dialog box appears.

21. Click the **Page Size** tab, and in the **Page size** area, select the **Custom size** option. In the **Custom size** area, type 13 in the first box.

22. Click **OK**.

Visio widens the drawing page.

23. On the **Shape** menu, click **Center Drawing**.

Visio centers the Gantt chart on the drawing page.

24. To add a background to the diagram, click the **Backgrounds** stencil, and drag the **Background web** shape onto the drawing page.

Visio creates a background for the diagram.

25. To add a title to the diagram, click the **Borders and Titles** stencil, drag the **Title block contemp.** shape onto the drawing page, and position it in the upper-left corner of the page.

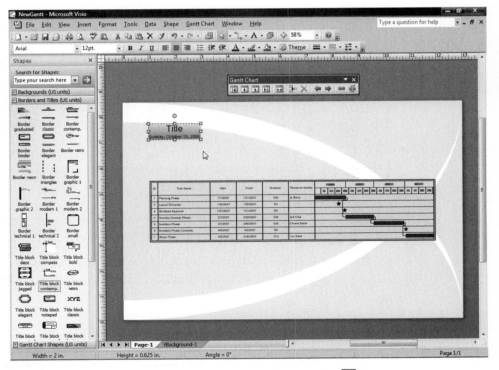

26. With the **Title block contemp.** shape selected, press the F2 key.

27. Highlight the word *Title*, and type a new title, Tradeshow Gantt Chart.

The shape expands to fit your title.

28. Click the pasteboard to close the text block and deselect the title shape.

29. Click the title shape, and drag it to align it with the left edge of the Gantt chart.

30. On the **Format** menu, click **Theme**.

The Theme – Colors task pane appears.

31. In the **Apply theme colors** list, scroll the theme color list until you see **Paper - Light**, and then click it.

Visio changes the theme color of the diagram.

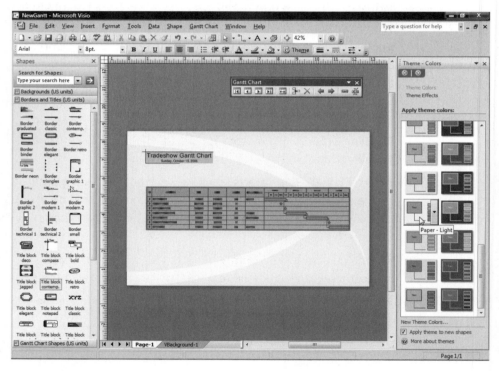

32. On the **File** menu, click **Save As** to open the **Save As** dialog box.

33. In the **File name** box, type GanttChart, and click the **Save** button to save the diagram.

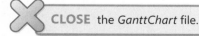 **CLOSE** the *GanttChart* file.

> **Tip** For more information on creating Gantt charts, type Gantt chart in the Type A Question For Help box in the upper-right corner of the Visio window.

Key Points

- A timeline is a graphic that represents a specific period of time and the events that occur during that time. Timelines are particularly good at showing an overview of a project—project status, a history of events, and what's to come. Use the Timeline template in the Project Schedule category to create timelines.

- Use expanded timelines to show a segment of the primary timeline in more detail.

- With Gantt charts, you can track the details of each project task, create task dependencies, see how changes to one task affect another, and quickly identify task owners and status. Use the Gantt Chart template in the Project Schedule category to create timelines.

- You can create timelines from scratch or from existing data. To import data to create timelines, open the Timeline template, and on the Timeline menu, click Import Timeline Data. To export data from a timeline, on the Timeline menu, click Export Timeline Data.

- You can create Gantt charts from scratch or from existing data. To import data to create Gantt charts, open the Gantt chart template, and on the Gantt Chart menu, click Import. To export data from a Gantt chart, on the Gantt Chart menu, click Export.

- When you export data from Visio timelines and Gantt charts, Visio saves the data in Microsoft Office Project file format so you can work with the data in Project.

- Right-click the shapes in timelines and Gantt charts to see their formatting options.

Chapter at a Glance

Store and display employee
information in organization charts —

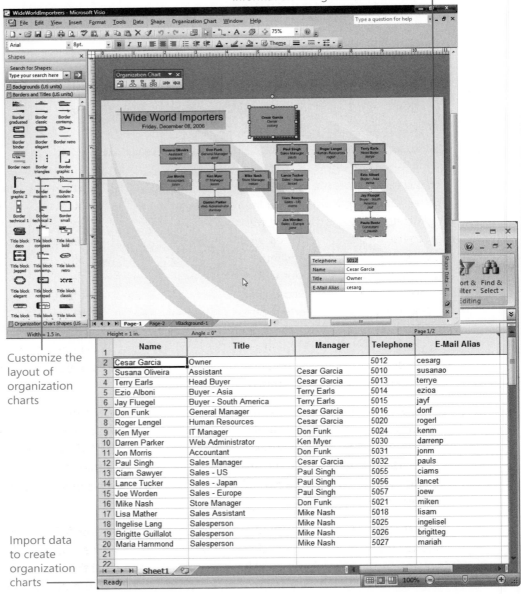

Customize the
layout of
organization
charts

Import data
to create
organization
charts —

	Name	Title	Manager	Telephone	E-Mail Alias
1					
2	Cesar Garcia	Owner		5012	cesarg
3	Susana Oliveira	Assistant	Cesar Garcia	5010	susanao
4	Terry Earls	Head Buyer	Cesar Garcia	5013	terrye
5	Ezio Alboni	Buyer - Asia	Terry Earls	5014	ezioa
6	Jay Fluegel	Buyer - South America	Terry Earls	5015	jayf
7	Don Funk	General Manager	Cesar Garcia	5016	donf
8	Roger Lengel	Human Resources	Cesar Garcia	5020	rogerl
9	Ken Myer	IT Manager	Don Funk	5024	kenm
10	Darren Parker	Web Administrator	Ken Myer	5030	darrenp
11	Jon Morris	Accountant	Don Funk	5031	jonm
12	Paul Singh	Sales Manager	Cesar Garcia	5032	pauls
13	Ciam Sawyer	Sales - US	Paul Singh	5055	ciams
14	Lance Tucker	Sales - Japan	Paul Singh	5056	lancet
15	Joe Worden	Sales - Europe	Paul Singh	5057	joew
16	Mike Nash	Store Manager	Don Funk	5021	miken
17	Lisa Mather	Sales Assistant	Mike Nash	5018	lisam
18	Ingelise Lang	Salesperson	Mike Nash	5025	ingelisel
19	Brigitte Guillalot	Salesperson	Mike Nash	5026	brigitteg
20	Maria Hammond	Salesperson	Mike Nash	5027	mariah
21					
22					

6 Creating Organization Charts

In this chapter, you will learn how to:

✔ Import data to create organization charts.

✔ Store and display employee information in organization charts.

✔ Customize the layout of organization charts.

Organization charts are used to visually document the groups within an organization—such as departments and teams—and their reporting relationships. Using the Organization Chart template in Microsoft Office Visio, you can easily create organization charts by dragging shapes, which represent people within an organization, onto the drawing page. By taking advantage of the intelligent behavior of these shapes, you can show employee relationships within an organization. For example, when you drag shapes on top of other shapes, Visio positions and connects the shapes for you, creating the reporting hierarchy as you add shapes to the drawing page. Shapes in organization charts can also store information about the people and relationships within the organization, and you can show as much or little of that information as you choose. You can also rearrange the shapes in a chart and create synchronized copies of departments without redrawing the hierarchy from scratch.

With the Organization Chart Wizard template, you have even more options. The template includes a step-by-step approach to building organization charts from information stored in data files or information that you enter in the wizard. If you already have organization data stored in a file and you don't want to create a chart from scratch, or if you prefer entering data into a wizard rather than dragging shapes onto a drawing page, this template is for you.

In this chapter, you import human resources data from a Microsoft Office Excel spreadsheet to create an organization chart for Wide World Importers. You view the additional data stored with each shape, modify the data, display some of the data in the chart, and then format the text in each shape. Finally, you change the layout of the chart, insert a hyperlink, and add color and a background to enhance the chart's appearance.

See Also   Do you need only a quick refresher on the topics in this chapter? See the Quick Reference entries on pages xxv–xliii.

> **Important**   Before you can use the practice files in this chapter, you need to install them from the book's companion CD to their default location. See "Using the Book's CD-ROM" on page xix for more information.

Importing Data to Create Organization Charts

Many organizations maintain human resources information in formats that aren't visual. With the Organization Chart Wizard template, you can create an organization chart by importing employee information already stored in corporate data sources such as databases and data files. If the organizational structure changes, you can simply update the chart rather than having to re-create it—a huge timesaver, especially for large organizations. You can import organization data from Microsoft Office Excel spreadsheets (*.xlsx*), text files (*.txt*), Microsoft Office Exchange Server directories, Microsoft Office Access databases (*.accdb*), or any ODBC-compliant (Open Data Base Connectivity) database application.

> **Important**   For the Organization Chart Wizard template to work, the source data must be properly formatted and include, at minimum, data identifying unique employee names and the managers to whom they report. In an Excel spreadsheet, columns of information represent data fields that can be imported to create an organization chart. For example, a human resources spreadsheet might include columns listing each person's name, manager, department, title, e-mail address, phone number, and office number.

With the Organization Chart Wizard template, you first specify the data source you want to use to import the data, and then you determine which columns contain the information for the organization chart. In a typical chart, Visio uses an Employee Name field and a Reports to field (the manager's name) to specify the reporting structure. That means that every employee name in the data source must be associated with the name of the manager to whom the employee reports (except the person at the very top of the organization). For example, if Jon Morris (employee) reports to Don Funk (manager), the data source must include both of those pieces of information so that Visio can structure the organization chart correctly.

Next, you select the data fields you want to appear in the organization chart and identify the additional fields you want to simply import as shape data (formerly custom properties) and store with each shape. *Shape data* is a category of information that is stored with each shape and that correspond to data. For example, a Manager shape might include a Telephone category, and the telephone number would be the shape data. Shape data for a shape might include Name, Manager, Department, Title, E-mail Address, Phone Number, and Office Number. However, your organization chart might display only each employee's name and title. The additional shape data can be viewed through the Shape Data window in Visio, but it doesn't appear in the organization chart unless you want it to.

> **Tip** Depending on the size and number of shapes in your organization charts, you might need to periodically zoom in to the drawing page to see the shapes and text more clearly.

In this exercise, you import data from an Excel spreadsheet to generate an organization chart for Wide World Importers. In addition to importing the Name and Reports To fields, you import data identifying the title, telephone number, and e-mail address for each employee.

> **Tip** For help creating organization charts, type organization chart in the Type A Question For Help box on the right side of the menu bar.

> **USE** the *Employees.xlsx* file located in Documents\Microsoft Press\Visio 2007 SBS \06_OrgCharts.

1. Start Visio. In the **Template Categories** list, click **Business**. Under **Other Templates**, double-click **Organization Chart Wizard**.

   The Organization Chart Wizard template opens a drawing page, three stencils, and the first page of the Organization Chart Wizard.

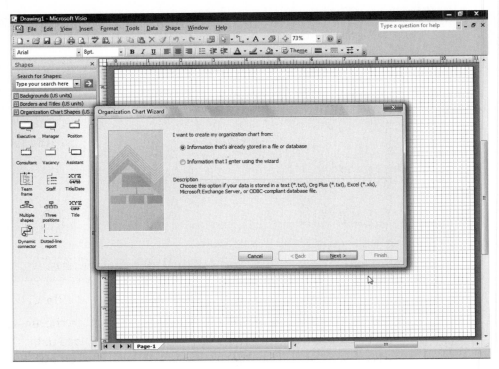

2. On the first page of the **Organization Chart Wizard**, make sure the **Information that's already stored in a file or database** option is selected, and then click **Next**.

The next page of the wizard appears, prompting you to identify the type of data source from which you are importing data.

3. Make sure the **A text, Org Plus (*.txt) or Excel file** option is selected, and then click **Next**.

The next page of the wizard appears, prompting you to locate the file that contains the organization information.

4. Click **Browse**, navigate to the **06_OrgCharts** folder, and then double-click **Employees.xlsx**.

The wizard displays the file and its path.

5. Click **Next**.

The next page of the wizard appears, prompting you to choose the columns in the spreadsheet that contain the information that defines your organization.

6. In the **Name** box, make sure **Name** is displayed, and in the **Reports to** box, make sure **Manager** is displayed. Click **Next**.

The next page of the wizard appears, prompting you to choose the fields you want to display in your organization chart.

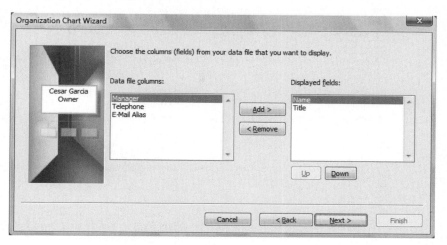

7. Make sure the **Displayed fields** list displays **Name** and **Title**. Click **Next**.

    The next page of the wizard appears, prompting you to choose additional columns (or fields) to import into your organization chart as shape data. The information doesn't appear in your organization chart, but it is stored with the shapes.

8. In the **Data file columns** box, click **Telephone**, and then click the **Add** button to move **Telephone** to the **Shape Data fields** box.

    Telephone is listed in the Shape Data fields box.

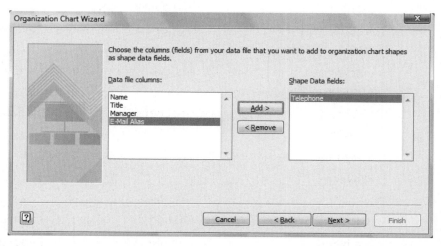

9. Repeat the previous step to add **E-Mail Alias** to the **Shape Data fields** box. Click **Next**.

The next page of the wizard appears, asking you whether you want Visio to break your organization chart across pages.

10. Make sure the **I want the wizard to automatically break my organization chart across pages** option is selected, and then click **Finish**.

The wizard imports the data according to the specifications you entered, and Visio creates the organization chart on the drawing page. The Organization Chart Wizard template also opens an Organization Chart menu and toolbar.

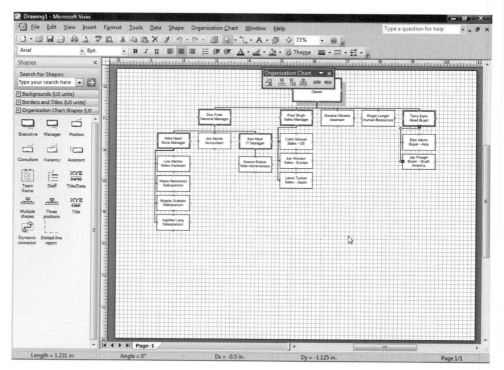

11. From the **Organization Chart Shapes** stencil, drag a **Consultant** shape onto the **Jay Fluegel** shape.

> **Tip** At this point in the exercise, you might need to periodically zoom in to the drawing page to see the shapes and text more clearly.

12. In the **Connecting Shapes** dialog box, select the **Don't show this message again** option, and then click **OK**.

Visio positions the Consultant shape below the Jay Fluegel shape and draws a connector between the two shapes.

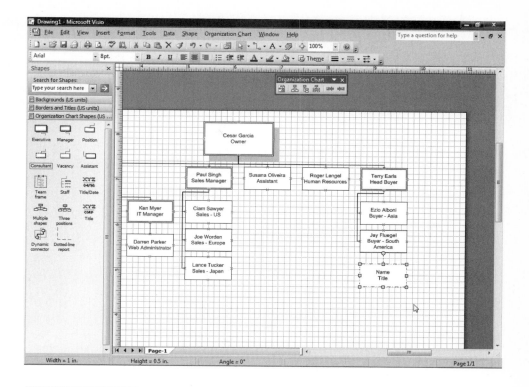

> **Tip** To create your own organization charts from scratch or revise existing ones, simply drag shapes on top of one another as you did in the previous step. Visio positions and connects the shapes to create the organization hierarchy for you.

13. With the shape selected, press F2 to open the shape's text block.

14. Type Paula Bento, press Enter, and then type Consultant.

Visio displays the employee's name and title in the shape.

> **Tip** You can also add up to 50 employee shapes to your organization chart at once by using the Multiple shapes shape on the Organization Chart Shapes stencil. Just drag it on top of the shape that represents the manager to whom all the employees report, and then in the dialog box, select the number of and type of shapes you want to add.

15. Click the pasteboard or a blank area of the drawing page to close the text block and deselect the shape.

Notice that this shape has a dashed-line border, which indicates that the shape represents a consultant.

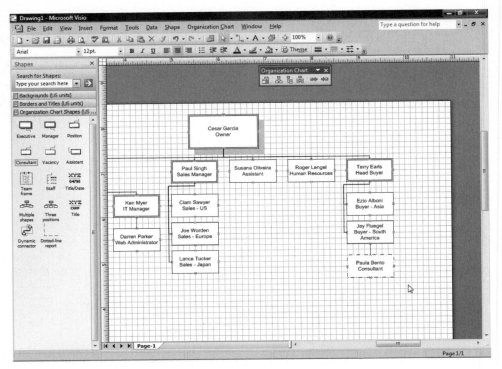

16. On the **File** menu, click **Close**, and then click **No** when Visio asks you if you want to save the changes to the drawing.

Visio and the drawing close.

Storing and Displaying Employee Information in Organization Charts

You can store shape data with shapes in any Visio diagram. In organization charts, you can use shape data for reports, reference, or as shape text in charts to store more descriptive detail about an employee. The default shape data for organization chart shapes are Department, Telephone, Name, Title, and E-mail. By default, the Name and Title properties are shown in the shapes in a chart.

Shape data for Name   Shape data for title

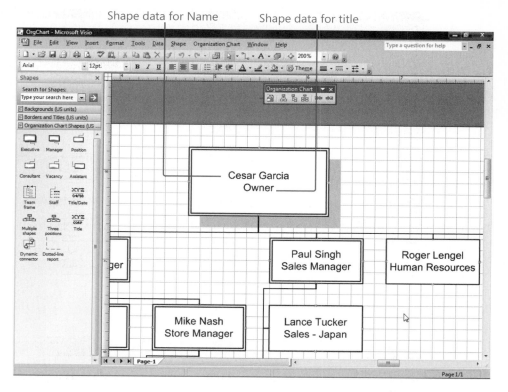

The other default shape data is stored with the shapes but not shown in the chart. You can display that data in your chart by clicking the Options command on the Organization Chart menu and then clicking the Fields tab in the Options dialog box. In Visio, you can view hidden shape data for any shape you select on the drawing page through the Shape Data window. Or, you can view the shape data for an individual shape by right-clicking the shape, pointing to Data, and then clicking Shape Data on the shortcut menu.

> **Tip** Visio Professional 2007 includes new data visualization features, which give you even more options for displaying data in your Visio diagrams. These features apply to any Visio diagram and are discussed in Chapter 9, "Visualizing Data in Diagrams."

You can also change shape data in the Shape Data window by selecting the data you want to change and typing new data. You can format the text in all the shapes at once by clicking the Options command on the Organization Chart menu and then clicking the Text tab in the Options dialog box. You can also format individual shapes by selecting the shape text and formatting it as you would any other text.

In this exercise, you open an organization chart. You view the shape data of a couple of shapes and change the data for one of them. You display e-mail alias data in all the shapes, and then format the text that appears in all the shapes.

OPEN the *OrgChart* file in Documents\Microsoft Press\Visio 2007 SBS\06_OrgCharts.

1. On the **View** menu, click **Shape Data Window**.

   The Shape Data window appears with no data displayed because a shape isn't selected.

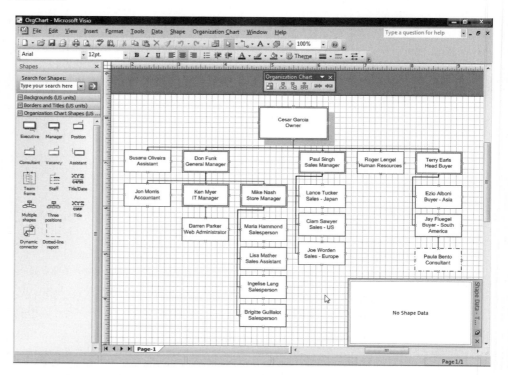

Shape Data Window

Tip You can also open the Shape Data window by clicking the Shape Data Window button on the View toolbar. To display the View toolbar, right-click the toolbar area, and click View on the shortcut menu.

2. Click the **Cesar Garcia** shape.

   The Shape Data window displays the telephone, name, title, and e-mail alias shape data for Cesar Garcia.

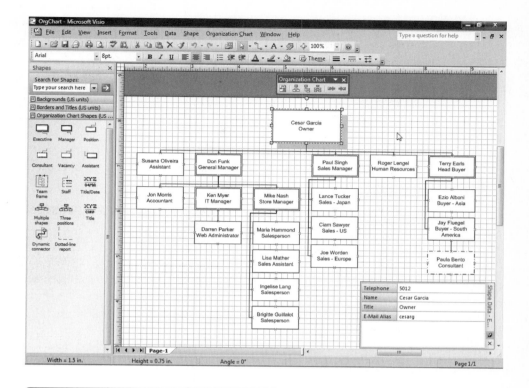

> **Troubleshooting** Zoom in to the drawing page to see the shapes and text more clearly. You can also move the Organization Chart toolbar if it obstructs your view of a shape. To move the toolbar, position the pointer over the toolbar's title, and then drag it to a different location.

3. Position the pointer over the left side of the Shape Data window, and when the pointer changes to a two-headed arrow, drag to the left to widen the window.

4. Click the **Maria Hammond** shape.

The Shape Data window displays the telephone, name, title, and e-mail alias shape data for Maria Hammond.

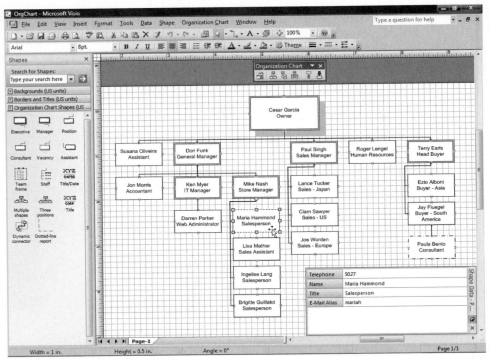

5. In the Shape Data window, click the **Telephone** box, type 5057, and press the Enter key.

The Telephone box displays the new number.

> **Tip** You can also view, change, and create new shape data fields in the Shape Data dialog box. To view this dialog box, right-click a shape, and then click Properties on the shortcut menu. Or point to Data, and then click Shape Data on the shortcut menu. To create new shape data fields, in the Shape Data dialog box, click the Define button.

6. Click the **Paula Bento** shape.

The Shape Data window displays the name and title shape data for Paula Bento.

7. In the Shape Data window, click the **Telephone** box, type 6025, and then press the Enter key.

The Telephone box displays the number.

8. In the Shape Data window, click the **E-Mail Alias** box, type c_paulab, and then press the Enter key.

The E-Mail Alias box displays the e-mail alias.

9. On the **Organization Chart** menu, click **Options** to open the **Options** dialog box.

10. In the **Options** dialog box, click the **Fields** tab.

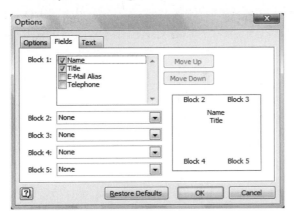

11. In the **Block 1** area, select **E-Mail Alias** to add a checkmark next to it.

    Notice that the preview area on the right side of the dialog box shows you where the e-mail alias data will appear in the shape.

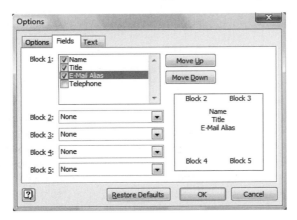

> **Tip** To add information to the other text blocks in the shapes in an organization chart, click the down arrow next to the block you want to use, and then click the shape data you want to display.

12. Click **OK**.

13. When a message box appears asking if you want the shape's height adjusted to accommodate the additional information and your drawing automatically arranged, click **Yes**.

The shapes in the chart enlarge to display the name, title, and e-mail alias for each position.

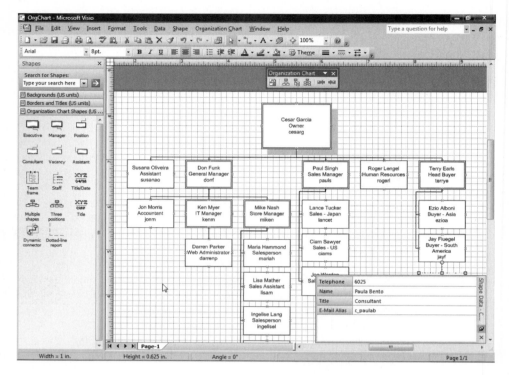

> **Tip** If the information in your organization chart shapes looks cramped, you can easily resize all the shapes at once using the Options dialog box. On the Organization Chart menu, click Options. On the Options tab, in the Shape display area, change shape dimensions.

14. On the **Organization Chart** menu, click **Options** to open the **Options** dialog box.

15. Click the **Text** tab.

16. In the **Fields** box, click **Name**, and then in the **Style** area, select the **Bold** check box to add that formatting to the names in the organization chart shapes.

17. In the **Fields** box, click **E-Mail Alias**, and in the **Style** area, select the **Italic** check box to italicize the e-mail aliases in the organization chart shapes.

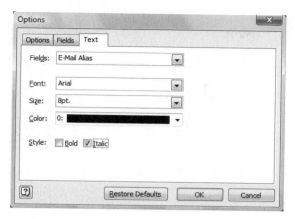

18. Click **OK**.

Visio formats the names and e-mail aliases in the shapes.

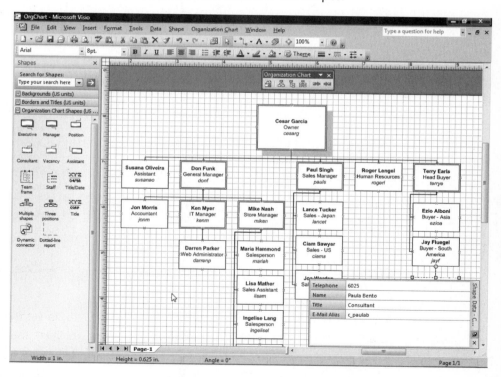

Tip You can add employee pictures to shapes in your organization chart. To insert a picture into a shape, right-click the shape, and then click Insert Picture on the shortcut menu.

19. Select the **Cesar Garcia** shape.

20. Right-click the shape, and then click **Show Divider Line** on the shortcut menu.

    Visio inserts a divider line under the owner's name.

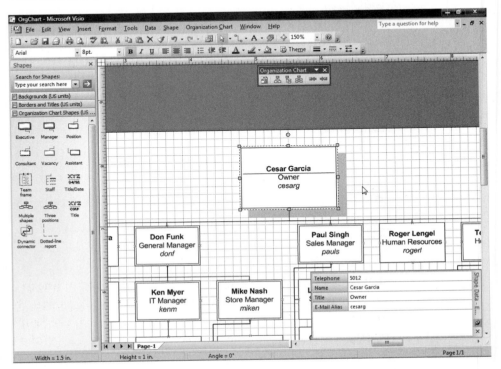

21. Right-click the shape, and then click **Hide Divider Line** on the shortcut menu to hide the line.

22. For an unobstructed view of the organization chart, click the **Close** button on the Shape Data window to close the window.

23. On the **File** menu, click **Close**, and then **No** so Visio doesn't save the chart.

    Visio and the chart close.

Customizing the Layout of Organization Charts

Visio includes a number of tools that you can use to rearrange the shapes in your organization chart, so you can modify the way the chart looks without wasting valuable time reconnecting the shapes in the reporting structure. You can change the location of individual shapes or the layout of all the shapes in a department by using the buttons on the Organization Chart toolbar. You can also change individual reporting relationships.

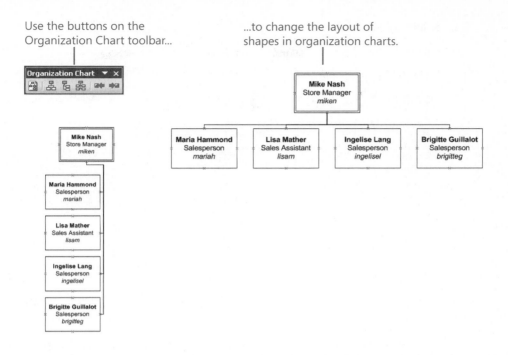

Use the buttons on the Organization Chart toolbar...

...to change the layout of shapes in organization charts.

Charts that represent large or complex organizations can be arranged on several pages so you don't need to crowd the entire chart onto one drawing page. You can quickly build a multiple-page organization chart by creating synchronized copies of departments on pages in the drawing file. For example, on the first page of a chart, select a manager shape with subordinate employees that make up a department or team, and then create a synchronized copy of it. Visio cuts the subordinates from the first page, creates a new page, and then places the manager and the subordinates on the new page. A shape representing the manager remains on the first page, indicating that a synchronized copy is on another page in the drawing file. Any changes you make to the text or shape data for any synchronized shape applies to all synchronized copies of it on other pages. If the manager changes her name and you update her name on the first page of the chart; that change ripples throughout all the synchronized copies of the shape on other pages. Synchronized copies save time, help you manage large organization charts, and make it easier to maintain accurate and consistent organization charts.

You can customize your organization charts further by adding hyperlinks to easily navigate between synchronized copies and pages of a complex organization chart. You could, for example, link the drawing page for a customer service department to the department Web site on the corporate intranet, making it easy to access more information about the group. To insert a hyperlink for a shape, select it, and then click Hyperlinks on the Insert menu. To insert a hyperlink for a drawing page, make sure nothing on the page is selected, and then click Hyperlinks on the Insert menu.

In this exercise you change the layout of some of the shapes in the organization chart. You create a synchronized copy of one department on a new page, and then insert a hyperlink linking the manager shape on the first page to its copy on the second page. Finally, you add a background to the chart, and change the color theme of the chart.

OPEN the *OrgChartLayout* file in Documents\Microsoft Press\Visio 2007 SBS \06_OrgCharts.

1. Select the **Mike Nash** shape.

Vertical Layout

2. On the Organization Chart toolbar, click the **Vertical Layout** button.

3. On the Organization Chart toolbar, click the **Align Right** button.

   The subordinates in Mike Nash's department are right aligned under the Mike Nash shape.

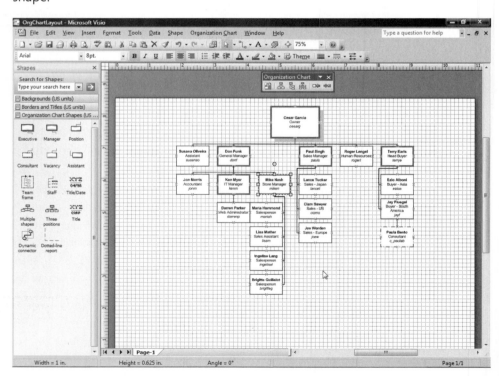

> **Tip** Another way to change the layout of all or part of an organization chart is to select the shape at the highest level of the staffing group you want to change, and then on the Organization Chart menu, click Arrange Subordinates. Click the layout style you want, and then click OK. You can also right-click the shape, and then click Arrange Subordinates on the shortcut menu.

4. With the **Mike Nash** shape selected, on the **Organization Chart** menu, point to **Synchronize**, and then click **Create Synchronized Copy**.

   The Create Synchronized Copy dialog box appears, asking whether you want the synchronized copy placed on a new page.

5. In the **Create Synchronized Copy** dialog box, make sure the **New page** option is selected. Select the **Hide subordinates on original page** check box, and then click **OK**.

   Visio inserts a second page in the chart and places Mike Nash's department on it.

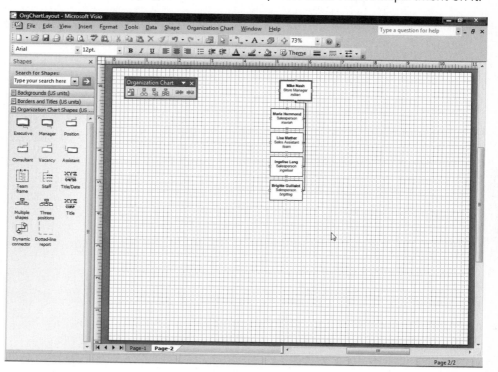

6. On the new page, select the **Mike Nash** shape.

> **Tip** You might want to zoom in so you can see the shapes in the drawing better.

7. On the Organization Chart toolbar, click the **Horizontal Layout** button.

8. On the Organization Chart toolbar, click the **Center** button.

    The subordinates in Mike Nash's department are center aligned.

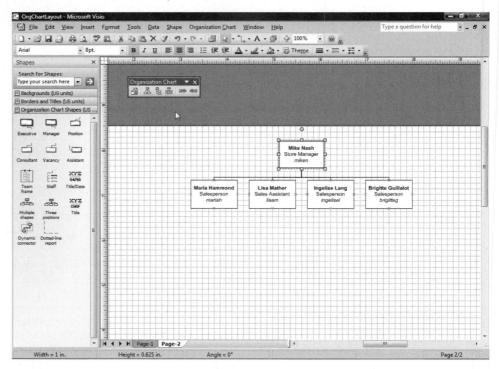

9. On the **View** menu, click **Shape Data Window**.

    The Shape Data window opens and displays the shape data for Mike Nash.

10. Click the **Telephone** box, type 5041, and then press [Enter] to change the telephone number.

    Visio changes the telephone number for Mike Nash.

11. Click the **Page-1** tab to go to the first page of the chart.

12. Select the **Mike Nash** shape to view the shape data for the shape.

    Visio displays the updated phone number for Mike Nash, and his subordinates are hidden from view on this page of the chart. Shape data for the Mike Nash shape is synchronized on both pages.

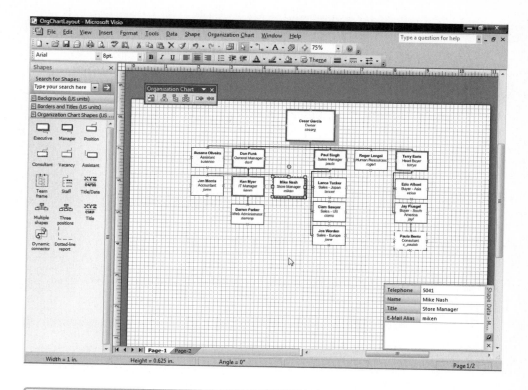

> **Important** Changes to shape text and data apply to all synchronized copies of the shape. However, changes such as adding, deleting, or moving a shape apply only to the page on which you are working; these changes aren't synchronized. If you want to show a manager's subordinates on the page where they're hidden, right-click the manager shape, and then click Show Subordinates.

13. With the **Mike Nash** shape selected, on the **Insert** menu, click **Hyperlinks** to open the **Hyperlinks** dialog box.

14. Click the **Browse** button next to the blank **Sub-address** box.

The Hyperlink dialog box appears.

15. In the **Hyperlink** dialog box, click the **Page** down arrow, and then click **Page-2**. Click **OK**.

The Hyperlink dialog box closes, and the Hyperlinks dialog box shows Page-2 in the Sub-address box.

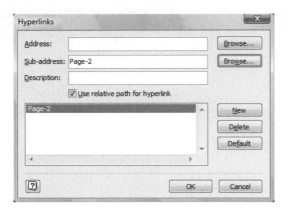

16. Click **OK** to close the **Hyperlinks** dialog box.

17. Pause the pointer over the **Mike Nash** shape.

Hyperlink pointer

A hyperlink pointer indicates that a hyperlink is associated with the shape. A ScreenTip identifies the name of the link as *Page-2*.

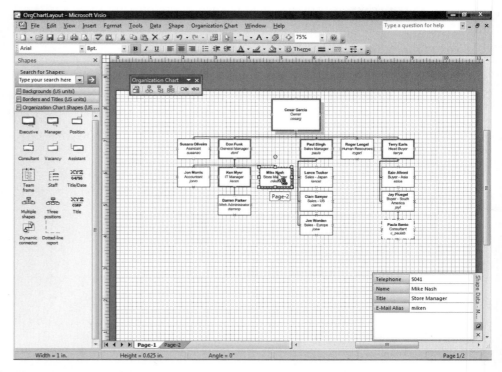

18. Right-click the **Mike Nash** shape, and then click **Page-2** on the shortcut menu.

Visio displays Page-2 of the chart.

> **Tip** You can also share an organization chart—or any type of Visio diagram—by saving it as a Web page and publishing it to a Web site, such as a corporate intranet site. Colleagues or team members in any location can easily view the chart with a Web browser at any time of day or night, making global collaboration easier. On the File menu, click Save as Web page.

19. Click the **Maria Hammond** shape to select it.

Move Right

20. On the Organization Chart toolbar, click the **Move Right** button.

Visio moves the Maria Hammond shape to the right.

> **Tip** You can also compare different versions of organization charts. Use the Compare Organization Data command on the Organization Chart menu to generate a report that lists the differences between current and previous versions of a chart.

Close

21. Click the **Close** button on the Shape Data window to close the window.

22. Click the **Page-1** tab to go to the first page of the chart.

23. Click the **Backgrounds** stencil, and then drag the **Background leaf** shape onto the drawing page.

Visio adds the background shape to the drawing page.

24. On the **Format** menu, click **Theme**.

The Theme – Colors task pane appears.

25. Click the **Office** theme.

Visio applies the color theme to the shapes on the drawing page.

26. Right-click the **Office** theme, and then click **Apply to All Pages** on the shortcut menu.

Visio applies the color theme to all the pages in your drawing.

27. Click the **Page-2** tab to go to the second page of the chart.

Notice that Page-2 has the same color theme as the first page, but it doesn't have a background.

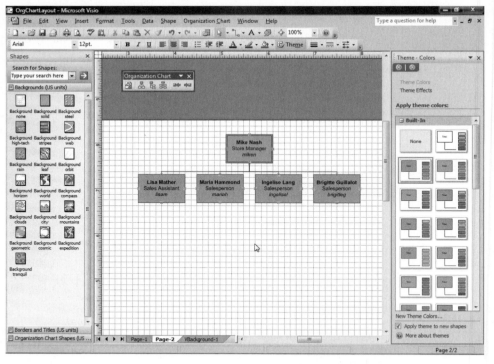

28. On the **File** menu, click **Page Setup**, and then click the **Page Properties** tab.

29. In the **Background** box, click the down arrow, and then select **VBackground-1**.

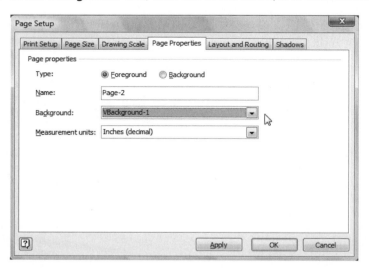

30. Click **OK**.

Visio adds the background to the second page and applies the color theme to it.

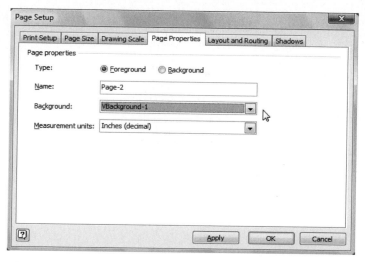

31. Click the **Page-1** tab to go to the first page of the chart.

32. Click the **Borders and Titles** stencil, and then drag the **Title Block contemp.** shape onto the drawing page.

33. Press [F2] to enter the text mode, highlight the title placeholder, and then type Wide World Importers.

34. Click the pasteboard to deselect the shape.

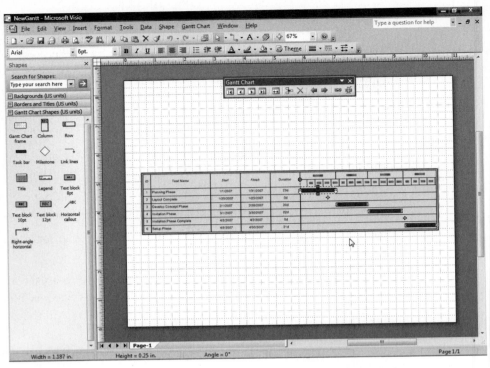

35. On the **File** menu, click **Close**, and then click **No** so you don't save the changes to the chart.

Key Points

- You can create organization charts from scratch by starting with the Organization Chart template and dragging shapes on top of one another to create reporting relationships.

- You can create organization charts from information stored in data files or information you enter in a wizard by using the Organization Chart Wizard template.

- You can use the Shape Data window to view shape data, such as e-mail addresses and telephone numbers, not shown in organization chart shapes.

- You can use the Options command on the Organization Chart menu to display shape data as text and format the text in all the shapes in a chart at once.

- You can use the Organization Chart menu and toolbar to rearrange shapes in an organization chart.

- You can create synchronized copies of departments or teams in large organizations to build multiple-page organization charts that show an overview of the organization on the first page and department details on the rest of the pages in the drawing file.

Chapter at a Glance

Create scaled office spaces

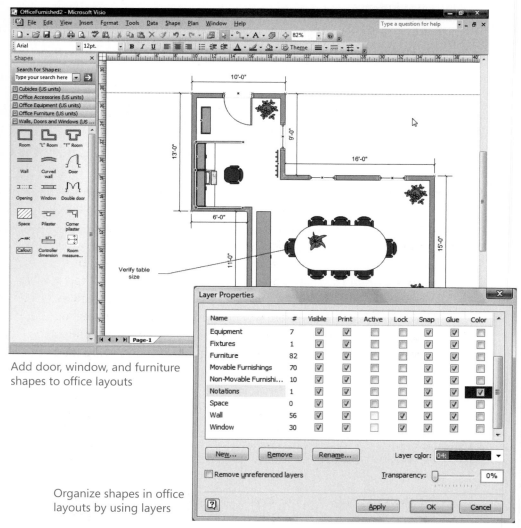

Add door, window, and furniture
shapes to office layouts

Organize shapes in office
layouts by using layers

7 Laying Out Office Spaces

In this chapter, you will learn how to:

In this chapter, you will learn how to:

✔   Create scaled office spaces.

✔   Add door, window, and furniture shapes to office layouts.

✔   Organize shapes in office layouts by using layers.

Think of something big—a house, an office building, or your backyard. Using Visio, you can diagram a large object on a small drawing page by use a *drawing scale*, which represents the relationship between the object's size in the real world and its size on the page. Like a map that depicts a 10-mile stretch of highway with a 1-inch line, a scaled diagram represents physical space and objects at a ratio or a fraction of their real size. A drawing scale isn't only for large objects—you can draw very small objects, such as watch mechanisms or printed circuits, at a larger scale as well. When you start a Microsoft Office Visio diagram with a scaled template, Visio sets up the drawing scale that's appropriate for the drawing type, and the shapes on the stencils included with the template conform to the scale automatically when you drag them onto the drawing page.

> **Important** This chapter demonstrates creating a scaled office layout. However, you can use the methods in this chapter to create any kind of scaled building plan—no matter how big or small it is. Visio Professional 2007 includes scaled templates that you can use to create everything from warehouses or industrial plants to plans for a home.

In this chapter, you create the layout for an office and conference space for Wide World Importers. You work with the Office Layout template to first create the walls, and then you add door, window, and furniture shapes to the diagram. Last, you organize the shapes in the office layout on layers, which is an efficient method for managing and differentiating categories of shapes.

See Also Do you need only a quick refresher on the topics in this chapter? See the Quick Reference entries on pages xxv-xliii.

Important Before you can use the practice files in this chapter, you need to install them from the book's companion CD to their default location. See "Using the Book's CD-ROM" on page xix for more information.

Creating Scaled Office Spaces

The Office Layout template makes it easy to create scaled office space diagrams with architectural details, such as pilasters (rectangular wall projections like columns) and door swing (the space needed to open or close a door). Because Visio creates diagrams with architectural and engineering precision, your scaled diagrams are as accurate as your measurements.

All Visio templates have a default drawing scale, but for most business diagrams, such as flowcharts or organization charts, that scale is 1:1—that is, no scale. In the Office Layout template, the default drawing scale is ½ inch to 1 foot, which means that a shape that is ½ inch wide on the drawing page represents an object that is 1 foot wide in the real world. Visio sets up the drawing page using the template's scale and *units of measure*, which are typically inches (although Visio includes metric templates as well). If you prefer to measure shapes in yards or meters or some other measurement unit, you can click the Page Setup command on the File menu, which is also how you change the drawing scale for a diagram. In addition, the Office Layout template adds the custom Plan menu, which includes commands specifically for working with floor plans.

When you start a diagram with a scaled template, the units of measure for the drawing scale appear on the rulers. Part of what you have to do when working in any scaled diagram is grow accustomed to measuring distance in real-world units. For example, if your drawing scale is ½ inch to 1 foot on letter-sized paper (11 by 8½ inches), the rulers show that the page represents a space that is 22 feet long and 17 feet wide.

The Plan menu appears on the menu bar

Rulers show the drawing scale

Guides help you align and move shapes

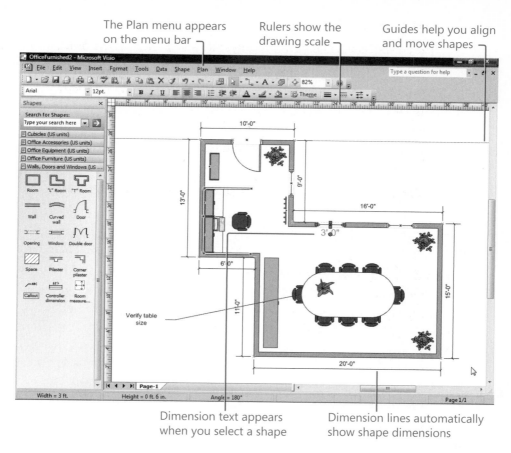

Dimension text appears when you select a shape

Dimension lines automatically show shape dimensions

You start an office layout by adding shapes that represent the structure of the office space. One way to do this is to drag wall shapes onto the drawing page and rotate them into position. Where two walls meet, Visio joins their corners for a smooth look. All the other structural shapes, such as doors and windows, are designed to snap to the wall shapes in an office layout. Alternatively, you can use the Space shape, which represents a 10-foot by 10-foot area, to create the office structure. For this technique, you first create a patchwork of space shapes, and then you unite them into a single area by using the Union command, which merges the shapes to create a new shape—that is, one that represents the entire office space. Last, you convert the new shape (the office space) into walls. This sounds time consuming, but most people find it faster and easier than dragging a lot of individual wall shapes—one at a time—onto the drawing page.

Create a patchwork of
space shapes, unite them...

...and then convert
them into walls

When you need to measure areas precisely, Visio offers several helpful shortcuts. Some shapes display their own dimensions—for example, the Space shape displays *100 sq. ft.* The status bar below the drawing page shows the real-world units of measure, so you can see at a glance how large shapes are in the real world. *Guides*—visual reference lines—help you align shapes to an exact point as well. Shapes connect to guides to ensure perfect alignment, and you can even drag a guide to move all the shapes connected to it. As you move or resize walls, the shape's dimensions and its dimension text and lines are updated automatically. To show the dimension text for a shape, select the shape. To add a dimension line to a shape, use the Controller dimension shape on the Walls, Doors and Windows stencil.

In this exercise, you start a new office layout with the Office Layout template and use the Page Setup command to change the drawing scale. You use Space shapes to build a scaled office space, unite the shapes to create a new space shape, and then convert the space shape to walls. Then you resize some of the shapes, add dimension lines to them, and connect them to guides that help you position them.

> **Tip** If you have Visio Professional 2007, you can insert AutoCAD drawings into your Visio architectural diagrams or start a diagram with a building shell already created in a CAD (computer-aided design) program. For more information about inserting and using AutoCAD drawings, type AutoCAD in the Type A Question For Help box.

1. Start Visio. In the **Template Categories** list, click **Maps and Floor Plans**. Under **All Templates**, double-click **Office Layout**.

   The Office Layout template opens a blank, scaled drawing page and the Walls, Doors and Windows stencil, Office Furniture stencil, Office Equipment stencil, Office Accessories stencil, and Cubicles stencil. The Plan menu is added to the menu bar. The rulers show the default architectural drawing scale (½" = 1'0") for the Office Layout template.

2. On the **File** menu, click **Page Setup** to open the **Page Setup** dialog box.

3. Click the **Drawing Scale** tab.

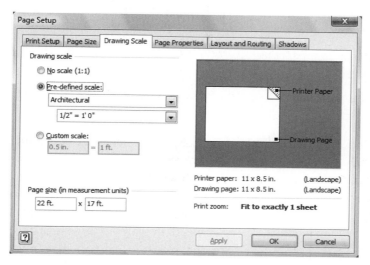

4. In the **Pre-defined scale** area, click the down arrow on the second box, scroll up, and then click ¼" = 1'0".

Visio changes the drawing scale for the diagram and recalculates the dimensions displayed in the Page size (in measurement units) boxes at the bottom of the dialog box.

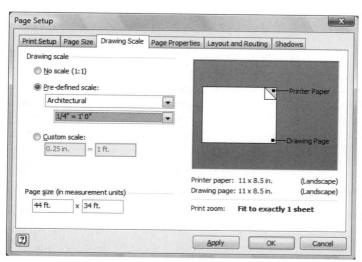

5. Click **OK**.

   The rulers display the new drawing scale and show that the drawing page represents an area 44 feet wide by 34 feet tall.

6. From the **Walls, Doors and Windows** stencil, drag a **Space** shape onto the drawing page and position it so that its top edge is at the 24-foot mark shown on the vertical ruler and its left edge is at the 10-foot mark shown on the horizontal ruler.

   The Space shape includes dimension text that is automatically updated when you resize the shape.

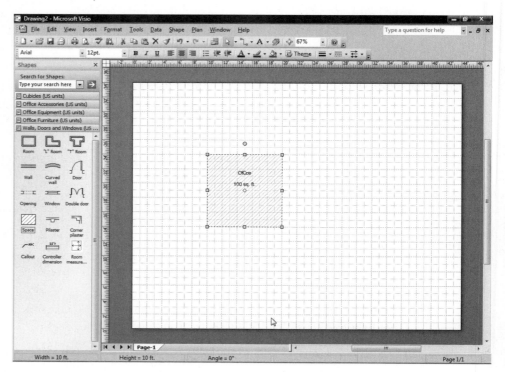

> **Tip** As you drag a shape, Visio displays dotted lines on the rulers and measurements in the status bar that show you the shape's exact position on the drawing page.

7. Drag a second **Space** shape onto the drawing page and position it so that its upper-left corner overlaps the lower-right corner of the first **Space** shape.

   The Space shape remains selected.

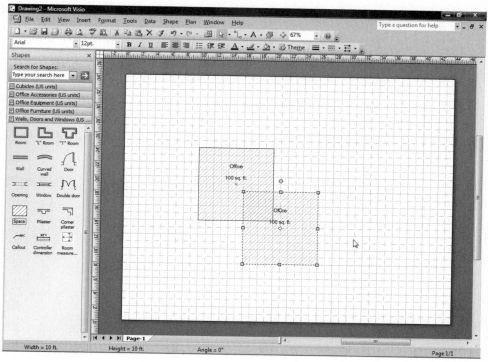

8. On the selected **Space** shape, drag the right-middle selection handle to the right to increase the width of the shape to 20 feet. Use the **Width** field in the status bar at the bottom of the drawing page window to determine the shape's width.

   Visio updates the measurement displayed on the shape to *200 sq. ft.*

9. On the same shape, drag the lower-middle selection handle down to increase the height of the shape to 15 feet. Use the **Height** field in the status bar at the bottom of the drawing page window to determine the shape's height.

   Visio updates the measurement displayed on the shape to *300 sq. ft.*

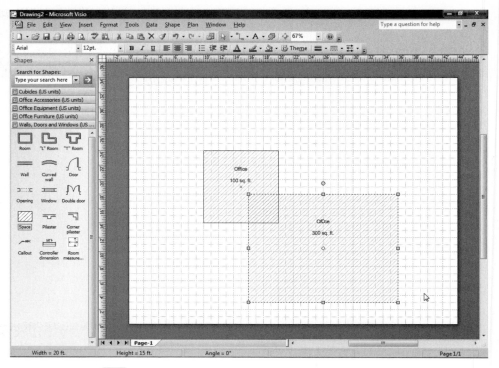

10. Hold down the [Shift] key while you select the other **Space** shape so that both shapes are selected.

11. On the **Shape** menu, point to **Operations**, and then click **Union**.

    Visio unites the two shapes into one shape.

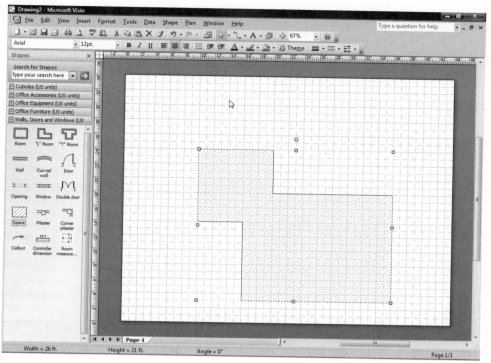

12. With the shape selected, on the **Plan** menu, click **Convert to Walls**.

The Convert to Walls dialog box appears.

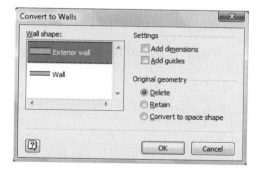

> **Tip** Another way to create walls is to use the Line or Rectangle tool to draw a rough approximation of the walls, and then use the Convert To Walls command.

13. In the **Settings** area, select the **Add dimensions** check box, and then click **OK**.

Visio displays a status bar as it converts the perimeter of the shape to wall shapes and adds dimension lines to each wall.

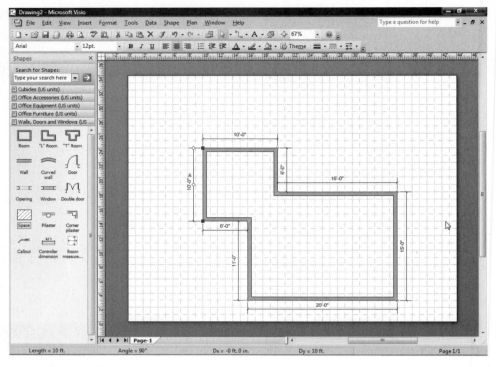

14. Select the top 10-foot wall.

    Visio displays the dimension text (*10'-0"*) for the wall.

15. Right-click the same 10-foot wall, and then click **Add a Guide** on the shortcut menu.

    Visio adds a guide to the wall shape's top edge and connects the other two adjoining walls to the guide so that you can move them together. The guide is selected and appears green.

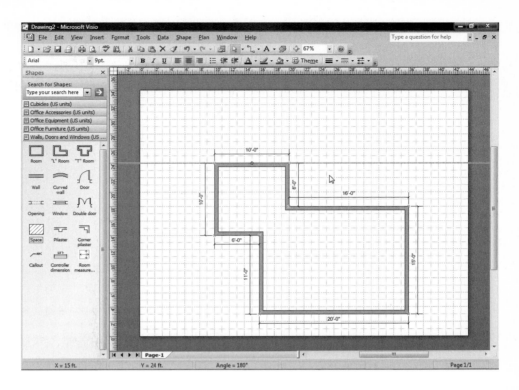

Two-headed arrow

16. Pause the pointer over the guide, and when a two-headed arrow appears, drag the guide up 3 feet to the 27-foot mark on the vertical ruler.

Visio moves the guide and all three walls that are connected to it to the new position and updates the dimension lines.

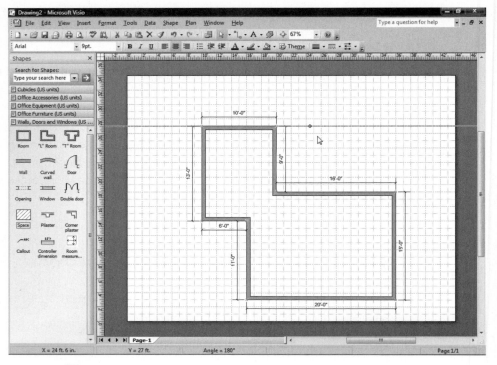

17. Press the [Esc] key to deselect the guide.

The deselected guide appears blue.

> **Tip** To select a guide, click it just as you would any shape. To add a guide to the drawing page, position the pointer over the horizontal ruler for a horizontal guide or the vertical ruler for a vertical guide, and then drag. As you drag, the guide appears on the drawing page. To delete a guide from the drawing page, select it, and then press the [Del] key.

Save

18. On the Standard toolbar, click the **Save** button to open the **Save As** dialog box.

19. In the **File name** box, type NewOffice, and then click **Save** to save the diagram.

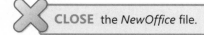

CLOSE the *NewOffice* file.

> **Tip** Although office layouts are a common type of scaled diagram, you can define a scale for any drawing type in Visio. For example, you can create maps, parts diagrams, and physical network diagrams to scale by using the Page Setup command on the File menu to define a drawing scale.

Adding Door, Window, and Furniture Shapes to Office Layouts

One of the many advantages of creating a scaled diagram with a scaled template is that the template includes shapes that are designed to work in the default drawing scale. The Office Layout template includes many specialized shapes that are designed to work in an architectural drawing scale and that have unique smart behavior. Wall shapes join together to form smooth corners. Door and window shapes snap into place on top of walls, rotating if necessary to match the wall's orientation. Dimension shapes display the dimensions of the shape they're connected to, and they stay connected to the shape when you move it.

Door snaps into place on a wall

Walls join to form smooth corners

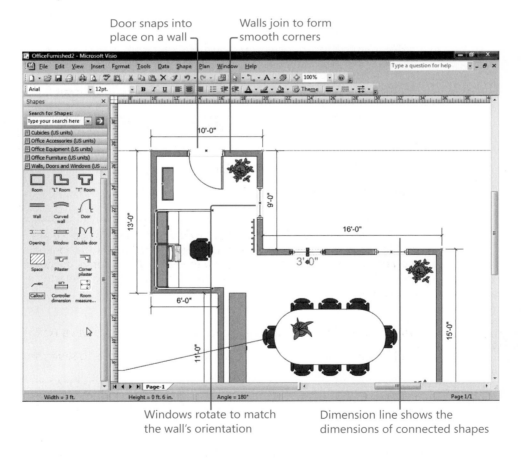

Windows rotate to match the wall's orientation

Dimension line shows the dimensions of connected shapes

Office Layout shapes are designed only in standard architectural sizes. Because of this, some shapes are locked to prevent you from manually resizing them with the pointer. To change their size, you must modify the property that controls the shape's dimensions. For example, a Door shape has a Door Width property that you can set to 24, 28, 30, 36, 48, 60, or 72 inches—standard door widths. Visio resizes the shape based on your selection. You can change a shape's properties by using the Properties command on shape's shortcut menu, which contains other specialized commands for modifying the shape. For example, you can't rotate or flip a door to change its orientation. Instead, you must use the Reverse In/Out Opening command or Reverse Left/Right Opening command on the shape's shortcut menu so that Visio rotates or flips the shape for you.

> **Tip** Right-click an office layout shape to see its shortcut menu of commands that you can use to modify the shape.

In this exercise, you add door, window, and furniture shapes to an office layout. You use shortcut menu commands to modify the door and window shapes. Last, you add furniture to the office and conference space.

 **OPEN** the *OfficeWalls* file in Documents\Microsoft Press\Visio 2007 SBS\07_OfficeLayouts.

1. From the **Walls, Doors and Windows** stencil, drag the **Door** shape onto the drawing page and position it in the middle of the top 10-foot wall.

   Visio connects the door to the wall. Red selection handles indicate that the shapes are connected, and gray handles indicate that the door is locked to prevent manual resizing. The door shape's dimension text appears while the shape is selected.

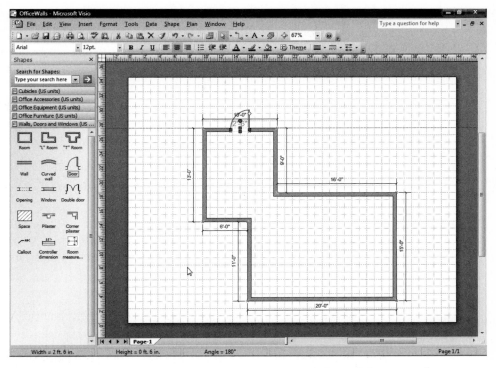

2. Right-click the door to display its shortcut menu, and then click **Properties**.

The Shape Data dialog box appears and lists properties for the door.

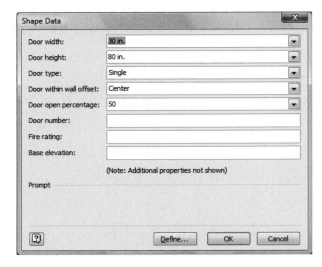

> **Troubleshooting** If you have trouble displaying the shape's shortcut menu, make sure you are right-clicking the shape and not the grid on the drawing page behind the shape. To ensure that you right-click the shape, position the pointer over the shape text, one of the shape's lines, or the white box that appears in the middle of the shape when it's selected, and then right-click.

3. In the **Door width** box, click the down arrow to display a list of dimensions, and then click **36 in**. Click **OK**.

Visio widens the door and updates its dimensions to *3'-0"*.

4. Right-click the door to display its shortcut menu again, and then click **Reverse In/Out Opening**.

Visio flips the door opening so that it swings down into the office.

5. From the **Walls, Doors and Windows** stencil, drag a **Window** shape onto the vertical wall to the right of the door.

Visio flips the window to match the wall's orientation and connects the window to the wall shape, displaying red and gray selection handles. The window shape's dimension text appears while the shape is selected.

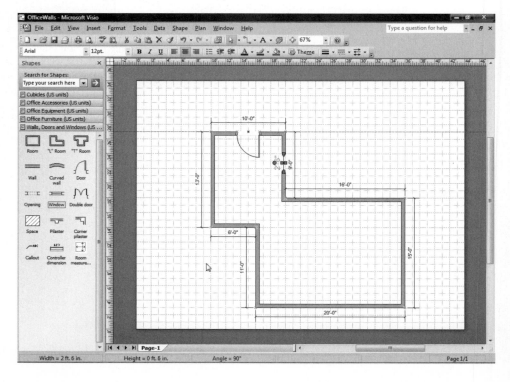

6. Drag the window's bottom selection handle until the shape is 3 feet wide. Use the **Width** field in the status bar at the bottom of the drawing page window to determine the shape's width.

   Visio widens the window and updates its dimensions to *3'-0"*.

   > **Tip** You might need to zoom in to specify exact dimensions.

7. From the **Walls, Doors and Windows** stencil, drag a **Window** shape onto the left area of the 16-foot wall.

   Visio connects the window to the wall shape, displaying red and gray selection handles. The window shape's dimension text appears while the shape is selected.

8. Drag the right selection handle on the window you just added to the wall to increase the width of the window to 3 feet. Use the **Width** field in the status bar at the bottom of the drawing page to determine the shape's width.

   Visio widens the window and updates its dimensions to *3'-0"*.

   > **Tip** You can set the display options for one or all the walls, doors, and windows in an office layout at once. For example, you can show or hide all the door frames and swings, window sills and sashes, and wall reference lines in a diagram. To set the display options for all the shapes in a diagram at once, on the Plan menu, click Set Display Options. To set the display options for a single shape, right-click the shape you want to change, and then click Set Display Options on the shortcut menu.

9. Hold down the Ctrl key while you drag the window to the right to duplicate the shape and position the copy on the wall to right of the original.

   Visio connects the duplicate window to the wall.

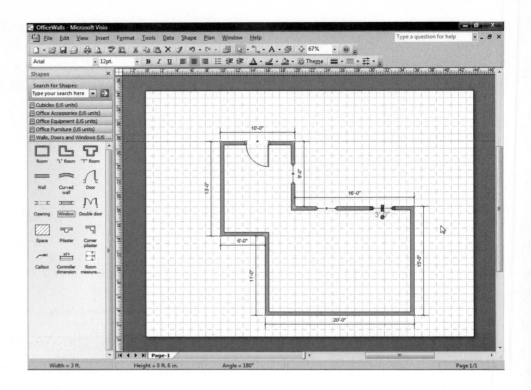

Troubleshooting If you move the window instead of copying it, press [Ctrl]+[Z] to undo your action, and then try again. Make sure you release the mouse button before you release the [Ctrl] key so Visio copies the window instead of moving it.

10. Click the **Cubicles** stencil to show it. From the **Cubicles** stencil, drag the **Straight workstation** shape into the corner of the office opposite and to the left of the door.

Visio adds the shape to the drawing page.

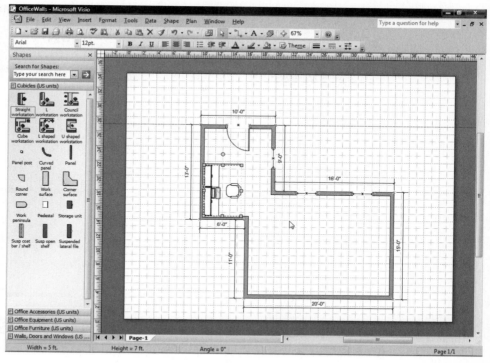

11. Click the **Office Furniture** stencil (at the bottom of the Shapes window) to show it. From the **Office Furniture** stencil, drag the **Multi-chair racetrack** shape into the empty room.

    Visio adds the shape to the drawing page. The shape is selected.

12. With the shape selected, on the **Shape** menu, point to **Rotate or Flip**, and then click **Rotate Left**.

    The shape rotates 90 degrees to the left.

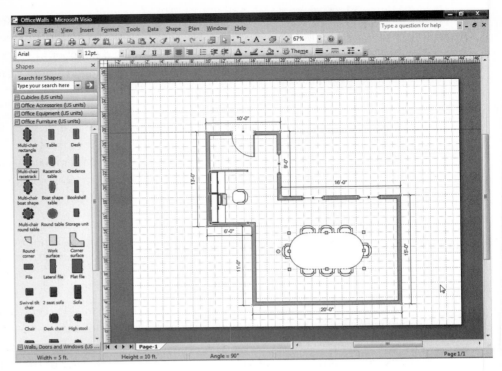

13. On the **File** menu, click **Close**, and then click **No** to close the drawing without saving the changes.

Organizing Shapes in Office Layouts by Using Layers

For some drawing types in Visio, shapes are preassigned to *layers*—categories that help you organize and manage related shapes. Visio can show, hide, lock, print, snap, glue, and color and change the transparency of shapes based on their layer assignment. Layers give you a great deal of flexibility over what you want to display and how you want categories of shapes to behave or look. For example, a space plan that hides everything except the electrical equipment and structural shapes, such as walls, doors, and windows, would be very helpful in determining the best cable routes for the office. You can accomplish this by hiding anything that's not on the electrical or structural layers, or setting particular layers as nonprinting layers. It's also common to lock the structural shapes, such as walls, doors, and windows, in a layout after they're in place so that you don't inadvertently move them while adding furniture to the office layout. You can temporarily hide all the annotation shapes, such as callouts and dimension lines, to make it easier to see and move furniture shapes. Layers open up all these options to you.

Layers are also used when more than one person revises or reviews a diagram. For example, in an office layout, the building shell can be locked and then handed off to an electrician, who adds wiring on one layer, and then to a plumber, who adds pipes on another layer. That way, each person can add to the diagram without disturbing another person's work. A shape can be assigned to a single layer, to several layers, or to no layer at all. For example, if you use the drawing tools to create a shape, that shape is not assigned to a layer. You can, however, choose to assign the shape to an existing layer or create a new layer. Fortunately, the shapes included with the Office Layout template are already assigned to predefined layers that are built into the template and added to your diagram—a feature that can save you a lot of time if you're working extensively with layers.

> **Tip** To quickly see which layers a shape is assigned to, display the Format Shape toolbar, and then view the Layer list. To display the Format Shape toolbar, right-click the toolbar area, and then click Format Shape on the shortcut menu.

Visio includes two commands for working with layers. The Layer command on the Format menu displays a shape's layer assignments and allows you to create and remove layers. The Layer Properties command on the View menu opens the Layer Properties dialog box, which you use to control the appearance and behavior of the shapes assigned to layers.

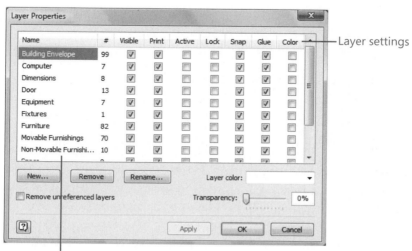

Predefined layers in a typical office layout

> **Important** This exercise demonstrates working with layers in an office layout. However, you can use the methods in this exercise to work with layers in any Visio diagram.

In this exercise, you determine which layers some shapes are assigned to, and then you change the layer properties for some layers. You add a callout to the diagram and color code it by using layer properties. Last, you create a new layer, assign shapes to it, and then change its properties.

OPEN the *OfficeFurnished* file in Documents\Microsoft Press\Visio 2007 SBS \07_OfficeLayouts.

1. Select the conference table that has eight chairs around it, and then on the **Format** menu, click **Layer**.

   The Layer dialog box appears and shows the layers to which the shape is assigned. In this case, the conference table (the Multi-chair racetrack shape) is assigned to the Furniture layer and Movable Furnishings layer.

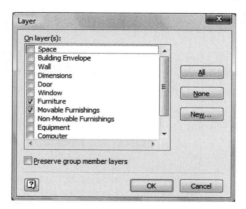

2. Click **Cancel** to close the **Layer** dialog box.

3. Select a wall shape, and then on the **Format** menu, click **Layer**.

   The Layer dialog box appears with the Building Envelope layer and the Wall layer selected, indicating that the wall shape is assigned to those two layers.

4. Click **Cancel** to close the **Layer** dialog box.

5. From the **Walls, Doors and Windows** stencil, drag a **Callout** shape onto the drawing page, and position it to the left of the lower-leftmost wall.

   Visio adds a callout to the diagram that points to the left. The shape is selected.

6. Drag the endpoint of the callout line and position it over the middle of the conference table.

As you drag the endpoint to the middle of the table, Visio highlights the table with a red border to indicate that you're creating a shape-to-shape connection. The callout text flips to the other side of the callout line, and the callout connects to the table so that when you move the table, the callout moves with it. The Callout shape remains selected.

7. With the **Callout** shape selected, type Verify table size.

Visio adds the text to the callout and resizes the text block so that the text fits within it.

8. Press the Esc key to close the text block.

The Callout shape remains selected.

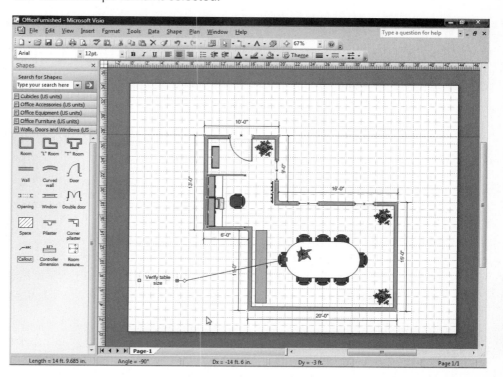

9. On the **View** menu, click **Layer Properties** to open the **Layer Properties** dialog box.

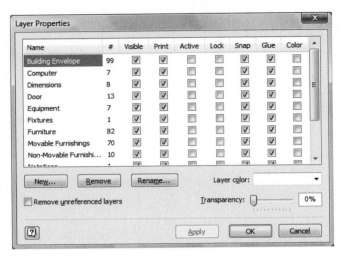

10. In the **Building Envelope** row, click the box in the **Lock** column.

    A check mark appears in the box in the Lock column in the Building Envelope row, indicating that all shapes on the Building Envelope layer are locked—in other words, you can't select them.

11. Click the corresponding box in the **Lock** column for the **Door**, **Wall**, and **Window** rows—one row at a time.

    Visio locks the shapes assigned to the Door, Wall, and Window layers and a check mark appears in the box in the specified rows.

12. In the **Notations** row, click the box in the **Visible** column to deselect it.

    There is no check mark in the box in the Visible column, indicating that all shapes on the Notations layer are hidden.

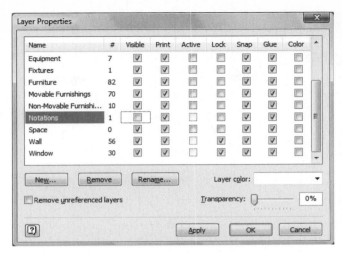

13. Click **OK**.

Visio updates the layers in the office layout with the new layer properties. The Callout shape is no longer visible.

14. Select a door shape.

Nothing happens—the shape is locked, so you can't select it. The walls and windows are also locked.

15. On the **View** menu, click **Layer Properties** to display the **Layer Properties** dialog box again.

16. In the **Notations** row, click the box in the **Visible** column to select it.

A check mark appears in the box in the Visible column in the Notations row, indicating that all shapes on the Notations layer are visible.

17. In the **Notations** row, click the box in the **Color** column.

A check mark appears in the box in the Color column in the Notations row, indicating that all shapes on the Notations layer are color-coded gray (the color that appears by default in the column and in the Layer Color box).

18. In the **Layer Color** box, click the down arrow, scroll up, and then click color **04:** (blue).

In the Notations row, the column is shaded blue to signify that the shapes on the Notations layer are color-coded blue.

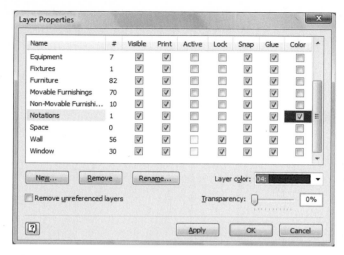

19. Click **OK**.

    Visio displays and changes the color of the Callout shape, which is on the Notations layer, to blue.

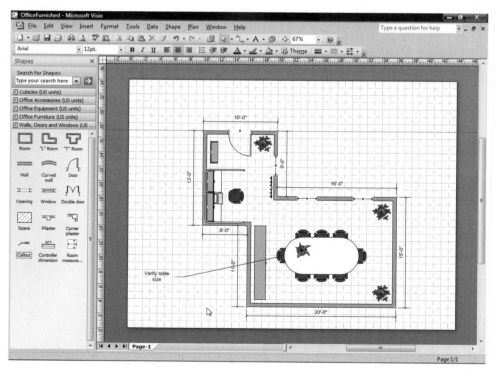

20. Select a plant.

21. Hold down the [Shift] key while you select the rest of the plants in the office layout.

All four plants in the diagram are selected.

22. On the **Format** menu, click **Layer** to open the **Layer** dialog box.

23. In the **Layer** dialog box, click **New**.

The New Layer dialog box appears.

24. In the **New Layer** dialog box, type Plants.

25. Click **OK**.

Visio closes the New Layer dialog box, adds the Plants layer to the layer list in the Layer dialog box, and selects the Plants layer to assign the selected plant shapes to it.

26. Click the **Furniture** layer to deselect it, and then click the **Movable Furnishings** layer to deselect it. Click **OK**.

Visio closes the Layer dialog box, removes the plant shapes from the Furniture layer and Movable Furnishings layer, and assigns the plant shapes to the Plants layer only.

27. On the **View** menu, click **Layer Properties** to display the **Layer Properties** dialog box again.

28. In the **Plants** row, click the box in the **Visible** column to deselect it. Click **OK**.

The plants in the office layout aren't visible.

29. Repeat steps 27 and 28, but *select* the **Visible** option to display the plants again.

Save

30. On the Standard toolbar, click the **Save** button to save the changes to the diagram.

> ✕ **CLOSE** the *OfficeFurnished* file.

> **Tip** Many of the shapes included with the Office Layout template are groups, such as the plant shapes on the Office Accessories stencil and the conference table shapes on the Office Furniture stencil. To add color to the individual shapes in the group, subselect the individual shapes, and choose a formatting option. For example, you can subselect a chair in the Multi-chair racetrack shape, and then click the Fill Color button on the Formatting toolbar to apply a color to that chair.

Key Points

- You can create a scaled diagram with a scaled template so that the drawing scale is already defined and the stencils that the template opens contain shapes appropriate for the drawing scale.

- You can change the drawing scale for a diagram by clicking Page Setup on the File menu, and then clicking the Drawing Scale tab.

- You can create walls by positioning Space shapes on the drawing page, uniting them by using the Union command, and then converting them to walls by using the Convert to Walls command on the Plan menu.

- You can easily add doors and windows to walls by dragging them on top of the walls. Visio orients the doors and windows for you.

- You can change the size of doors and windows by either dragging a shape's end-point or right-clicking the shape, clicking Properties on the shortcut menu, and specifying the shape's width.

- You can set the display options for all the spaces, walls, doors, and windows in an office layout at once by clicking Set Display Options on the Plan menu. You can set the display options for a single shape by right-clicking it and then clicking Set Display Options on the shortcut menu.

- You can see a shape's dimensions by selecting it. To add a dimension line to a shape, use the Controller dimension shape on the Walls, Doors and Windows stencil.

- You can create a new layer and assign a shape to it at the same time by selecting one or more shapes on the drawing page and then clicking Layer on the Format menu.

- You can change the properties for all the shapes assigned to a layer by clicking Layer Properties on the View menu.

Chapter at a Glance

Connect shapes in network diagrams   Store information with network shapes

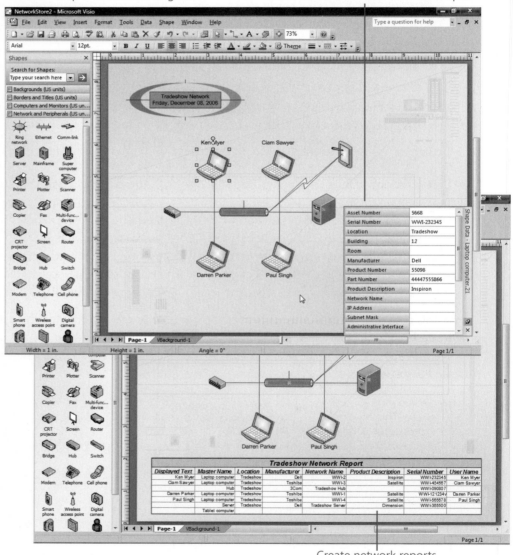

Create network reports

8 Creating Network Diagrams

In this chapter, you will learn how to:

✔ Connect shapes in network diagrams.

✔ Store information with network shapes.

✔ Create network reports.

Organizations of any size can use network diagrams to plan, document, and trouble-shoot network infrastructures. Using the Basic Network Diagram template in Microsoft Office Visio, you can diagram a wide variety of computer and network equipment and their physical and logical relationships. You can also store data, such as serial number, location, manufacturer, network name, product description, and so on, with the equipment shapes in a network diagram. You can then use that data to create your own network reports that you can store in spreadsheets or display in your network diagrams.

In this chapter, you create a diagram of the proposed network infrastructure for the tradeshow hosted by Wide World Importers. You add information to the network equipment shapes in the diagram, and then use that information to create a hardware report for the network.

> **Note** This chapter covers basic methods for manually entering shape data. Visio Professional 2007 provides new functionality and more advanced methods for integrating and visualizing data with the shapes in any Visio diagram. These methods are covered in Chapter 9, "Visualizing Data in Diagrams."

See Also Do you need only a quick refresher on the topics in this chapter? See the Quick Reference entries on pages xxv-xliii.

> **Important** Before you can use the practice files in this chapter, you need to install them from the book's companion CD to their default location. See "Using the Book's CD-ROM" on page xix for more information.

Connecting Shapes in Network Diagrams

You can quickly and easily create a network diagram that includes information such the type of equipment in the network, how it is connected to the network, and the most effective network configuration, by using the Basic Network Diagram template. You simply drag shapes onto the drawing page and experiment with their arrangement until you achieve the result you want.

The first step in creating a network diagram is to determine which type of *network ring* or *backbone*—the part of the network that handles the major data traffic—you want to use. Then you drag the backbone shape onto the drawing page, followed by each hardware shape in the network. After you position the network equipment shapes around the backbone, you drag control handles from the backbone shape to connect the hardware shapes to the backbone. Finally, you add text to the shapes as you would any other Visio shape. It really is that easy.

In this exercise, you diagram the Wide World Importers local area network (LAN) for the tradeshow they're hosting. You drag an Ethernet shape (the backbone of the network) onto the drawing page, connect laptop computers and other components directly to the backbone, and then add descriptive text to some of the network equipment shapes. Finally, you add a background, title, and color theme to the diagram.

1. Start Visio. In the **Template Categories** list, click **Network**. Under **Featured Templates**, double-click **Basic Network Diagram**.

   The template opens a blank drawing page and the Network and Peripherals stencil, Computers and Monitors stencil, Borders and Titles stencil, and Backgrounds stencil.

2. From the **Network and Peripherals** stencil, drag an **Ethernet** shape just to the left and below the center of the drawing page.

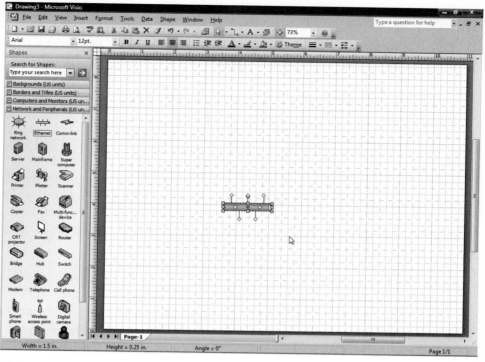

3. Click the **Computers and Monitors** stencil to show it.

4. From the **Computers and Monitors** stencil, drag a **Laptop computer** shape onto the drawing page, and position it above the **Ethernet** shape.

5. From the **Computers and Monitors** stencil, drag another **Laptop computer** shape onto the drawing page, and position it above the **Ethernet** shape and to the right of the other **Laptop computer** shape.

> **Tip** You can align the shapes using the grid.

6. Repeat steps 4 and 5, this time positioning the two **Laptop computer** shapes below the **Ethernet** shape.

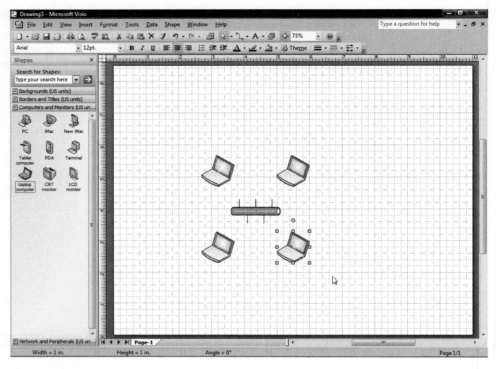

7. Select the **Ethernet** shape.

Four-headed
arrow

8. Position the pointer over the yellow, upper-left control handle on the **Ethernet** shape, and then when the pointer changes to a four-headed arrow, drag the control handle to the connection point in the middle of the upper-left **Laptop computer** shape.

   Visio connects the two shapes. The connector remains selected and the endpoint is red, indicating that it is glued to the Laptop computer shape.

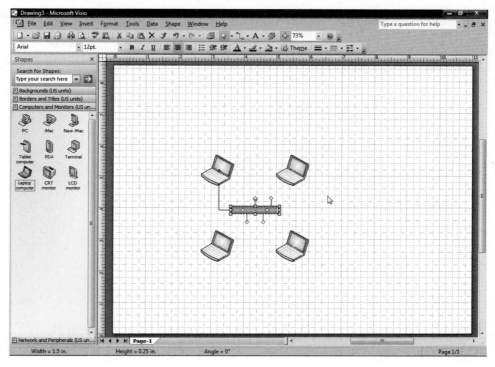

9. Repeat step 8 to create connections from the **Ethernet** shape to each of the remaining **Laptop computer** shapes. Each time, drag a different control handle to a **Laptop computer** shape.

All four laptop computers are connected to the Ethernet shape.

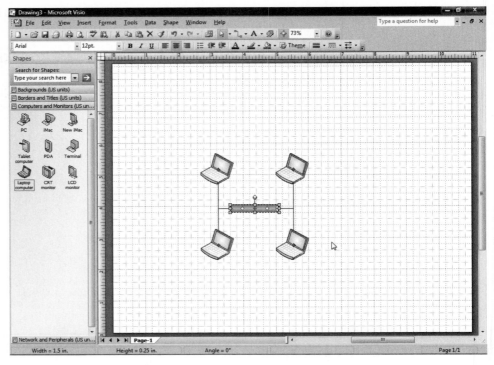

10. Click the **Network and Peripherals** stencil to show it.

11. From the **Network and Peripherals** stencil, drag a **Server** shape onto the drawing page, and position it to the right of the **Ethernet** shape.

12. From the **Network and Peripherals** stencil, drag a **Hub** shape onto the drawing page, and position it to the left of the **Ethernet** shape.

13. Select the **Ethernet** shape.

14. Position the pointer over one of the control handles (represented by a yellow diamond) on the **Ethernet** shape, and when the pointer changes to a four-headed arrow, drag the control handle to the connection point in the middle of the **Server** shape.

    Visio connects the two shapes. The connector remains selected and the endpoint is red, indicating that it is glued to the Server shape.

15. Position the pointer over one of the control handles (represented by a yellow diamond) on the **Ethernet** shape, and when the pointer changes to a four-headed arrow, drag the control handle to the connection point in the middle of the **Hub** shape.

Visio connects the two shapes. The connector remains selected and the endpoint is red, indicating that it is glued to the Hub shape.

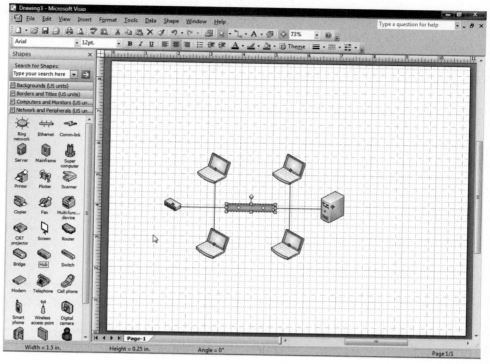

16. Click the **Computers and Monitors** stencil to show it.

17. From the **Computers and Monitors** stencil, drag a **Tablet computer** shape onto the drawing page, and position it above and to the right of the **Server** shape, and slightly higher than the laptop shapes.

18. Click the **Network and Peripherals** stencil to show it.

19. To indicate the transmission of data from the **Tablet computer** shape to the network, drag a **Comm-link** shape onto the drawing page, and position it anywhere in the top half of the diagram.

20. Drag the **Comm-link** shape's right endpoint to the middle connection point on the **Tablet computer** shape.

    Visio connects the two shapes. The connector remains selected and the endpoint is red, indicating that it is glued to the Tablet computer shape.

21. Drag the **Comm-link** shape's left endpoint to the right connection point on the **Ethernet** shape.

Visio connects the two shapes. The connector remains selected and the endpoint is red, indicating that it is glued to the Ethernet shape.

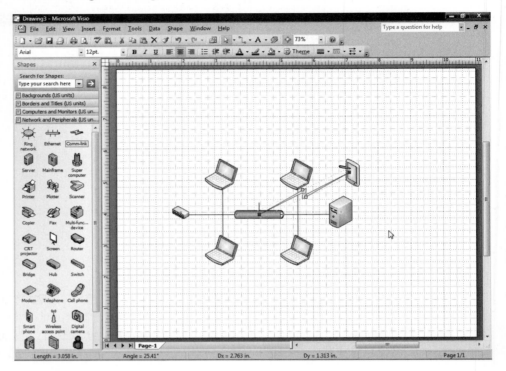

22. Double-click the upper-left **Laptop computer** shape to open the shape's text block.

23. Type Ken Myer, and then press the [Esc] key to close the shape's text block.

    The shape remains selected and a new yellow control handle appears on top of the shape text.

24. Drag the new control handle above the **Ken Myer** shape to position the text above the shape.

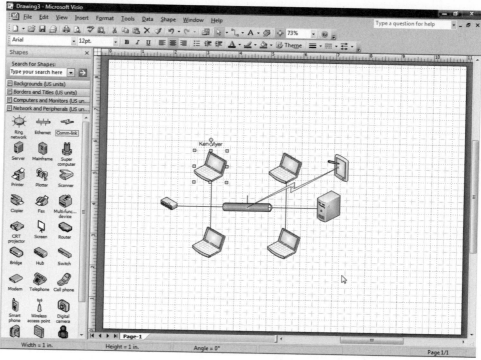

25. Double-click the lower-left **Laptop computer** shape to open the shape's text block, type Darren Parker, and then press the [Esc] key to close the shape's text block.

26. Double-click the lower-right **Laptop computer** shape to open the shape's text block, type Paul Singh, and then press the [Esc] key to close the shape's text block.

27. Double-click the upper-right **Laptop computer** shape to open the shape's text block, type Ciam Sawyer, and then press the [Esc] key to close the shape's text block.

    The shape remains selected and a new control handle appears on top of the shape text.

28. Drag the new control handle above the **Ciam Sawyer** shape to position the text above the shape.

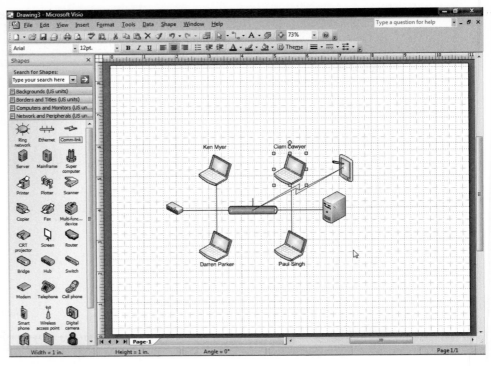

29. Click the **Backgrounds** stencil to show it.

30. From the **Backgrounds** stencil, drag the **Background high-tech** shape onto the drawing page.

    Visio adds a *VBackground* page to the drawing file and places the background shape on it.

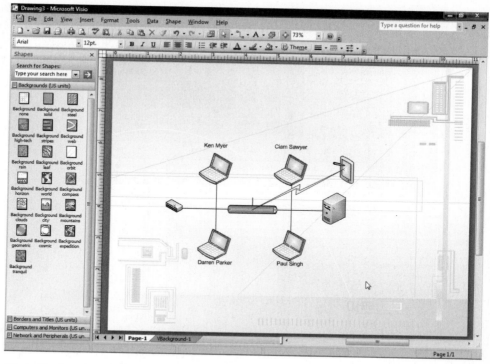

31. Click the **Borders and Titles** stencil to show it.

32. From the **Borders and Titles** stencil, drag the **Title block sphere** shape onto the drawing page, and position it in the upper-left corner of the drawing page.

33. With the shape selected, press [F2] to open the shape's text block.

34. Highlight the placeholder text, *Company Name/Title*, and then type Tradeshow Network to replace it.

35. Click the pasteboard to deselect the shape.

36. On the **Format** menu, click **Theme** to open the **Theme – Colors** task pane.

37. In the **Apply theme colors** list, click **Concourse - Light**.

Visio applies the color theme to the entire diagram.

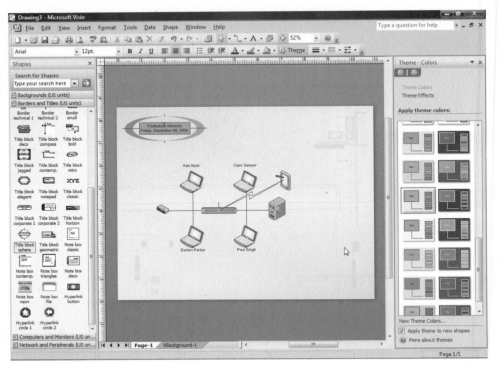

38. On the **File** menu, click **Save**.

39. In the **Save As** dialog box, in the **File name** box, type Network.

40. In the **Save As** dialog box, click the **Save** button to save the diagram.

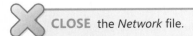

CLOSE the *Network* file.

Storing Information with Network Shapes

Network equipment shapes have default *shape data fields*, which you can use to store *shape data* with the shapes. These fields include manufacturer, product number, part number, product description, and serial number. You can also define new shape data fields for a specific shape or for all the instances of a shape in a diagram.

To view shape data for a shape, on the View menu, click Shape Data Window, and then select the shape. The shape's data appears in the Shape Data window. Alternatively, you can right-click a shape, and then click Properties on the shortcut menu, or point to Data, and then click Shape Data. You can define a new shape data field for all the instances of a shape in a diagram by using the Document Stencil, which includes all the shapes you've added to your diagram. If you edit a shape on the Document Stencil, the changes ripple throughout all the instances of the shape in the diagram.

> **Tip** You can also create shape data *sets* for shapes in a diagram. A shape data set is a set of related data. To create a shape data set for a shape, right-click the Shape Data window, and then click Shape Data Sets on the shortcut menu. In the Shape Data Sets window, define the set. For more information about defining and working with shape data sets, type shape data set in the Type a question for help box.

In this exercise, you view the shape data assigned to several of the network equipment shapes in your network diagram. You also create a new shape data field for all the Laptop computer shapes in the diagram to identify which employee uses each computer.

 **OPEN** the *NetworkStore* file in Documents\Microsoft Press\Visio 2007 SBS\08_Networks.

1. On the **View** menu, click **Shape Data Window**.

   No shape data appears in the Shape Data window because a shape isn't selected.

2. Select the **Ken Myer** shape.

   The Shape Data window displays a list of the blank data fields for the shape, including Asset Number, Serial Number, Location, Building, Room, Manufacturer, and Product Number.

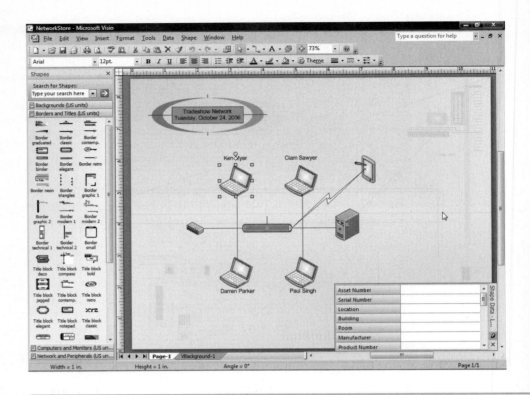

> **Tip** To see more data fields, scroll the Shape Data window. Or, drag the top border of the window up to increase the height of the window.

Shapes

3. On the Standard toolbar, click the **Shapes** button, and then click **Show Document Stencil**.

The Document Stencil appears in the Shapes window and displays each shape in your diagram.

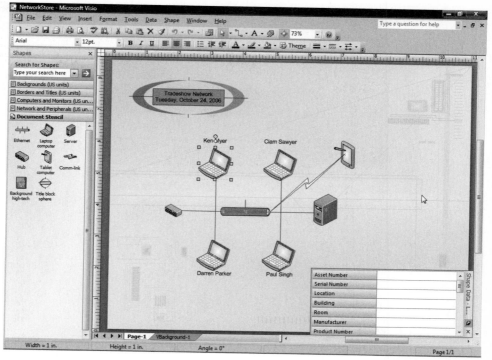

4. In the **Document Stencil**, right-click the **Laptop computer** shape, point to **Edit Master**, and then click **Edit Master Shape**.

   The Laptop computer shape appears in a drawing window that covers your entire diagram. No shape data fields appear in the Shape Data window because the shape isn't selected.

5. Select the **Laptop computer** shape.

   The shape data fields for the shape appear in the Shape Data window.

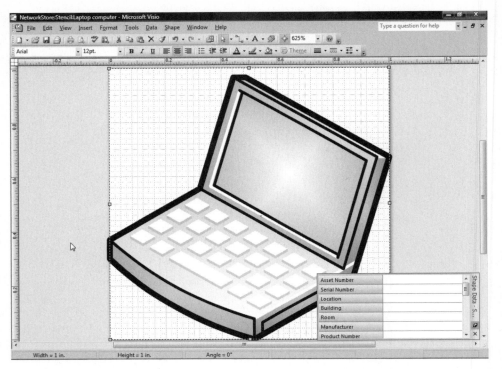

6. Right-click the Shape Data window, and then click **Define Shape Data** on the short-cut menu.

The Define Shape Data dialog box appears.

7. In the **Define Shape Data** dialog box, click **New**.

A data field labeled *Property25* is added and highlighted in the Properties box at the bottom of the dialog box.

8. In the **Label** box, type User Name, and then click in the **Prompt** box.

9. In the **Prompt** box, type Enter the name of the person who uses this device. to create a ScreenTip for the new data field.

10. Click **OK**.

The Define Shape Data dialog box closes.

11. Scroll to the end of the list in the Shape Data window to see the new **User Name** data field at the end of the list.

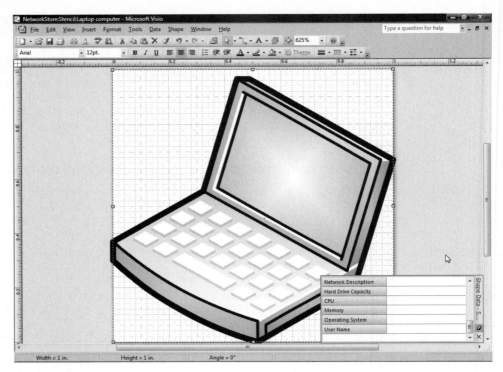

Close Window

12. Click the **Close Window** button to the right of the **Type a question for help** box in the upper-right corner of the drawing window.

13. When a message appears asking if you want to update the **Laptop computer** shape and all of its instances on the drawing page, click **Yes**.

    The Laptop computer shape drawing window closes and Visio adds the new shape data field to all the Laptop computer shapes in the diagram and on the Document Stencil.

14. Right-click the **Document Stencil** title bar, and then click **Close**.

    The Document Stencil closes.

15. Click the **Darren Parker** shape, and then scroll to the bottom of the list in the Shape Data window to see the new **User Name** data field.

    The User Name box has been added to the Darren Parker shape. Now you could document the individuals who use each laptop computer in the diagram.

> **Tip** You can quickly create a data field for a single instance of a shape. Rather than editing the shape in the Document Stencil, select the shape on the drawing page. Right-click the Shape Data window, and then click Define Shape Data on the shortcut menu. In the Define Shape Data dialog box, click New, and then enter the information for the new data field.

16. Position the pointer over the **User Name** box to see the ScreenTip that appears for the data field.

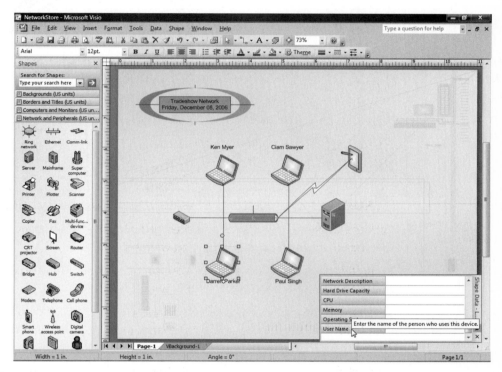

17. In the Shape Data window, click the **User Name** box, and then type Darren Parker. Visio stores the new shape data with the Darren Parker shape.

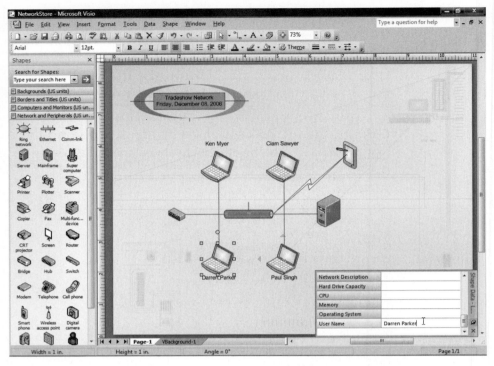

18. On the **File** menu, click **Close**, and then click **No** when Visio asks you if you want to save the changes to the drawing.

Visio and the drawing close.

Creating Network Reports

You can create a report on the equipment in your network diagrams by using the shape data stored in the diagram. Visio includes several standard report types, such as the Inventory report and Network Device report. You can also define your own report by creating a *report definition*—a set of criteria that specifies which shapes and custom properties are included in the report, as well as the format to use. You create report definitions or modify existing ones by using the Report Definition Wizard, which guides you through the process of specifying the criteria for your report. You run the report by clicking the Reports command on the Data menu. You can save the results in a spreadsheet, an XML file, or a Web page, or you can display the report as a Visio shape—a specialized shape that displays the report data directly on the drawing page in your network diagram.

In this exercise, you create a new report definition, specifying which shapes and shape data to include in it, and then you display the report as a Visio shape in the network diagram.

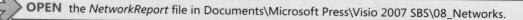

OPEN the *NetworkReport* file in Documents\Microsoft Press\Visio 2007 SBS\08_Networks.

1. Click one of the network equipment shapes in the diagram, then hold down the [Shift] key, and click all the other network equipment shapes except the **Ethernet** shape.

2. On the **Data** menu, click **Reports** to open the **Reports** dialog box.

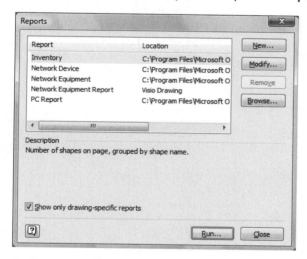

3. In the **Reports** dialog box, click **New**.

   The first page of the Report Definition Wizard appears.

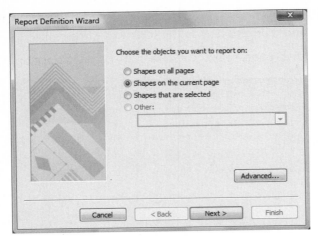

4. On the first page of the **Report Definition Wizard**, select **Shapes that are selected**, and then click **Next**.

   The second page of the wizard appears, asking you to select the shape data fields you want to include as columns in your report.

5. Select the **<Displayed Text>**, **<Master Name>**, **Location**, **Manufacturer**, **Network Name**, **Product Description**, **Serial Number**, and **User Name** check boxes.

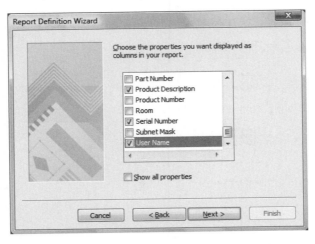

6. Click **Next**.

   The third page of the wizard appears, asking you to title the report.

7. In the **Report Title** box, type Tradeshow Network Report, and then click **Next**.

   The fourth page of the wizard appears, asking you to name the custom report definition you're creating.

8. In the **Name** box, type Tradeshow Equipment Report. In the **Description** box, type Includes all network equipment and is sorted by shape name.

9. On the same wizard page, select the **Save in this drawing** option.

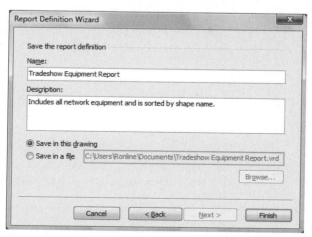

10. Click **Finish**.

    The Reports dialog box reappears, listing the Network Equipment Report in the Report column.

11. In the **Reports** dialog box, make sure **Tradeshow Equipment Report** is highlighted.

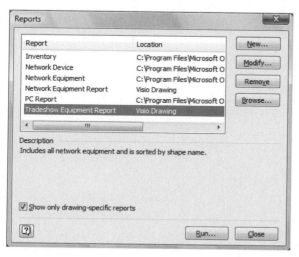

12. Click **Run**.

    The Run Report dialog box appears.

> **Tip** To run an existing report, on the Data menu, click Reports. Click the report you want, and then click Run. In the Run Report dialog box, select the format for the report, and click OK.

13. In the **Run Report** dialog box, in the **Select report format** box, click **Visio shape**, and then click **OK**.

Visio generates the report and places it at the bottom of the drawing page in a Visio shape that looks like a table.

14. Drag the shape to the bottom of the drawing page.

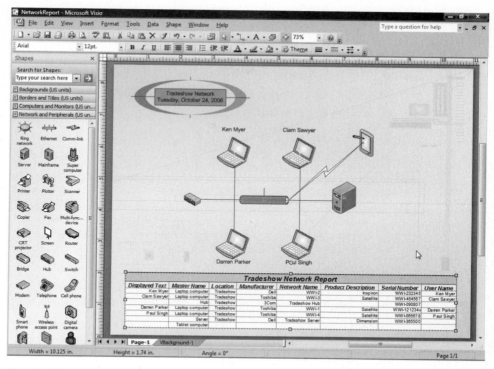

15. On the **File** menu, click **Close**, and then click **No** so you don't save the changes to the diagram.

Key Points

- You can connect network equipment shapes to backbone shapes, such as Ethernet or Ring network shapes, in network diagrams by dragging control handles from the backbone shape to the middle of the network equipment shape.

- You can store network equipment information with shapes by using shape data fields. To view a shape's data, select the shape, and then on the View menu, click Shape Data Window. You can also right-click a shape, point to Data, and then click Shape Data on the shortcut menu.

- You can define a new data field for all the instances of a shape in your diagram. Open the Document Stencil, and then on that stencil, double-click the shape to which you want to add the data field. Select the shape in the drawing window, and then add the data.

● You can define a new shape data field for a single shape. Select the shape, right-click the Shape Data window, and then click Define Shape Data on the shortcut menu.

● You can run a predefined network report or create your own network report definition. On the Data menu, click Reports. To create your own report definition, click New in the Reports dialog box.

A Chapters on the CD

Glossary

attributes Qualities of text or shapes that you can format, including text font and color; line color, ends, weight, and pattern; and fill color, pattern, and shadow, and so on. See also formatting.

background A background is a shape that appears behind a diagram and looks like a pattern, much like the background of a Microsoft Office PowerPoint slide.

background page Another drawing page that appears behind a drawing page in a diagram and usually contains background shapes.

backbone The physical network configuration, or topology, that you can depict in a network diagram by using a shape such as the Ethernet shape on the Network and Peripherals stencil. See also network ring.

begin point The selection handle that appear at the start of a selected 1-D shape and is marked by ×. See also endpoints; end point.

breakdown shape A shape in a PivotDiagram that shows the name of the category that's broken down, or shown, on the drawing page. A breakdown shape is positioned on the connector between the parent node and child node. See also parent node; child node.

child node The shape(s) below a parent node in a PivotDiagram. Typically child nodes are connected to parent nodes. A parent node can have multiple child nodes; however, a child node has only one parent node. See also parent node.

closed shape A 2-D shape, such as a box, with a solid border to which you can apply a fill color and pattern. See also open shape.

color theme A set of coordinated fill colors that you can apply to an entire diagram and its shapes. Choose color themes from the Theme – Colors task pane.

connection point A point on a shape where you can attach a connector or 1-D shape. Each connection point appears as a blue mark on a shape when the Connection Points command is selected on the View menu.

connectors 1-D shapes designed to connect other shapes. The Connectors stencil in the Visio Extras folder contains a variety of connector shapes for use in any drawing type.

control handles Yellow diamond-shaped handles that control a shape's behavior in special ways. Depending on the shape, a control handle might adjust the position of a line, reshape an arrow, or connect to other shapes. To find out what a control handle does, point to the handle to display a ScreenTip.

control point The circular handle that appears on a line or arc when you select it with the Pencil tool. You can drag a control point to change the curve of an arc or ellipse.

crop To reduce the size and cut out a portion of an imported picture. You use the Crop tool to drag one of the picture's selection handles to the desired size, and then drag the picture inside the selection box to view the portion of the picture you want to use.

custom properties See *shape data*.

data graphics Visio shapes that include visual elements designed specifically for visualizing data. You build your own data graphics using the Data Graphics task pane.

data legend A rectangular shape in a PivotDiagram that's placed next to the top node and contains details about the data source linked to the top node.

deselect To click the pasteboard or a blank area of the drawing page, or press the [Esc] key so a shape's selection handles don't appear.

dock To attach a window to a side of the drawing page window. For example, stencils are docked by default in the Shapes window on the left side of the drawing window. See also *float*.

drawing file A file that contains a Visio drawing or diagram. Drawing files have a .vsd file extension.

drawing page The printable area in the Visio window that contains a drawing. Each drawing page has a size, which usually corresponds to a standard printer paper size, and other properties that you can change with the Page Setup command on the File menu.

drawing scale A measure of the relationship between real-world sizes or distances and the sizes represented in a Visio drawing. For example, an office layout might have a drawing scale of one foot of actual distance to one inch in the drawing. To set a drawing scale, click the Page Setup command on the File menu. Then, click the Drawing Scale tab.

dynamic grid The dotted line that appears on the screen when you drag a shape near another shape. The dynamic grid shows the optimal alignment. To turn on the dynamic grid, click the Snap & Glue command on the Tools menu.

effect theme A set of coordinated text, line, fill pattern, shadow, and connector colors and styles that you can apply to an entire diagram and its shapes. Choose effect themes from the Theme – Effects task pane.

embed To paste or insert an object, such as text or a group of shapes, from one program into a file created in another program. The embedded object becomes part of the file, but you can double-click it to modify it in its original program. See also *link*.

end point The selection handle that appear at the end of a selected 1-D shape and is marked by +. See also *begin point*; *endpoints*.

endpoints Either of the selection handles that appear at the beginning or end of a selected 1-D shape. The endpoint at the beginning of the shape (begin point) is marked by ¥. The endpoint at the end of the shape (end point) is marked by +. See also *begin point*; *end point*.

expanded timeline A linear graphic that represents and is synchronized with a segment of a larger timeline. See also *timeline*.

field Placeholder text that Visio uses to display dates or other information in a shape. You can insert a field into a shape with the Field command on the Insert menu.

fill The color and pattern inside a shape.

float To display and move a window anywhere within the Visio window. For example, you can drag a stencil onto the drawing page to display it in a floating window. See also *dock*.

formatting A combination of attributes that make up the appearance of a shape, diagram, or text. For example, you can format a shape to change the thickness and color of its lines, the color and pattern inside the shape, its font, and so on. See also *attributes*.

Gantt bars Bars in a Gantt chart that represent the duration of a task.

Gantt charts Diagram types you create in Visio with the Gantt Chart template that describes the discrete tasks associated with a project. In a Gantt chart, bars represent the duration of each task within a timescale that is displayed in the chart.

glue Shape behavior that causes one shape to stay connected to another, even if the shape to which it is glued moves.

grid Nonprinting horizontal and vertical lines displayed at regular intervals on the drawing page. The grid makes it easier to align shapes and position them precisely.

group A shape composed of one or more shapes. A group can also include other groups and objects from other programs. You can move and size a group as a single shape, but its members retain their original appearance and attributes. You can also subselect individual shapes in the group to modify them. See also *subselect*.

guides Visual reference lines that you can drag from the horizontal or vertical ruler onto the drawing page in order to help position and align shapes precisely. Guides do not appear on the printed page.

interval markers A shape used to designate a period of time in a diagram created with the Timeline template.

landscape orientation A printed page or drawing page that is wider than it is tall. You can change page orientation in Visio with the Page Setup command on the File menu. The orientation of the printed page and drawing page can differ. See also *portrait orientation*.

layers Named categories to which shapes are assigned in some diagram types, such as office layouts and network diagrams. You can organize shapes in your drawing by selectively viewing, editing, printing, or locking layers, and you can control whether you can snap and glue shapes on a layer.

line caps Style of a line end: round or square.

line ends Patterns, such as arrowheads, that can appear on the end of a 1-D shape.

link To create a dynamic link from one file to another so that the contents of the original file appear in the linked file. When changes are made to the original file, you can update the link so that the most recent version of the object appears in the linked file. See also *embed*.

locked A setting that limits the ways you can modify a shape. For example, this setting can prevent you from resizing a shape using a selection handle. When you select a locked shape, the shape handles appear gray.

measurement units The type of measurement system used in a drawing and displayed on the rulers. You specify the measurement units (inches, centimeters, points, miles, and so on)

with the Page Setup command on the File menu.

merge To create a new shape by combining or splitting apart existing shapes using an Operations command, such as Union or Combine, on the Shape menu.

milestones A shape from the Timeline Shapes stencil that shows a significant date in a timeline.

network ring The physical configuration or topology of a network that refers to the configuration of cables, computers, and other peripherals. To create a network diagram, start with the Basic Network Diagram template. See also *backbone*.

node A shape in a PivotDiagram that represents data. Breakdown shapes and connectors in a PivotDiagram aren't nodes. See also *breakdown shape*; *connector*.

object linking and embedding In Microsoft Windows, the ability to link or embed a shape or other object created in one program, such as Visio, into a document created in a different program, such as Word.

one-dimensional (1-D) shape A shape, such as a line, that has only one dimension and two endpoints. See also *two-dimensional shape*; *connector*; *endpoint*.

open shape A shape that does not have a continuous border, such as a line or arc. You cannot apply fill color or patterns to an open shape. See also *closed shape*.

page breaks Gray lines that appear on the drawing page when you click the Page Breaks command on the View menu. Page breaks show you where the page will break when you print a large diagram.

pan To change the view by moving the drawing page. You can use the horizontal and vertical scroll bars in the Visio window to pan a drawing, or you can use the keyboard shortcut: Hold down `shift` + `Ctrl` as you drag with the right mouse button.

parent node The shape above a level containing one or more child nodes in a PivotDiagram. Typically child nodes are connected to parent nodes. A parent node can have multiple child nodes; however, a child node has only one parent node. See also child node.

pasteboard The blue area around the drawing page, which you can use as a temporary holding area for shapes. Shapes on the pasteboard are saved with a drawing but aren't printed.

picture A graphic file created in another program that you can add to a Visio diagram. To insert a picture, click the Picture command on the Insert menu.

PivotDiagram A diagram that shows collections of shapes arranged in a tree structure that helps you analyze and summarize data in a visual format. Nodes in PivotDiagrams can show data counts, sums, averages, minimums, and maximums.

point-to-point connection A connection between shapes in which the endpoint of a connector stays attached to a particular point on a shape, even when the shape is moved.

portrait orientation A printed page or drawing page that is taller than it is wide. You can change page orientation in Visio with the Page Setup command on the File menu. The orientation of the printed page and drawing page can differ. See also landscape orientation.

primary shape The first shape you select in a multiple selection, which can affect the outcome of a command, such as the Align Shapes and Operations commands on the Shape menu.

primary timeline

read-only A setting that prevents you from modifying a file, such as a stencil.

report definition The settings and shape properties included in a report, which you can customize with the Reports command on the Data menu.

rotation handle The round handle that appears above a 2-D shape. Drag it to rotate a shape.

rulers The horizontal and vertical rulers that appear on the top and side of the drawing page, which you can hide and show by clicking Rulers on the View menu. The rulers display the units of measurement specified by the Page Setup command on the File menu. See also measurement units.

ScreenTip Descriptive text that appears when you pause the pointer over a button on a toolbar, a shape on a stencil, handles on a shape, the rulers, and so on.

secondary shapes The shapes you select after the primary shape in a multiple selection. See also primary shape.

select To click a shape so that it becomes the focus of the next action. Selected shapes display handles. Selected text is highlighted.

selection handles Handles that appear on a selected shape. Visio displays different types of selection handles depending on the tool you used to select a shape.

selection box The dotted line that surrounds a shape and shows that it is selected.

selection net The dotted line that appears when you drag using the Pointer Tool. Selection nets are used to select more than one shape; anything within a selection net is selected.

shape data Information about a shape, which appears in the Shape Data window. For example, a shape that represents office furniture can have shape data that identify its inventory number, owner, and location. To see the shape data stored with a shape, right-click the shape, point to Data, and then click Shape Data on the shortcut menu. To easily see the shape data for any shape you select on the drawing page, use the Shape Data window. To open it, on the View menu, click Shape Data Window.

shape data fields Fields that contain shape data values. You can create your own shape data fields. See shape data.

shape data set A collection of shape data. Shape data sets usually include related data, such as IP address, Manufacturer, Model, CPU, Memory, all of which could be included in a Network Asset data set. See shape data.

shapes Objects that you drag onto the drawing page to assemble diagrams and that you create using the Visio drawing tools. Most shapes used in Visio diagrams are pre-drawn symbols stored in Visio stencils. See stencils.

shape-to-shape connection A connection between shapes in which the endpoint of a connector stays attached to a shape at the closest point, even when you move the shape.

shortcut menu The menu that appears when you right-click an object, such as a shape, stencil, or the drawing page. Many Visio shapes have special commands that appear only on a shortcut menu.

snap The way a shape aligns itself automatically with the nearest grid line or guide.

stencils Visio files that contain shapes you can drag onto a drawing page. Stencil files have a .vss file extension.

style A set of formatting attributes, which typically include fill, line, and text attributes. To apply a style to a shape, select the shape, and then on the Format menu, click Style.

subselect To select an individual shape within a group. Select the group, and then select the individual shape. See also group.

task panes Panes, or windows, that open to the right of the Visio drawing page and contain task-oriented or diagram-specific information. To view task panes, on the View menu, click Task Pane.

template A Visio file that includes all of the tools, settings, and shapes you need to assemble a particular type of drawing or diagram. A template opens a drawing page and, usually, stencils. Template files have a .vst file extension.

text block The text area associated with a shape that appears when you click the shape with the Text tool or Text Block tool, or select the shape and start typing. You can size a text block and move a text block in relation to its shape using the Text Block tool.

text-only shape Independent text that's not associated with a shape, but behaves like a shape. Create a text-only shape by using the Text Tool.

theme A set of coordinated colors and effects that Visio applies to all the shapes and text in a diagram, including backgrounds and borders. See also effect theme and color theme.

timelines Linear graphics that represent a specific period of time and the events that occur during that time. You create a timeline in Visio using the Timeline template.

top node The top shape in the tree structure in a PivotDiagram that's linked to an external data source.

two-dimensional (2-D) shape A shape, such as a rectangle or ellipse, that has length and width. A 2-D shape has eight selection handles and one rotation handle.
See also one-dimensional shape.

units of measure See measurement units.

vertex A diamond-shaped handle that appears when you select a shape with the Pencil tool. Each vertex defines a point at the beginning or end of a line segment.

weight The thickness of a 1-D shape or the border around a 2-D shape.

zoom The degree of magnification of a drawing. A zoom of 100% displays the drawing page at the same size it will be when it is printed.

About the Authors

Judy Lemke (*www.judylemke.com*) is an award-winning writer with more than ten years of experience writing, editing, and designing everything from developer documentation and tutorials to product manuals and marketing collateral. Ms. Lemke specializes in documentation, marketing collateral, and training for Microsoft Office Visio products.

Resources Online (*www.ronline.com*) has been creating and delivering content for companies and organizations via electronic and print media for more than fifteen years. The company provides content architecture and management services; Web and application development; and content development including writing, editing, and media production. In addition to creating books and training materials about Microsoft Visio, Resources Online uses Visio extensively to model and build protocols for their health care products.

Index

> **Note** Can't find what you're looking for? A fully searchable version of this book is included on the CD-Rom.

What do you think of this book?

We want to hear from you!

Do you have a few minutes to participate in a brief online survey?

Microsoft is interested in hearing your feedback so we can continually improve our books and learning resources for you.

To participate in our survey, please visit:

www.microsoft.com/learning/booksurvey/

...and enter this book's ISBN-10 number (appears above barcode on back cover*).
As a thank-you to survey participants in the United States and Canada, each month we'll randomly select five respondents to win one of five $100 gift certificates from a leading online merchant. At the conclusion of the survey, you can enter the drawing by providing your e-mail address, which will be used for prize notification only.

Thanks in advance for your input. Your opinion counts!

* Where to find the ISBN-10 on back cover

ISBN-13: 000-0-0000-00000-0
ISBN-10: 0-0000-00000-0

0 0 0 0 0

0 000000 000000

Example only. Each book has unique ISBN.

Microsoft
Press

No purchase necessary. Void where prohibited. Open only to residents of the 50 United States (includes District of Columbia) and Canada (void in Quebec). For official rules and entry dates see:

www.microsoft.com/learning/booksurvey/